The Garland Library
of Medieval Literature

General Editor
James J. Wilhelm, Rutgers University

Literary Advisors
Ingeborg Glier, Yale University
Thomas R. Hart, University of Oregon
Guy Mermier, University of Michigan
Lowry Nelson, Jr., Yale University
Aldo Scaglione, University of North Carolina

Art Advisor
Elizabeth Parker McLachlan, Rutgers University

Music Advisor
Hendrik van der Werf, Eastman School of Music

The Writings of Medieval Women

translation and
introductions by
Marcelle Thiébaux

Volume 14
Series B
GARLAND LIBRARY OF MEDIEVAL LITERATURE

Garland Publishing, Inc.
New York & London
1987

Library of Congress Cataloging-in-Publication Data

The Writings of medieval women.

(Garland library of medieval literature ; v. 14.
Series B)
Bibliography: p.
1. Literature, Medieval.   2. European literature—
Women authors.   I. Thiébaux, Marcelle.   II. Series:
Garland library of medieval literature ; v. 14.
PN667.W75   1987   808.8′99287   83-49069
ISBN 0-8240-9417-4 (alk. paper)

Printed on acid-free, 250-year-life paper
Manufactured in the United States of America

To My Parents

Anna and Martial

Acknowledgements

I owe thanks to friends and colleagues who gave advice, assistance, and support, notably Stanislaus Akielaszek, Adelaide Bennett, Anna Donnelly, Nancy Kandoian, Patrick Otte, Pamela Sheingorn, and James J. Wilhelm. Anthony Papale deserves special credit for setting this book in type. My deepest gratitude is to my husband, Cameron Bloch, for his constant encouragement as well as his practical assistance in the book's design. St. Johns University has been most generous in granting me necessary time for research and writing.

Preface of the General Editors

The Garland Library of Medieval Literature was established to make available to the general reader modern translations of texts in editions that conform to the highest academic standards. All of the translations are original, and were created especially for this series. The translations attempt to render the foreign works in a natural idiom that remains faithful to the originals.

The Library is divided into two sections: Series A, texts and translations; and Series B, translations alone. Those volumes containing texts have been prepared after consultation of the major previous editions and manuscripts. The aim in the editing has been to offer a reliable text with a minimum of editorial intervention. Significant variants accompany the original, and important problems are discussed in the Textual Notes. Volumes without texts contain translations based on the most scholarly texts available, which have been updated in terms of recent scholarship.

Most volumes contain Introductions with the following features: (1) a biography of the author or a discussion of the problem of authorship, with any pertinent historical or legendary information; (2) an objective discussion of the literary style of the original, emphasizing any individual features; (3) a consideration of sources for the work and its influence; and (4) a statement of the editorial policy for each edition and translation. There is also a Select Bibliography, which emphasizes recent criticism on the works. Critical writings are often accompanied by brief descriptions of their importance. Selective glossaries, indices, and footnotes are included where appropriate.

The Library covers a broad range of linguistic areas, including all of the major European languages. All of the important literary forms and genres are considered, sometimes in anthologies or selections.

The General Editors hope that these volumes will bring the general reader a closer awareness of a richly diversified area that has for too long been closed to everyone except those with precise academic training, an area that is well worth study and reflection.

James J. Wilhelm
Rutgers University

Lowry Nelson, Jr.
Yale University

Contents

Introduction

There were always women throughout the Middle Ages who could read and write. In the eleven centuries between the legalizing of Christianity and the beginning of the Renaissance, women's individual names appear in the documents of educated men, their clerics and mentors. From the crabbed eloquence of a medieval Latin sentence, a feminine name — a Burgundian, a Gothic, a Toulousan woman — will shine like a tiny point of light in a thicket. The isolated name sheds a glimmering, tantalizing hint of a story and a life. Theudelinda, we discover, was able to write her name and received letters from Pope Gregory, who also sent her a sumptuously ornamented Gospel lectionary for Adaloald, her little son. Adelperga, daughter of an eighth-century Lombard king, had the keen ability to grasp with ease the golden rhetoric of the philosophers and the jeweled sayings of the poets.

In the ninth century, Irmingard, wife of Boso of Provence, had a tutor and read the Scriptures. Matilda, sister to Burchard of Worms in the tenth century, protested she couldn't be an abbess because the only book she knew was the Psalter. Hedwig, whose uncle was the emperor Otto the Great, spent her time after her husband died reading the Latin poets. Beatrice of Burgundy, Frederick Barbarossa's second wife, was said to have studied poetry and composed an epitaph for herself in eight verses of Latin. We can picture Ricarda, wife of Charles the Fat, borrowing books from the Saint Gall library. Or Cunegonde, wife of the last Saxon Emperor, Henry II, with her nose always in a book or listening to someone else reading, and later teaching her niece Uta, who would become the first abbess of Kaufungen. Or Almode, countess of Toulouse inscribing two words with her own hand in a deed of confirmation to an abbey in 1066.[1] The tenth-century queen Mathilda buries her face in the book she is reading when she learns of her son's death. The nun Elisabeth fretfully flings away her Psalter.

Medieval paintings and illuminations show women at their books; many of these depictions have been gathered by Susan Groag Bell.[2] Sometimes the woman reading is a queen sitting by her window overlooking the garden. She may be the Virgin Mary, a poor woman reading while riding a donkey on the flight into Egypt. By examining wills, library catalogues, household inventories, and dedications to patrons, Susan Bell has also identified women who acquired and collected books, tabulating 242 women book-owners from the ninth to the fifteenth centuries. It should no longer come as a surprise that in addition to reading and acquiring books, women were also writers during the Middle Ages.

Perhaps the mass of anonymous medieval writing included some women authors. We are free to conjecture that a woman's imagination could have produced a work like *Aucassin and Nicolette* — with its fanciful country where men bear the babies and women go to war. Women whose names do survive often subscribe to equally subversive notions. But the women authors whose names we know are apt to come from privileged circumstances, from royal and noble households, with the requisite wealth and leisure for study. Many, though not all, would have been destined for monastic life. It was not unusual for a woman to spend time in the cloister before marriage or after it.

---

[1] James Westfall Thompson, *The Literacy of the Laity in the Middle Ages* (Berkeley, 1939). Examples cited are from pp. 15-16, 36, 88, 139, 37, 85, 130.

[2] "Medieval Women Book Owners: Arbiters of Lay Piety and Ambassadors of Culture," *Signs: Journal of Women in Culture and Society* 7 (Summer 1982), 742-768.

In the early Middle Ages — before the twelfth century — literacy meant a knowledge of Latin; there is ample evidence that queens and noblewomen could write Latin well enough for literary composition and for the addressing of letters, private and public. And here is a most telling point. Of all the forms available to women writers, none has been so necessary and so congenial over the centuries as the letter. A literate woman would always find the need and opportunity to write letters without having to apologize for presuming to authorship. Women's letters were purposeful, their audiences immediate and pressing — a son, nephew, beloved, a sister in God, a powerful ruler to be placated. Maintaining ties, expressing friendship, love, or parental concern could be especially urgent during these turbulent ages, with the movement of migrating peoples, of continual travel from estate to estate, of princes holding court in different residences, of parlays and councils, of exiles, pilgrimages and crusades, raids and military campaigns. Women were apt to be less mobile than men; the separations between men and women or between women bound by kinship or common interest impelled the flow of letters.

It would be tempting to say that the writing of letters was for women a most "normal" form of authorship. In the fourteenth century, Chaucer describes how both Troilus and Criseyde individually write letters. Troilus labors over his, blotting it with many a tear, and struggling to get the rhetoric right — of course he's in love. But Criseyde, who declares she's never written a letter in her life, sits down to compose her missive with little ado.

This doesn't mean that a medieval woman might not have to wrestle with the art of a complicated letter. Dhuoda, writing a letter that stretches to a treatise to her hostage son William, coins a word "agonizatio" for her literary efforts. Any letter, however private and familiar, always afforded the writer opportunities for rhetorical flourishes in a context that could be stuffed with learning — culled perhaps from available guidebooks on how to quote Scripture in an edifying fashion. But not all familiar letters were so ambitious as Dhuoda's; many exist chiefly as expressions of concern for an absent relative. Brunhild in the sixth century, Herchenefreda in the seventh, are anxious mothers writing to or on behalf of children. Letters could serve as veiled autobiographies. A letter from a loved one, as Radegund says, painted the writer's portrait.

There are several letters in the present volume. An anonymous sixth-century woman writes to another woman she admires. Elisabeth of Schönau, the twelfth-century German mystic, writes to Hildegard of Bingen — who is a kind of model for Elisabeth — justifying herself, explaining the sources of her visions. At times when autobiographies and journals are rare, both letters give intimate glimpses of their subjects. Amalasuntha, the beleaguered Gothic queen, writes letters of political necessity to the Emperor Justinian and the Roman senate in a desperate try to save herself. To the Empress Theodora, she suggests that letters might create a spiritual bond that even transcends the physical meeting of friends. Matilda of England writes letters to her adored Anselm, who is like a father to her, but together with the affection she shows him there is also a shrewd sense of political realism, as she frames proposals and pleas on behalf of the realm and her husband Henry I.

As Giles Constable has observed in his *Letters and Letter-Collections,*[3] there are letters that turn into treatises, and books that take on epistolary form. Once a letter-writer got started, she or he might feel it worth extending the document to make a volume for a circle of readers, while apologizing — not too sincerely — for a lack of *brevitas.* Dhuoda instructs her son to share her letter — really a compendium of feudal conduct and obligation — with his brother and assumes there will be further readers.

The mideast travelogue of the restless Egeria is actually an ongoing letter to the women in her community. One of the treasures she promises to bring back with her is — another epistle! This is a document of the sort termed a "fictional letter," though genuine to her, purporting to be a correspondence between Jesus and a contemporary king. To her male relatives Radegund addresses autobiographical poems in the style of those famed fictional letters, the

---

[3]Turnhout, 1976.

Heroides of Ovid. As the writing of letters reached a peak of activity in the twelfth century, even the lyrics of the troubadours — men's and women's — echo the new epistolary note, with their salutations, special pleading, farewell closings (*envois* and *tornadas*), and directions to a messenger.⁴ Christine de Pizan, also a writer of actual letters, includes in her tale of thwarted lovers a delightful fictional letter that looks forward to the epistolary novel.

The writings of many of the women in this volume are letters or pseudo-letters reaching out to bridge physical distances or to express unanimity. Sisterly bonding informs exchanges between the troubadour women, between Radegund and Caesaria, Elisabeth and Hildegard. The sense of female community generates descriptions of the building of new structures for women and all Christians alike, perhaps on the order of the City of God. As a metaphor and a reality, too, building cities or cloisters appears in the writing of Hrotswitha of Gandersheim, Hildegard of Bingen, Julian of Norwich, and Christine de Pizan.

Other recorded experiences are intensely private, composed — their authors say — under extreme pressure to glorify God and benefit the faithful. These writers are the mystics and ecstatics: Hildegard of Bingen, Elisabeth of Schönau, Julian of Norwich, Mechthild of Magdeburg. But what marvelous productions issue forth — visions, prophecies and cosmologies, erotic lyrics patterned on *Minnesang* and the troubadours!

Hrotswitha also views herself as an historian. Both Hrotswitha and Anna Comnena have left us an epic poem apiece, celebrating a strong, dynastic male figure to whom each woman was closely connected. One in the west, one in the east, one in Latin, one in Greek, they sing respectively of the deeds of Otto of Saxony and Alexius of Constantinople. But each woman uses the epic form to interject the praises of heroic and appealing women. The creation of near-hagiographical portraits as idealized models occupied

---

⁴Raymond Gay-Crosier, *Religious Elements in the Secular Lyrics of the Troubadours* (Chapel Hill, 1971), p. 31.

Hrotswitha and Anna, as they did other women writers. Baudonivia commemorates Radegund. Hildegard leaves us her visions of celestial virgins, transparent with light and treading on air. Elisabeth of Schönau spins from a fevered imagination a whole troop of saintly women including her own particular friend and protector, "St. Verena," one of the 11,000 virgins whom St. Ursula led from Britain to Rome to Cologne. Elisabeth's visions achieved such notoriety as to attract pictorial artists who created cycles of the Ursula legend and perpetuated the virgins' images.

A few writers, connected to royal courts, may be termed professional — that is, they wrote for patrons and on commission. Marie de France, a Frenchwoman in England, and Christine de Pizan, an Italian-born woman in France, entertained their princely betters with narratives of sexual love, whether carefree, pathetic, or tragic. Perhaps Hrotswitha in the tenth century and the women troubadours in the twelfth can be counted among the professionals, for their dramas and lyrics seem to have enjoyed court performances.

The writings of medieval women contribute generously to our understanding of women's lives and history, their centuries, and all of medieval literature. Many of the selections offered here are translated into English for the first time. The bibliography that follows this Introduction includes the valued work of other scholars and translators in this endeavor; several of the listed works also treat the women writers in the present anthology. Brief bibliographies of further reading accompany each of my selections of individual writers.

Select Bibliography

Derek Baker, ed. *Medieval Women*. Oxford, 1978.

Caroline Walker Bynum. *Jesus as Mother: Studies in the Spirituality of the High Middle Ages*. Berkeley, 1982.

Peter Dronke. *Women Writers of the Middle Ages*. Cambridge, 1984.

Lina Eckenstein. *Women Under Monasticism*. Rpt. New York, 1963.

Christine Fell, with Cecily Clark and Elizabeth Williams. *Women in Anglo-Saxon England and the Impact of 1066*. Bloomington, 1984.

Joan M. Ferrante. *Woman as Image in Medieval Literature from the Twelfth Century to Dante*. Rpt. Durham, N.C., 1985.

———. "The Education of Women in the Middle Ages in Theory, Fact, and Fantasy." In P.A. Labalme, ed. *Beyond Their Sex: Learned Women of the European Past*. New York, 1980.

Frances Gies and Joseph Gies. *Women in the Middle Ages*. New York, 1978.

Penny Schine Gold. *The Lady and the Virgin: Image, Attitude, and Experience in Twelfth Century France*. Chicago, 1985.

Sybille Harksen. *Women in the Middle Ages*. New York, 1975.

Barbara Kanner, ed. *The Women of England from Anglo-Saxon Times to the Present*. Hamden, Conn., 1979.

Alice Kemp-Welch. *Of Six Medieval Women*. Rpt. Williamstown, Mass., 1972.

Julius Kirshner and Suzanne F. Wemple, eds. *Women of the Medieval World. Essays in Honor of John H. Mundy*. New York, 1985.

Angela M. Lucas. *Women in the Middle Ages: Religion, Marriage, and Letters.* New York, 1983.

Jo Ann McNamara. "Sexual Equality and the Cult of Virginity in Early Christian Thought." *Feminist Studies* 3 (1976), 145-148.

Rosemary T. Morewedge, ed. *The Role of Women in the Middle Ages.* Albany, 1975.

John A. Nichols and Lillian Thomas Shank, eds. *Medieval Religious Women.* Kalamazoo, 1984.

Régine Pernoud. *La femme au temps des cathédrales.* Paris, 1980.

Elizabeth Alvilda Petroff. *Medieval Women's Visionary Literature.* New York, 1986.

Eileen Power. *Medieval Women.* M.M. Postan, ed. Cambridge, 1975.

Douglas Radcliff-Umstead, ed. *The Roles and Images of Women in the Middle Ages and Renaissance.* Pittsburgh, 1975.

Beryl Rowland, ed. and tr. *Medieval Woman's Guide to Health.* Kent, Ohio, 1981.

Shulamith Shahar. *The Fourth Estate: A History of Women in the Middle Ages.* Tr. Chaya Galai. London and New York, 1983.

Pauline Stafford. *Queens, Concubines and Dowagers: The King's Wife in the Early Middle Ages.* Athens, Ga., 1983.

Susan Mosher Stuard, ed. *Women in Medieval Society.* Philadelphia, 1976.

Susanne Fonay Wemple. *Women in Frankish Society: Marriage and the Cloister, 500-900.* Philadelphia, 1981.

Katharina Wilson, ed. *Medieval Women Writers.* Athens, Ga., 1984.

The Writings of
Medieval Women

1   A Pilgrim to the Holy Land

Egeria of Spain (fl. 382-396)

Late in the fourth century a woman of means and leisure traveled from Galicia in northwest Spain to Asia Minor, Palestine, and Egypt. She left a record in simple Latin of her three-year journey that is striking for its immediacy and detail.

The persecutions of Christians had ended with the Council of Nicaea in 325. Tombs, shrines, and churches were being built, rebuilt, or embellished by the Emperor Constantine, who urged Christians to visit the holy places throughout the Middle East. Many who flocked to the Holy Land in this great age of pilgrimage were women. The adventures of Silvia and Poemenia, of Melania and her granddaughter were recorded by others.

Of first-hand accounts the only one earlier than Egeria's is that of the Bordeaux Pilgrim in 333, whose record informs us of sites, distances, and stopping places. The letter Paula and Eustochium sent from Jerusalem to their friend Marcella in Rome is perhaps contemporary with Egeria's. The fuller memoir of Egeria displays energy and personal responsiveness to the idea of the sacred as localized in geographical space. Throughout, the indefatigable Egeria treks, climbs mountains on foot, traverses sandy wastes on muleback, and follows the shoreline where her animals walk through the sea. At times her party needs the armed escort of Roman soldiers. She marvels at the sight of vineyards, orchards, cultivated fields, fountains, fruitful gardens, ruins, tombs, and palaces.

Who was Egeria? Later historians considered her a nun, but there is no clear hint of this in her writing. Perhaps she belonged to a community of consecrated women of which there were many kinds and orders, not yet cloistered and still mobile. She greets the deaconess Marthana at St. Thecla's shrine as a dear friend. She addresses her book to ladies (*dominae*) in her own country, and one in particular as "Your Grace" (*affectio vestra*). Because she makes Constantinople a focus of her journeying, arriving there in time for the Council of Constantinople in 381, Egeria may have had some connection to the imperial circle in that city. Both Egeria and the Emperor Theodosius were members of the pious Spanish aristocracy; possibly she had friends at court.

The *Itinerarium* of Egeria falls into two parts, one that covers distances and the other localized in Jerusalem. In the first part Egeria ranges from Sinai and Egypt, tracing the steps of the Israelites in Exodus, going northward through Palestine, Syria, and Mesopotamia before heading back toward Constantinople. She examines the Burning Bush, still budding, the stone where the Golden Calf was worshipped, and the spot where Lot's wife became a pillar of salt. Egeria visits the desert monks, renowned for their mission of hospitality toward pilgrims. She passes the Red Sea at Clysma. As she moves north, her many stops include the graves of Job and Moses, the pool of John the Baptist near Salem, and Abraham's house at Carrae. Her visits to King Abgar's palace at Edessa in the province of Osrhoene, and to Thecla's shrine at Seleucia in Isauria — both from this part of the *Itinerarium* — are the sources of the first two passages given below.

The Abgar Epistles were a Christian document of popular renown. Although Pope Gelasius eventually declared them apocryphal in 494, they continued to be rewritten with fresh miracles added. Eusebius recorded the texts of both letters in his *History of the Church*. Abgar, writing to Jesus, invites Jesus to the palace in Edessa, hoping to be cured of an illness. Jesus replies in a letter that he cannot come since he must fulfill his mission, but promises to send a disciple. Legend had it that Jesus entrusted his letter — and a portrait of himself — to the messenger Ananias. After the Ascension of Jesus, the Apostle Thomas sent Thaddeus, one of the 70 designated disciples, to Edessa. Egeria preserves a lively account of her visit to the palace, where she learns how Jesus' epistle miraculously foiled the city's enemies. She secures copies of the letters from the bishop of Edessa; their authenticity interests her, and she is convinced that she has received the most complete version.

Soon after leaving Edessa, Egeria headed for the shrine of St. Thecla. The saint's tomb was thought to be at Meriamlik, just outside Seleucia, in the Roman province of Isauria. This Isaurian sanctuary was Thecla's most important; hordes of pilgrims frequented it. Thecla had a devout following, as the many versions of her legend show: they exist in Greek, Latin, Syriac, Armenian, Slavonic, and Arabic. Her fifth-century *Life* by Basil of Seleucia was based on the *Acts of Paul and Thecla,* current in the second century. Its main events are:

A highborn virgin of Iconium in Asia Minor, Thecla overheard St. Paul preaching in a neighbor's house. Smitten by the apostle's words with a fervor for virginity and asceticism, Thecla refused her fiancé. When Paul was arrested for hindering the young from lawful marriage, Thecla visited him in prison, sitting at his feet and listening to his doctrine. Paul was beaten and driven from the city, while the girl was ordered to be burned alive. Numerous adventures and escapes followed, with Thecla's continually seeking out Paul. Finally, Thecla spent her last years as an anchoress dwelling in caves near Seleucia. A surprising feature of the narrative is that Thecla baptized herself on the last day of her life. Her feast was September 23 or 24.

Despite the romance elements of her legend, some factual core is likely. Tertullian, Athanasius, Jerome, and Ambrose regarded Thecla as an actual person. The discounting of her legend over the centuries undoubtedly stems from a general unwillingness to accept Thecla's claim of self-baptism.

The reading of the *Acts of Thecla* in Egeria's presence must have provided festive entertainment. As Thecla's cult grew, the emperor Zeno had her basilica magnificently rebuilt a century after Egeria's visit. Basil's *Life* describes the grandeur of the ceremonies at that time and the pilgrims' eagerness despite the heat, dust, and confusion created by jostling mobs.

The second part of Egeria's *Itinerarium,* after her wider

travels, concentrates on buildings and sites in and around Jerusalem, and forms a smaller pilgrimage. She tells of the Churches of the Nativity at Bethlehem, and of Lazarus at Bethany. On the Mount of Olives she describes the holy site of the Ascension, called "Imbomon," where a church would soon be built, as well as the church called "Eleona," built over the grotto where Christ taught the apostles after his Ascension. Inside Jerusalem she speaks of the Church of Sion, on the site where the Last Supper was eaten in an upper room. She elaborately describes the sanctuaries of the Holy Sepulchre on Golgotha.

From this segment of her adventures, Egeria gives a vivid Easter Week scene. She is the first to mention the veneration of the cross — the *adoratio crucis* — an Eastern ceremony conducted in Jerusalem and already well developed at this date. It was not adopted in Rome until the seventh century. This act of devotion formed the basis of the liturgical custom that eventually entered the drama of the medieval church. The candlelight processional of the groaning faithful through the city, commemorating the agony, arrest, scourging and crucifixion of Jesus, also contributed to the spectacle.

Egeria opens this portion by explaining how on Holy Thursday the people have held vigil from midnight to cockcrow on the hill of the Ascension on the Mount of Olives. They then move on to an elegant church, built on the site where Jesus prayed after he had parted from his disciples and just before his betrayal. The people will remain in this church for prayer, hymns, and gospel readings. The Good Friday ceremony leading to the veneration of the Cross is the subject of the third passage.

1. King Abgar's Letters

The holy bishop of the city[1] was a truly religious man,

---

[1]Egeria's party of pilgrims has arrived in the city of Edessa (mod. Urfa). For Egeria, Edessa meant a 25-day journey from Jerusalem, but no Christian coming to the Holy Land, she writes,

both monk and confessor.[2] He cordially welcomed me, and said to me, "I see, daughter, that because of your piety you have imposed upon yourself the great hardship of traveling to these places from the far ends of the earth. So if you wish, we shall show you the places the Christians rejoice to see." Giving thanks first to God, I begged him to be good enough to do what he had promised.

He led me first to the palace of King Abgar[3] where he showed me a huge statue of the king. Everyone said it was a very good likeness, fashioned of a marble as lustrous as pearl. It was evident, when one confronted those features face to face, that Abgar had been a wise and distinguished man. The holy bishop told me, "That is King Abgar, who, even before he saw the Lord, believed in him as the true son of God." Next to the statue was another one made of similar marble, which he said was a statue of Magnus, the king's son. The expression of the features had also something pleasing about it.

Next we entered an inner part of the palace, where we saw pools full of fish. I have never encountered fish of such great size, so hallowed, and so delicious.[4] There is no other

---

failed to visit the city. Rich in sculptures and mosaics, Edessa was the stronghold of Syriac-speaking Christendom, and the location of the first Christian edifice. Egeria's party had already visited the city's most treasured relic, the remains of St. Thomas the Apostle, buried outside the walls.

[2] A confessor was a Christian who had heroically acknowledged and suffered for the faith without having attained martyrdom.

[3] Aggar, or Abgar V, called Ukkama (the Black), either because he was blind or dark-skinned, was one of a Mesopotamian dynasty of kings that had lasted 375 years in Edessa. A contemporary of Jesus, Abgar reigned between 4 B.C. and 50 A.D. The story of his correspondence with Jesus gained currency in the late 2nd century.

[4] The famous fishpools of Edessa, surviving to this day, and

source of water inside the city, except for this one that flows from the palace. It is like an immense silver river. The holy bishop then told me about this water:

"King Abgar wrote to the Lord, and some time afterward the Lord wrote back to Abgar, sending the letter by his courier Ananias, just as it is written in this same letter. Time went by. The Persians swooped down and encircled the city. Abgar immediately took the Lord's epistle to the city gate, together with his entire army, and he prayed before the people. He said, 'Lord Jesus, you promised us that no enemy should invade this city, but now the Persians are attacking us.' When he had said this, he held the open letter high in his upraised hands. Suddenly thick darkness fell outside the city, clouding the eyes of the Persians, who were packed around the city at a distance of three miles. They were quickly disoriented by the darkness, and could hardly set up their camp, let alone encircle the entire city at that distance of three miles.

"The Persians were so disorganized that they could find no way of gaining entrance to the city to launch their attack, so they posted guards around the locked city and held it under siege for several months. Eventually, when they saw there was no way of their getting to the city, they thought of forcing the inhabitants to die of thirst.

"Now, daughter, in those days, that little hill you see above the city furnished the city's water. Realizing this, the Persians diverted the water course away from the city and made it flow in a different direction, toward their own camp. Suddenly, on the very day and hour that the Persians diverted the flow of water, this fountain you see here in this spot gushed forth by God's command. From that day to this it has continued, by the grace of God. But at that very moment, the stream the Persians had diverted dried up, so that those who

---

the springs that fed them, were the subject of ancient lore and practice. The sacred wells of healing waters surrounded by statuary were the scene of rites honoring the Syrian mother goddess Atargatis (the Greek Hera). Mermaid effigies can be seen today in the museum at Urfa.

were besieging the city could not drink from it even for one day. It is that way now, for no drop of moisture has ever been seen flowing from it to this day.

"And so by the will of God who had promised it, they were forced to return at once to their home in Persia. Since then, whenever an enemy has wanted to attack the city, the letter has been brought out and read before the gate. Immediately, according to God's wish, all the enemy has been driven out."

The holy bishop informed me that these springs had gushed forth where formerly there had been a field within the city. The field lay below Abgar's palace. "It had been built, as you can see, on higher ground, for so it was customary to build palaces in those days. But after the fountains gushed forth here, Abgar built the palace for his son Magnus, whose statue you see beside his father's, so that the fountains might be enclosed within the palace walls. . . ."

It was particularly pleasing to me that I acquired these same letters from Abgar to the Lord and the Lord to Abgar, which the holy bishop read to us there. For although I have copies of them at home, it seemed to me quite a favor to receive these from him, in case the ones at home are lacking something. Certainly, the copy I was given here seems to have more in it. You will read them yourselves, ladies of my heart, when I return to our country, if Jesus our God wills it.

2. St. Thecla's Shrine

St. Thecla's shrine, in Isauria, that is, requires a three-day journey from Tarsus.[5] We were extremely happy to go there, especially as it was so close. I left Tarsus, still in the province of Cilicia, and arrived at a city called Pompeiopolis[6]

---

[5]Tarsus, capital of the province of Cilicia, was St. Paul's birthplace (Acts 21.39).

[6]This ancient seacoast city of Soloi was destroyed in 91 B.C. The refuge of pirates, it was rebuilt in 63 B.C. by Pompey. Its ruins and long row of Corinthian columns can still be seen not far from the

which is on the sea. From there I crossed the border into Isauria, where I stayed at the city of Corycus.[7] On the third day I reached a city called Seleucia of Isauria.[8] As soon as I arrived I visited the bishop, a very holy man who had been a monk. I also saw a most beautiful church in that city.

St. Thecla's is just outside the city on a flat hilltop about fifteen hundred paces away, and as I needed a place to sleep, I chose to go on and stay there. Near the holy church there is nothing but countless numbers of individual monastic cells for men and women both. And there I came upon a very dear friend of mine, a holy deaconess named Marthana.[9] Everyone in the East attests to her way of life. I had known her in Jerusalem when she had come up on pilgrimage for the purpose of prayer. Now she was supervising the cells of apotactites[10] or virgins. When she saw me, her pleasure and

---

beach of Viransehir in Turkey.

[7]The modern Turkish city of Korykos. Cicero, when governor of Cilicia, lived there between 52 and 50 B.C.

[8]Founded in the 3rd century B.C., and so called to distinguish it from several other cities of the same name. The modern Silifke is about three miles north of the old city.

[9]Deaconesses in the 3rd and 4th centuries were charged with charity, hospitality, the care of the poor and sick, and the supervision of ecclesiastical widows and virgins. Eastern deaconesses fulfilled clerical functions, administering the sacraments to women in particular. In the absence of clergy they would have read the sacred texts and attended to the lamps and oil of the altar. Like deacons, they were expected to assist bishops. Marthana, the only living person named in Egeria's book, was praised by Basil in his *Life of St. Thecla*.

[10]The name for ascetic sects in the 3rd and 4th centuries in Cilicia, as well as Pamphylia and Phrygia. These men and women aspired to special purity of life by practicing rigorous fasts and other

mine were so great — could I ever describe it?

But let me get back to my subject. There are a great many monastic cells all about that same hill. In the middle a huge wall surrounds the church which contains the shrine. The shrine itself is extremely beautiful. The reason for the wall's having been built is to protect the church against the Isaurians. They are a bad sort who often turn to banditry and must be prevented from trying anything against the monastery that is established there.

In the name of God, I arrived at the shrine where they conducted both prayer and a reading of all the Acts of St. Thecla. I gave boundless thanks to Christ our God that he deigned to fulfill my desires in all things, unworthy and undeserving though I am.

And so I remained two days, visiting the monks and the apotactites, both the men and women who were there. After prayer and communion, I turned back to Tarsus to resume my journey. I made my quarters there for three days; then in God's name I set out from there to continue my route. Then on the very day I set out, I arrived at a resting place called Mansocrene, at the foot of Mount Taurus.[11] There I put up for the night.

The next day we went up Mount Taurus. We resumed a route that was familiar to us, since on our way out we had already crossed through each province, namely Cappadocia, Galatia and Bithynia. I reached Chalcedon, where there is a shrine much talked about, that of St. Euphemia.[12] I had long

---

penances. Egeria seems to use the term synonymously with "virgins" as those given to renunciation.

[11]Mansocrene or Mopsucrene was a usual stopping place between Tarsus and the Cilician Gateway (mod. Gulek Pass) through the Taurus slopes. The latter is a mountain range along the southern coast of Turkey.

[12]Chalcedon, the modern Turkish city of Kadiköy, was colonized in the 7th century B.C. just opposite Byzantium on the Bosphorus. The cult of St. Euphemia, the Bithynian martyr (d. 307) was founded in

known about it, and I stopped there.

On the following day I crossed the sea and arrived at Constantinople. I thanked Christ our God, who deigned to grant me such grace despite my lack of worth and merit. For not only did he deign to grant me the will to go on this journey, but the ability to ramble everywhere I wished, and finally to return to Constantinople. When I got there, I never ceased giving thanks in all the churches, the shrine of the apostles, and those many martyrs' shrines, to Jesus our God, who so deigned to grant me his mercy.

From here, ladies — light of my eyes — once I have sent this letter to Your Grace, it is my plan to go up, in Christ's name, to Ephesus in Asia. I want to pray at the shrine of the blessed apostle John.[13] If indeed after this I am still alive and

---

Egeria's own time. Her feast (September 16) was one of the most popular in both East and West. Bishop Asterius of Amasea, who would have been Egeria's contemporary, described in about 400 a series of tablets or paintings showing stages of St. Euphemia's martyrdom. She stands before the judge, she has her teeth drawn with hammer and auger, and is finally burned. The Council of Chalcedon in 451 attributed its success to her protection. Her relics were later transferred from her church in Chalcedon to St. Sophia in Constantinople. Venantius Fortunatus (6th c.) singled her out in his poem on virgins.

[13]The tomb of John the Apostle was the chief pilgrim attraction of Ephesus, rich in history, and Egeria is the first to mention it. As late as 416, as St. Augustine reports, John was supposed not to be dead but asleep, awaiting Christ's Second Coming. Revered since the 2nd century, the tomb was the site in Egeria's day of the construction of a great church, to be finished in 420. Ephesus owed some of its ancient fame to its cult of Artemis. The issue of Artemis's cult had occasioned the great theater riot noted in St. Paul's Acts 19.20-41. The partly restored temple of Artemis was still used in Egeria's time. Now a major Christian center, the capital of the proconsular province of Asia and the wealthiest city of Roman Asia Minor, Ephesus was a seaport strategically placed for travel and

able to learn about other places, I shall either tell you about them myself when I am with you — God willing — or I shall report them to Your Grace. Certainly, if anything else occurs to my mind, I shall write about it. I beg you, ladies, light of my eyes, to deign to remember me, whether in this bodily life or beyond the body hereafter.[14]

3. Good Friday in Jerusalem and the Adoration of the Cross

Then all the people, even the smallest children, go down to Gethsemane[15] on foot, together with the bishop. They sing hymns. There is such a great crowd of people, and they are so worn out with their nightlong vigil and weakened from each day's fasting, that they descend the steep hill to Gethsemane very slowly. They sing hymns as they go. More than two hundred church candles light their way.[16]

When everyone has arrived in Gethsemane, first the proper prayer is read, then the hymn is sung. The gospel passage is read recounting the Lord's arrest. During the reading there is such howling and roaring among the people, along with weeping, that it is likely that the people's groans can be heard at the far end of the city. And now they walk, singing hymns, and they arrive at the gate at an hour when

---

trade. In 431 it would be the site of the Third Ecumenical Council.

[14]This section, occurring midway through the *Itinerarium*, imparts a sense of conclusion with its expressions of thanksgiving and farewell. It ends the "itinerary" itself, for Egeria proceeds next to her description of Jerusalem.

[15]The garden to which Jesus went with the disciples after the Last Supper, immediately before his betrayal and arrest. He withdrew a stone's throw from them to pray that the cup might be taken away from him (Luke 22.41; Matthew 26.36-42).

[16]Candles provided light as well as commemorating Jesus' arrest by a band of men with lanterns and torches (John 18.3).

they can recognize one another. From there they go through the middle of the city together. Old and young, rich and poor, all appear there on this special day when no one leaves the vigil before morning. In this manner the bishop is escorted from Gethsemane to the gate, and from the gate through the entire city to the Cross.

When they have arrived before the Cross, the day is already beginning to grow light. There, finally, they read the whole gospel account of how the Lord was led before Pilate and all that was written that Pilate said to the Lord and to the Jews.

After this the bishop speaks to the people, comforting them, since they have suffered such exertions through the night and will continue to do so during this day. He urges them not to be weary but to hope in God, since their exertions will be richly rewarded. Comforting them as much as he can, he tells them, "Go, for now, each of you to your homes, and sit down a while. Then at the second hour of the day [8 o'clock] be back here so that until the sixth hour [noon] you will be able to see the sacred wood of the Cross, trusting that it will assure future salvation for each of us. From that hour of noon on, when we must gather here again before the Cross, we must conduct readings and prayers until nightfall."

The sun has still not yet risen when the people are dismissed from the Cross. Those who are stalwart go on to pray at Sion, at the pillar where the Lord was scourged.[17] Then people go back home to rest for a little while, but before long everyone is back. A bishop's throne is set up on Golgotha, behind the Cross which now stands there.[18] The bishop is

---

[17] Jesus was scourged here by Pilate. In 404 St. Jerome wrote that the pillar, still stained with Jesus' blood, supported the church at Sion.

[18] Golgotha is the Aramaic name meaning skull — from the shape of the hill — of the place later called Calvary, outside the ancient city of Jerusalem. The Cross standing there is not the "true" Cross, which will be brought forward later.

seated on his throne and a linen-covered table is placed before him. Deacons stand around the table. The silver coffer, ornamented with gold, is brought which contains the sacred wood of the true Cross. The coffer is opened and the wood of the Cross, together with the superscription,[19] are laid on the table.

While the Cross is on the table, the bishop, remaining seated, holds down the ends of the holy wood with his hands. The deacons also guard it as they stand around him. They all now guard it this way for it is customary for the people to approach the table one by one, both the faithful and the catechumens. They bow to the table, kiss the sacred wood, and then move along. I don't know when it was, but someone is said to have bitten off a piece of the sacred wood and stolen it. For this reason it is guarded now by the deacons who surround it, so that no one will dare to do this again.

Now all the people pass before it one by one, bowing and touching it first with the forehead, then with the eyes. Then they kiss it before they move on. No one, however, reaches out a hand to touch it.

Further Reading on Egeria

Text: E. Franceschini and R. Weber, eds. *Itinerarium Egeriae.* Corpus Christianorum, Series Latina, Vol. 175. Turnhout, 1965.

George E. Gingras, tr. *Egeria: Diary of a Pilgrimage.* Ancient Christian Writers. New York, 1970.

E.D. Hunt. *Holy Land Pilgrimage in the Later Roman Empire A.D. 312-460.* Oxford, 1982.

Hélène Pétré, ed. *Ethérie: Journal de voyage.* Sources chrétiennes, Vol. 121. Paris, 1948.

John Wilkinson, tr. *Egeria's Travels.* London, 1971.

---

[19]The mocking and condemnatory "Jesus of Nazareth, The King of the Jews" (John 19.19) is variously worded in Matthew 27.37, Mark 15.26, and Luke 23.38.

2   An Ill-Fated Gothic Queen

Amalasuntha of Italy (d. 535)

A queen whose main court was at Ravenna, Amalasuntha held sway in Italy beginning August 30, 526, after her father's death. He was Theodoric the Great, the Ostrogoth who had defeated Odovacar (who himself had driven out the last Roman emperor). Her mother Audefleda was a sister of Clovis. Amalasuntha's own reign of nine years ended with her murder, treacherously strangled in her bath on the small island where she was held prisoner.

The life of Amalasuntha can be seen against two historic events: the half-century of Gothic control in Italy (494-553 A.D.), and the efforts — ultimately successful — of the Byzantine emperor Justinian to reconquer Italy and bring it back under the imperial Roman administration. During Amalasuntha's reign, there was unrest in the Italian kingdom. Rivalries and suspicions between ruling Goths and subject Romans riddled court life.

Like her father, Amalasuntha retained an immense admiration for Roman culture, learning and law. She tried to keep order and dispense justice, seeing to it for instance that Gothic soldiers' salaries and bonuses were paid out of tax revenues and not from wrested Roman properties. One of her significant acts was to restore to the children of Boethius, and of Symmachus his father-in-law, the estates which Theodoric had confiscated when he had for somewhat unclear reasons put these two to death. It will be recalled that the execution of Boethius, author of *The Consolation of Philosophy,* remains a blot on Theodoric's generally humane record. Amalasuntha's tendency to protect those Romans

15

whom she saw wronged by predatory Goths would, unfortunately, prove her undoing.

Her biographers, both men, accord high praise to Amalasuntha for her fair-mindedness, strength of will, intellect, and learning. Her secretary, Cassiodorus, says she knew Greek and Latin as well as her native Gothic tongue. Procopius[1] points out her wisdom and high sense of justice, while praising her "masculinity." However capable she may have been, the hostility and misogyny of her Gothic nobles and advisers were such that she did not have a chance.

When her father died, Amalasuntha was a widow with two children — a girl named Matasuntha, and Athalaric, a boy of 8 or 10. Amalasuntha served then as regent for her son. She wanted to mold Athalaric on the lines of a Roman ruler, and sought to oversee his education by engaging Roman tutors. This plan ran counter to the Gothic conviction that the pursuit of letters was unmanly. Enforced study would cause a boy to cower before his teachers — old men at that. The nobles prescribed riding, hunting, and skill at weaponry, practiced among young companions. Amalasuntha's relationships with her Gothic advisers were poor; yielding to their importuning, she gave the boy over to a life that proved to be his destruction: drunken routs and other excesses led to Athalaric's wasting illness and death before he reached twenty. This left Amalasuntha at the head of the state.

But the Goths would not accept a woman's rule. When she uncovered a plot against her, Amalasuntha ordered the deaths of three ringleaders. Seeing herself surrounded now and helpless, she attempted to build support both at home and abroad. Her anxiety during her son's illness had impelled her to turn to her married cousin Theodahad. When the son died she named Theodahad co-ruler with herself, and asked for approval from Justinian, the Byzantine emperor. Theodahad was an older man with a taste for Roman letters,

---

[1]Procopius of Caesarea was secretary to Belisarius, Justinian's general. He wrote a *History of the Wars* (Persian, Vandal, and Gothic), *The Buildings of Justinian,* and *The Secret History.*

and not at all a soldier. He had formerly shown a rapacious inclination to enrich himself in Tuscany by taking over his Roman neighbors' estates, and affected the style of the landed Roman gentry. Unfortunately, Theodahad was one of those avaricious Goths whom Amalasuntha had brought to justice earlier. Now she forced herself to gloss over her kinsman's peccadillos in a letter to the Roman Senate, drawing attention to a supposedly regenerate and deeply bookish Theodahad.

At the same time Amalasuntha prudently sent messages to Constantinople, written letters accompanied by verbal amplification carried on the persons of trusted envoys, in case the arrangement with Theodahad fell through. She had kept up friendly relations with Justinian, and now made preparations — with loaded ships should she have to flee — to place herself under his protection. If need be she would hand over the kingdom of Italy as well. Justinian, it seems, eagerly encouraged these dealings with Amalasuntha. But Theodahad, still rankling against Amalasuntha over the matter of the Tuscan estates, had also made overtures to Justinian, tendering offers to yield up estates to Constantinople in the hopes of retiring in honorable comfort to the Byzantine court.

Justinian must have dealt a double game, negotiating with Amalasuntha and Theodahad both, playing one against the other until the time was ripe. Within seven months of her son's death on October 2, 534, Theodahad took Amalasuntha into custody and held her captive at Martana, an island on the lake of Bolsena near Orvieto. Theodahad indicated to Justinian that he was treating her well there, considering her high-handedness with his Tuscan estates. Meanwhile, Theodahad allowed Amalasuntha to be slain by the relatives of those same three Goths she had earlier ordered killed as traitors.[2]

After Amalasuntha's death, Theodahad's wife Gudeliva,

---

[2]Procopius suggests that the Empress Theodora, Justinian's jealous spouse, urged the murder through a conspiracy with Peter, imperial envoy to Italy.

now assuming the title of Queen of Italy with her husband
as King, sent two letters to Theodora in Constantinople,
gratefully confirming her new position. Eventually, the Goths
grew dissatisfied with Theodahad and had him murdered. His
successor, an old soldier named Witigis, tried to consolidate
his hold on the throne by taking Amalasuntha's daughter
Matasuntha as his wife. In the eighteen years that followed,
Justinian managed to drive the Goths out of Italy, completing
the reconquest by 554.

Four letters by Amalasuntha have been preserved among
the writings of Cassiodorus. She wrote the first of these
translated below in 534, soon after the death of her adolescent son at the age of 15 or 17. Here she informs Justinian
that she has offered a share of the rule of Italy to her kinsman
Theodahad, and looks to Justinian for his sanction. In the second letter, Amalasuntha addresses the Roman Senate,
praising Theodahad for his good qualities, including a love
of literature, while alluding in glancing terms to his past
misdeeds. The third letter thanks Justinian for a gift of
statues, while the fourth addresses the Empress Theodora
with amicable reverence, showing concern for her health,
seemingly during a pregnancy.[3]

1. Queen Amalasuntha to the Emperor Justinian

Until now, most merciful prince, we have put off the
disclosure of the death of our son, of glorious memory, so as
not to wound the heart of a loving friend with a sorrowful
message. But now, with the help of God — who always turns

---

[3]Procopius's *History* preserves two other letters of Amalasuntha's
over the Byzantine use of the Sicilian port of Lilybaeum (mod.
Marsala), one to Belisarius and one to Justinian. Belisarius wanted
to occupy the ports as a vantage point in his war against the Vandals.
It is thought that these letters, too, contained implicit negotiations
with Justinian in preparation for Amalasuntha's possible flight from
Italy.

Letters in Athalaric's name are probably Amalasuntha's compositions as well, since he was only 8 or 10 when Theodoric died.

harsh mischance into good fortune — we have chosen to bring to your attention matters over which you may be able to rejoice with us, and share our exultation. It is always pleasing to acknowledge the gifts of divine providence to those who love us.

We have brought to the sceptre one who is closely connected to us by brotherly kinship, a man who may uphold the royal rank together with us by the strength of his counsel, so that he may be resplendently clothed in the purple glory of his ancestors. In this way the solace of a prudent man may lift up our spirits.

Join together now your propitious prayers. For just as we eagerly hope that all things will turn out favorably in the empire of Your Beneficence, so we will be the living proof of the kindness that you bestow upon us.

And so we add the service of a most friendly ambassador to the message which has been sent, and which we trust that you, with your inborn clemency, will look upon as the fulfillment of a vow. By this means, we hope that the peaceful relations which you maintain toward us — and which you continue to uphold for my sake especially — may be extended for the protection of my people.

For although the concord of princes is always an adornment, yours wholly ennobles me, since whoever harmoniously shares in your glory is made more fully sublime.

But since everything cannot be adequately settled in the brief space of a letter, we have, in sending our respectful greetings to you, entrusted to our envoys certain appropriate matters to be made known to you verbally. Please be willing to accept these in the accustomed manner of Your Serenity.

It is agreed then, that I may without any doubt count on you, since we are doing those things that we recognize you have expected us to do, concerning those people you have recommended, in fulfillment of your wishes.

2. Queen Amalasuntha to the Senate of the City of Rome

After mourning for the death of our son, of blessed memory, our concern for the people's common good has conquered a dutiful mother's heart, so that it dwells not upon the cause of her own grief but upon your prosperity. We have searched into the kind of help we might obtain to strengthen the kingdom's administration. But that Father of purity and unique mercy, who was to deprive us of a son in his young manhood, has kept alive for us the affection of a brother ripe in years.

We have chosen by God's grace the blessed Theodahad as the consort of our reign, so that we who have until now borne in solitary deliberation the burden of the commonwealth, may now carry out the achievement of all things by united counsels. We shall be seen to be two persons in mutually working out the administration of the State, but one person in purpose. The stars of heaven themselves are controlled by the aid they give to one another — and having been made partners by their shared labor — guide the world with their lights. Heavenly power has assigned to men two hands, companion ears, and twin eyes, so that the function which was to be fulfilled by the allied pair might be more efficiently carried out.

Rejoice, Fathers of the Senate, and commend to the heavenly powers what we have accomplished. We have desired to do nothing blameworthy, we who have — in conjunction with each other's counsel — commanded all things to be put in order. We of course preserve with liberality the kingdom's tradition, since one who is demonstrated to have a partner in her exercise of power is rightly seen to be compassionate.

With God's help, therefore, we have unbarred the imperial residence to an illustrious man of our family, who, descended from the race of the Amals, has a royal worthiness in his actions. He is patient in adversity, restrained in his prosperity, and possesses what is the most difficult kind of control — a self-control of long standing. His literary erudition adds to these good qualities, and excellently adorns an already praiseworthy nature. For it is through books that the prudent man discovers how he may become wiser. There the warrior finds how he may become staunch in his greatness of soul; there the prince learns in what manner he may control diverse peoples under an equal rule. No fortune in the world can exist which the glorious knowledge of literature does not enhance.

Welcome, too, that greater thing which the prayers of the commonwealth have gained. Your prince is even learned in ecclesiastical letters. By these we are reminded of whatever pertains to the well-being of humanity: to adjudicate correctly, to know the good, to revere the divine, and to be mindful of the Judgment to come. Indeed it is necessary — for one who believes that he will have to plead his case on account of his own actions — to follow in the footsteps of justice.[4] And so, I may observe that while reading sharpens the intelligence, divine reading continually works to perfect a dutiful person.

Let us come to that most generous sobriety of his private life, which has amassed such an abundance of gifts, such a wealth of feasts, that in the light of his former activity he will be seen to require nothing further in conducting the realm.[5] He is prompt in hospitality and most dutiful in compassion, so that although he has spent much, his worth has kept increasing through heaven's reward.

The whole world ought to hope for such a man as the one we are seen to have chosen, who — managing his own belongings reasonably — does not crave the belongings of other people. For the necessity of committing excesses is removed from princes who are accustomed to being moderate in their own expenses. The view that enjoins moderation is, of course, being praised, since too much of even what is considered to be a good thing is not acceptable.

Rejoice, then, Fathers of the Senate, and render thanks to the Heavenly Grace on our behalf, since I have ordained

---

[4]Perhaps a significant though veiled allusion to the past insolence of Theodahad. While this line can be taken to mean the Last Judgment, it is also a reminder that Theodahad in fact had once been prosecuted for unlawful seizure of properties. He indeed refers, in his companion speech before the Senate, to the fact that Amalasuntha had caused him to plead his case publicly, prior to naming him her co-regent.

[5]Amalasuntha suggests, not so subtly, that since Theodahad has already enriched himself he probably won't see the need to continue his grasping ways.

such a prince with me who will perform the good deeds that flow from our justice, and make his own good deeds manifest through his own sense of duty. For the virtue of his ancestors will admonish this man, and Theodoric as his uncle will effectually inspire him.

3. Queen Amalasuntha to Justinian Augustus

The kindness of Your Piety delights us so much in permitting us freely to ask for whatever we may desire from among your share of belongings in order to enhance our glory. For the heavenly powers have assigned such treasures to you that you richly abound in their gifts, and you grant with a benevolent spirit things which are necessary to those who hope for them.

And so, reverently saluting Your Clemency, I have directed the bearer of these letters to the favor of Your Excellency. In this way you may command, with God's grace, that the marble statues and other necessary items which we previously ordered Calogenitus to secure for us shall reach us by means of the present bearer. We therefore may acknowledge ourselves to be esteemed by Your Revered Piety.

You cause our prayers to be fulfilled; we are adorned with your glory. For it is known that you surpass whatever praises we can address to you.

It is fitting that, with your help, the Roman world of yours should also shine brilliantly — that world which Your Serenity's love embellishes.

4. Queen Amalasuntha to Theodora Augusta

Since it is characteristic of our way of life to seek those things which are considered to pertain to the glory of pious princes, it is appropriate to venerate you in written words — you who all agree are continually enhanced in your virtues.

Harmony exists not only between those who are in each others' presence; indeed, those joined together in the charity of the spirit have an even greater respect for each other.

For this reason, rendering to the Augusta the affection of

a reverent greeting, I hope that when our legates return — those whom we have sent to the most clement and glorious prince — you will make us rejoice in your safety. Your propitious circumstances are as welcome to us as our own. It is essential to make your safety our heartfelt concern. It is well known that we hope for this unceasingly.

Further Reading on Amalasuntha:

Text: *Monumenta Germaniae Historica: Auctorum Antiquissimorum,* Vol. 12. Cassiodorus, *Variae,* Book X, pp. 296; 298-299; 303; 304. Berlin, 1894.

Norman H. Baynes. "Justinian and Amalasuntha." *English Historical Review* 40 (1925), 71-73.

Eleanor Shipley Duckett. *The Gateway to the Middle Ages.* "The Gothic Rule in Italy: Cassiodorus, Secretary of Theodoric the Great," pp. 58-100. New York, 1938.

Procopius of Caesarea. *History of the Wars.* H.B. Dewing, tr. Vol. II, pp. 252-255; Vol. III, pp. 12-43. Loeb Library: London and New York, 1914-1928.

3 Early Convent Life: Three Women of Merovingian Gaul

Radegund of Poitiers (520-Aug. 13, 587)
Caesaria of Arles (d. 559)
Baudonivia of Poitiers (fl. 610)

Radegund of Poitiers

What we know of Radegund, the royal founder of one of the earliest religious houses for women in Gaul, can be gathered from her autobiographical poems, written as letters, and from three other sources in her own time. Gregory of Tours[1] and Venantius Fortunatus[2] wrote accounts of her, Fortunatus having also honored her with his graceful courtly

---

[1] Gregory of Tours (538-594) was born in France, classically trained, and known for his *History of the Franks,* in which there is a great deal about Radegund. He came to Tours in search of a cure at St. Martin's tomb. Eventually he became St. Gregory, Bishop of Tours. Often at odds with the Merovingian kings, he tended to excuse those who, like Clovis, Clothar, and Guntram, protected the Church.

[2] Venantius Fortunatus (530-609) was an Italian poet and rhetorician who had traveled to France. He resided at various courts, including that of Sigibert and Brunhild, for whom he wrote a wedding song. He went to Tours to be cured of an eye ailment; there he enjoyed the friendship of Gregory and Radegund. He became a priest, then Radegund's chaplain, and eventually Bishop of Poitiers. His works include occasional pieces, verse epistles, saints' lives, and hymns, notably the one to the Cross that Radegund brought to Poitiers.

lyrics. In the next generation, Baudonivia, a nun of Radegund's convent, received an assignment to write a life to supplement the one by Fortunatus.

Radegund was born at Erfurt in the kingdom of Thuringia in about 520 during the reign of the Eastern emperor Justinian. Berthar, her father, had shared Thuringia with his brothers Hermenefred and Baderic. Radegund and her younger brother were brought up in the household of her aunt Amalaberga and uncle Hermenefred after he had killed her father and Baderic. Radegund remembers with tearful affection her cousin and childhood playmate Hamalafred in *The Fall of Thuringia* and the *Letter to Artachis*.

The assault on Thuringia in 531 was the deed of two of Clovis's sons — Theodoric I, king of the Austrasian Franks, and his half-brother Clothar I (511-561), king of Neustria in Northwestern France. After the brutal sack of Thuringia, Clothar won Radegund and her brother by lot or combat as his share of the spoils. He took them to his royal estate at Athiès on the Somme River. There he had Radegund educated until she should reach an age to marry. When she was eighteen or twenty their wedding took place at Soissons, Clothar's capital city. Through her marriage, Radegund became related to the recently deceased Amalasuntha, since Clothar and Amalasuntha were cousins.

As the son of the first Christian king of the Franks, Clothar was nominally a Christian. His mother, St. Clothild, had founded a nunnery at Chelles near Paris and another small house at Tours. Radegund's biographer Baudonivia states that Clothar converted Radegund to Christianity. Clothar, however, had gained a reputation for cruelty and sensuality. When he married Radegund he had other wives and concubines; it seems she was the fifth of his seven wives.

Clothar's political motive for marrying Radegund was to legitimize his claim to Thuringia. To Radegund the marriage was repugnant. As a wife she provoked the king's annoyance for her many pieties and mortifications. He is said to have accused her of being more nun than queen, when she avoided the conjugal bed to keep nocturnal vigils. She also arrived late at the dining table where she was expected to preside. Radegund may have wished for some time to escape from Clothar, but when in her absence from the court he had her younger brother murdered she felt she could no longer live with him. Allowing Clothar to think she would return, Radegund fled to Noyon, where she persuaded Bishop Médard to consecrate her as a deaconess. Despite his unwillingness to thwart Clothar — who had sent soldiers to threaten him physically — Médard acquiesced after Radegund placed her jewels and richly ornamented robes on the altar and demanded consecration.

From Noyon Radegund traveled to Tours as a pilgrim to St. Martin's tomb there. She then went to live at the villa Clothar had given her at Saix, where she tended and administered baths to the sick. Perhaps it was St. Hilary's shrine that drew her to Poitiers. Finally she was able to elude her husband, who had traveled to Tours with Bishop Germanus of Paris to try to get her back. Germanus instead dissuaded Clothar from this hope; old now, Clothar was induced to donate the buildings for Radegund's monastery of Notre Dame of Poitiers, where she founded her community of women. In her letter of foundation to the Bishops, Radegund wrote: "I asked myself, with all the ardor of which I am capable, how I could best forward the cause of other women, and how, if our Lord so willed, my own personal desires might be of advantage to my sisters."[3] In 552 Bishop Germanus consecrated the buildings and professed the nuns.

After Clothar's death Radegund, not wanting to be trammeled by administrative responsibilities and desiring to be free for her devotions, transferred her authority to her young friend Agnes, naming her abbess. She obtained a copy of the first monastic Rule designed for women. It was the work of St. Caesarius, Bishop of Arles, for the house of his sister Caesaria. The Rule provided for strict enclosure and a requirement of literacy. The reading and copying activity that went on, as well as the friendship of Venantius Fortunatus, who exchanged poems with Agnes and Radegund, created an unusual literary ambience and made the monastery a center of Christian and humanist letters.

---

[3]Letter in Gregory of Tours, *History of the Franks*, IX, 42, tr. Lewis Thorpe (New York, 1974), p. 535.

Fortunatus, for his part, acknowledged Radegund's poems with the words: "You send me splendid songs on little tablets; to their dead wax you restore the honey!"

The secure refuge, even the comforts of monastic life — there were baths and backgammon for some of the women — were preserved in a period of bitter and bloody political turmoil. Clothar's sons, Sigibert, Chilperic, Guntram, and Charibert, wrangled among themselves; several of their wives were murdered. During this period of court intrigue, violence, and war, Radegund felt the need of divine protection over the stability of the realm. She began to collect relics. With the help of Sigibert, with whom she enjoyed a friendly relationship, she was able to secure fragments of the Holy Cross from Constantinople. She also had blood relatives there to whom she could appeal, for it was to Constantinople that the survivors of the Thuringian war had fled. The Cross and other relics arrived in Tours between 566 and 573. Fortunatus celebrated the occasion with his famous hymn *Vexilla regis prodeunt*, "The banners of the King come forth." The monastery was renamed Sainte-Croix, or Holy Cross.

Because of her energetic piety, political and ecclesiastical connections, and the special status of her convent, Radegund probably represented a threat to her local prelate, Bishop Maroveus of Poitiers. The arrival of her relics stirred his resentment, and he left for his country house, refusing to provide the suitable ceremonies for receiving them. Radegund then turned to her friends Sigibert and Bishop Euphronius of Tours, who conducted the procession with Psalms, censers, and candlelight. Neither could Maroveus be counted on to bury Radegund when the time came at last; Gregory of Tours both performed the funeral ceremony and wrote her eulogy.

Radegund's biographers praise her piety and learning: she would deprive herself of sleep at night to read the Scriptures. She labored as a motherly teacher of her conventual flock. As a healer and miracle worker among the sick and poor, she had the aid of her physician, Reovalis. A tireless ascetic, she imposed mortification and drudgeries on herself that she did not expect of others: harsh fasts, cooking and housekeeping, bathing the unfortunate and cleaning their shoes. In times of extreme stress she chastened her body with burning irons and chains.

The numerous miracles attributed to Radegund — her ability to feed, clothe, and care for ...er flock as well as the needy who came to her doors — are not just marvels of inventiveness, but are rooted in certain economic realities during a time of upheaval and scarcity. Radegund's high-ranking connections, the royal wealth and the land she had been able to secure for her monastery as well as her bounty of relics, had made Sainte-Croix a center of stability and near-opulence, serving to attract other well-born women with fortunes to the community.

Radegund's two poems, *The Fall of Thuringia* and the *Letter to Artachis*, reveal her literary affinities as well her capacity for love and sorrow as she recalls her childhood and expresses longing for her lost family. *The Fall of Thuringia* gives a strikingly detailed memoir of the little girl's passionate devotion to her older cousin. Hamalafred. Since the sack of their family's home and city, he has taken refuge with their relations in Constantinople. The letter also grieves for her brother, slain by her husband Clothar; Radegund feels responsible since she had begged the boy to stay with her when he had wanted to leave to join Hamalafred. Radegund moreover directs that timeless epistolary complaint to Hamalafred — "Why don't you write more often?" The *Letter to Artachis* addresses a nephew, now that Hamalafred, too, has died.

Both poems contain a *planctus*, a lament for the dead. *The Fall of Thuringia*, a miniature epic that speaks of Troy, sounds especially the notes of exile and elegy heard in early Germanic poetry — notably Old English laments like the *Wanderer* and the *Seafarer*. The decay of a great hall, the deaths of companions, the risk and loneliness of a wintry sea voyage all belong to this genre and tradition, echoing the kinds of songs Radegund might have heard in her uncle's house in Thuringia. In addition she borrows a common persona from the *Heroides* of Ovid, letters of the bereft daughters of heroes who utter the female viewpoint of classical epic. Skillfully Radegund adapts all these conventions to herself, transcending convention, however, in the vivid, yearning accents of a consecrated woman separated from those she loves.

1. The Fall of Thuringia

The harsh nature of war! The malevolent fate of things! How proud kingdoms fall, suddenly in ruins! Blissful housetops that had held up for long ages now lie torched, consumed beneath a huge devastation.

This hall that once flourished in imperial splendor is covered now — no longer with vaulted arches — but with wretched cinders. A pall of pale ashes buries the steep shining roof that long ago gleamed with red-gold metal. Its potentate has been sent into captivity, subject to an enemy lord. Its former glory has fallen into lowliness. The attendant crowd of striving retainers, all of whom served at the same time, lies filthy with the dust of death. Their life is over. The brilliant thronging circle of court dignitaries lies unsepulchred, deprived of the honors of death.

My beloved father's sister lies stretched on the ground, her milk-white body outshining the flame-spewing, red-gold glow of her hair. Ah, the foully unburied corpses have covered the field, and so the whole nation lies in one tomb.

Let Troy no longer be the only city to lament her ruin. The land of Thuringia also endured an equal massacre. From this place the married woman bound in chains was dragged by her mangled hair, not able to bid a sad farewell to the gods of her hearth. The captive was not allowed to imprint kisses on his doorpost, or turn his eyes once more to the places he would never see again. The wife walked barefoot through her husband's blood, and the charming sister stepped over the fallen brother. The child, torn from its mother's embrace, still hung on her lips, and there was no one to accord them a flood of mourning tears. It was not enough that a harsh fate deprived her of her child's life; the mother, all breath gone, had also lost her son's affectionate weeping.

But I, a barbarian woman, cannot weep enough, even though in all my wretchedness I were to swim in a lake of tears. Each person had an individual lament. I alone pour forth laments for all, since the public grief is a private grief for me. Fortune took care of those men whom the enemy forces cut down. But I endure as a sole survivor in order to mourn them all. I am forced to weep not only for dear ones slain; I weep as well for those whom kindly life has preserved. Often I press my eyes shut, my face wet with tears. My sighs lie quelled, but my cares are not silent!

Eagerly I look to see whether a breeze will carry some greeting. Yet not a single shadow from among all my kinsmen comes to me. Unfriendly fate has torn from my embrace the one whose look used to console me with tender love.

Since you are so far from me, doesn't my grief torment you? Has bitter misfortune taken away sweet affection? At least remember, Hamalafred, how from your earliest years of youth I used to be your Radegund, and how much you loved me when you were a sweet baby and the son of my father's brother, beloved cousin. You alone were for me what my dead father, what my mother, what my sister or brother could be thought to be.

Grasped by your loving hands, ah, and hanging on your sweet lips when I was a little girl, I used to be caressed by your gentle words. There was scarcely an interval of time when an hour would not bring you back; now ages fly by and I receive no words from you. I used to churn my savage griefs within a beating breast, as if you, my cousin, could be summoned back at any time, from any place. If your father, or your mother, or some cares of the realm detained you, then — even when you hastened back — you already seemed to me to be too slow! Fate was a warning sign that I should soon be deprived of you, my dear. Cruel love does not know how to wait a long time. I used to be tormented with anxiety if one and the same house did not shelter us: if you were going out of doors, I would believe that you had gone far, far away.

Now the East hides you too in the shadows, as the West hides me. The waves of the Ocean keep me here as the Red Sea detains you. The whole globe is thrown between the two of us who love each other. A world separates those whom no lands had parted before. All that earth holds forces loving ones asunder. If earth possessed more regions, your journey from me would be even more distant!

Be more fortunate, however, there where the good wishes

of your family are keeping you, more fortunate than the land of Thuringia allowed you to be!

Here, on the contrary, I am tormented, burdened by strong griefs. Why are you unwilling to send me any sign of yourself? If only a letter would paint the features of him I long for but do not see! Or if only a picture would bring me the man whom faraway places detain! You restore your forebears to life by your own excellence, you revive your kinsmen by your good name. It is as if the rose color of your father's beauty plays in your own cheek. Be assured, cousin, if you would send a message you would not be altogether absent from me. The speaking pages you sent would act the part of a brother to me.

All people have a share of good things; I have only the solace of weeping. Oh, the outrage, that the more I love the less I receive! If other people, bound by the law of affection, pursue their servants, why, I ask, am I passed over by those to whom I am joined by the blood of kinship?

Often, in order to recover a household slave, a master will force a passage through the Alps congealed with ice and snow. He bursts into a gloomy cave hewed out of the rocks; no frost or snow hinders him in his burning desire. A lover, he runs barefoot, needing no guide; he seizes his prey despite the enemy's opposition. He braves hostile weapons and his own wounds in order to capture what he desires — nor does his love spare itself!

But I, in suspense at every moment on your account, enjoy scarcely a moment of time with a free and tranquil mind. If a breeze rustles, I want to know the places that detain you. If clouds are hovering, I seek your whereabouts. Do the warlike trumpets of Persia or Byzantium claim you? Are you a ruler of rich Alexandria? Do you live in the neighborhood of the citadel of Jerusalem, where Christ was born of his virgin mother? Not a single letter with your writing discloses this, and ah — my sorrow grows heavier and takes on greater force. Therefore, if neither lands nor seas will send me a message from you, at least let a bird of good omen bring me news!

If the monastery's sacred cloister did not hold me, I would come unannounced to wherever you are dwelling. Swiftly, over the wave-smashing tempests, I would set sail and would navigate happily through seas driven by wintry winds. Hanging above the waves, and stronger than the driven waves, I would control them. What the sailor fears would not terrify her who loves you. If the waves should break up my vessel with angry storms, I would seek you out, carried over the sea by an oarsman on a plank. And if by some mischance I were prevented from grasping the wood, I would come to you weary, swimming with my hands. When I should see you again, I would deny all the dangers of the voyage. You, sweet cousin, would soon ease the woes of my shipwreck. Or, if my final fate should rob me of my querulous life, at least your hands would raise my sandy burial mound. I would pass before your sweet eyes as a sightless corpse. And you, at least, would be moved to perform my funeral rites — you who begrudge the living woman your tears! You who refuse words now would grant me a song of funeral lament!

Why, cousin, do I avoid mentioning my brother, and why do I put off my weeping? Why do you keep silent about his death — O the deep sorrow! — how guiltless he fell by vile treacheries, and how, having misplaced his trust, he was snatched from the earth? Unhappy me, I begin my weeping afresh when I remember his death, and suffer again while I speak of these grievous things:

He hastens away, eager to see your face, but his love is not fulfilled as long as my love stands in his way. To avoid inflicting harsh wounds on me, he stabs himself! Because he feared hurting me, he now becomes the reason for my grief. A tender, downy-bearded youth, he is cut down. I, his sister, being absent, did not see his terrible death. Not only did I lose him, but I did not close his dear eyes, nor did I throw myself upon him, nor did I speak words of farewell. I did not warm his cold breast with my scalding tears, nor did I receive kisses from his dear dying lips. I did not cling tearfully to his neck in a wretched embrace, or gasping, cherish his unhappy body to my breast. Life was denied him — why could not his dying breath as a brother be caught from his lips and be given to his sister? The little gifts I fashioned for him while he was alive, I would have sent as an offering for his bier. Is it not at least permitted that my love should deck his dead body? Wicked me — believe me, I am answerable, brother, for your safety. All I was to him was the cause of his death, and I did not provide him a sepulchre!

I, who left my homeland once, have twice been captured: when my brother lay felled, I suffered the enemy again. This sorrow has returned so that I may weep for father and mother, uncle and kindred at their tomb. After my brother's death there is no day free of tears; he has taken my joy with him to the dwelling of the shades.

Was it for this that my sweet kinsmen — wretched woman that I am — achieved the highest honors, for this their royal blood and birth descended in an unbroken line? I wish that my lips did not need to describe the evils I myself have suffered, or that, troubled as I am, I did not need to be consoled by you. At least, fair cousin, I ask that your letter may hasten now, so that your kind utterance may soothe my heavy grief.

As for your sisters, I am similarly concerned, for I cherish them with the heartfelt love of a blood relation. I am not permitted to embrace their persons, those kinswomen I love, nor even as a sister eagerly kiss each of their eyes. If, as I hope, they are yet alive, I ask that you give them my greetings and that you bear back kisses in answer to my yearning. I beg that you remember me to the kings of the Franks, who cherish me with the affection due a mother.

Enjoy life-giving breezes for many long years, and may my own safety flourish through your good office. Christ grant my prayers: let this page reach loving ones, and may a letter painted with sweet messages come to me in return, so that this woman — whom lingering hopes have long tormented — may be refreshed by a swift rush of attendant prayers.

2. Letter to Artachis

My homeland was ravaged by fire, and my family's high houses fell in the destruction that the land of Thuringia suffered by the enemy sword. If after this I should speak — a wretched woman driven by the war's unlucky strife — what sorrows shall I, a captive woman, be drawn to first? What is left for me to mourn? Is it this nation crushed by death? Or my sweet family, ruined by diverse misfortunes?

My father was cut down first, and my uncle followed: both their deaths struck me a grievous blow. One honored brother remained, but a heinous destiny causes the sandy earth to heap heavily on his tomb — and on me. All of them are dead. Ah, the tearing inward pain of her who mourns!

You, Hamalafred, were the only one left — and now you lie lifeless! Do I, Radegund, ask for this after so long a time? Has your letter come to me — unhappy woman — to say this? Have I long awaited such a gift from one who loves me? Do you send me these reinforcements as your soldierly service? Do you send me these silken skeins[4] as my daily spinning portion, so that I as a sister may be consoled as I spin? Is this the way your care comforts my sorrow? Should your first and last message bring such things? Have we not hastened with our gushing tears, wishing for something different?

This galling sweetness should not have been offered to reward my hopes. Full of anguish I have racked my heart with violent feeling. Is so great a fever of spirit to be cooled by these tears? I was not entitled to see him alive, nor to be present at his tomb. Now I bear both these losses in addition to your funeral rites.

Dear foster-child Artachis, why do I mention these things, adding your own weeping to mine? I ought instead to have offered a kinswoman's solace, but grief for the dead forces me to say bitter words. He was close to me — not bound by distant ties, but as a cousin, child of my father's brother. My father was Berthar, his was Hermenefred: we were the children of brothers, and now we are worlds apart.

You, at least, dear nephew Artachis, take the place of that gentle cousin, and be mine in love as he once was. I beg you — ask me to send messages often from my monastery. Let that house continue to be your champion with God, so that this unceasing care may render you — together with your

---

[4]Radegund's *serica vellera,* skeins of Chinese silk, create a charming double image. They hint at the stuff spun by the lovesick woman who sings at her spinning; hers becomes the lyrical voice of the "chanson de toile." But for Radegund — since the convent's rule forbade weaving and needlework — the skeins refer more likely to the silk paper (or paper with a silky surface) of the letter she receives. Papyrus from Egypt, waxed wooden tablets, and the recently introduced vellum were the more usual writing materials in Radegund's day; paper of Chinese silk probably works poetically here to suggest the distant East where Artachis lives.

dear mother — worthy rewards upon a starry throne. Now may the Lord grant you, blessed ones, abundant safety for the present, and glory in the world to come.

Caesaria of Arles

Eager to have a rule of monastic living for her women, since she was unable to count on guidance from the unfriendly Maroveus, Bishop of Poitiers, Radegund turned for help to the abbess Caesaria of the monastery of St. Jean in Arles. This was the younger Caesaria, the older having been sister to the Bishop Caesarius who had composed the Rule for her house, the first female monastery in Gaul. Its church had been dedicated on August 26, 513. After 567, the year the Cross came to Poitiers, Radegund procured a copy of the Rule.

Caesarius's Rule for Women was the first of its kind. It contained 41 articles, a recapitulation in 19 articles, and a prologue. The nuns were to be completely enclosed. Male visitors were forbidden, except for the clergy. Meals with visitors were also not allowed, nor were the receiving of clothing from outsiders or the exchanges of gifts and letters. Only the sick could eat meat. The women slept in dormitories, although Radegund was privileged to have her own cell. Clothing had to be plain in color, or else of milk-white woolen, spun and woven on the premises. The Rule tolerated neither black nor bright colors. There was to be no silver or ornamentation. Tapestries and lavish bed coverings, pictures, decorations, and individual armoires were likewise proscribed.

Housekeeping chores were done in common, with exemptions from kitchen and laundry duty allowed to the abbess — although as Fortunatus lovingly observed, Radegund chose to scrub pots and vegetables as a special mortification. There were offices for particular tasks: the *praeposita,* or deputy abbess, the *formaria* in charge of novices, the cellarer, gatekeeper, and sicknurse. The women were not to embroider or make elaborate woven coverlets; the only needlework allowed were embroidered handkerchiefs and towels which the abbess ordered.

The important work was literary. The women had to be able to read and write. They read or listened to the divine service; they copied manuscripts; they devoted two hours each day to books.

Caesaria's letter to Radegund and Richild speaks out with welcoming warmth, while maintaining a rather uncompromising tone about conventual behavior. These are new sisters: they can benefit from her affectionate harangue. She has a realistic awareness of the necessary adjustments ladies of rank will have to make to the enclosed and disciplined life. She knows about the wealth Radegund has at her disposal, and even anticipates the presence of poor or disinherited women among the convent's number. She mentions items in the Rule that Radegund would receive, stressing the business of reading and writing. Her array of biblical allusions gives solid backing to this aspect of the Rule, and demonstrates the priority Caesaria herself gave to study. While the Rule was strict about diet, Caesaria advises Radegund against fasting to extremes, lest her health suffer.

On the matter of male visitors Caesaria speaks severely — has she heard rumors of the friendship between Fortunatus and Radegund? She exhorts the women to avoid male protectors, and to conduct themselves like men, as she holds up masculine examples of strength and worth: men listen to their rulers' commands; men fight in battle to save their bodies from injury. She sees the women as combatants; let them emulate men, but in the spiritual sense.

The numbering of the letter's scriptural verses refers to the Douai-Rheims Bible, from the Vulgate of St. Jerome.

3. Caesaria to Radegund and Richild

To the sainted ladies Radegund and Richild, from the humble Caesaria:

I was filled with spiritual joy beyond measure when your letter arrived, for I recognized that you have chosen to hold to the decision by which you are preparing — with God's grace — for life everlasting. You do this so that you may gain eternal riches and exultation with the saints — which are without end. May "our lord God, who raised up those who were cast down, released those who were in chains, and gave

sight to the blind" (Psalm 145.7,8) himself guide you along
the right path. May he himself teach you how to do his will,
and may he grant you to walk in his ways, guard his
teachings, and meditate on his law. Just as the Psalmist has
said: "And he will meditate on his law both day and night"
(Psalm 1.2). And again, "The teaching of the Lord il-
luminating the souls of those without blame" (Psalm 18.9,8).

You must pay attention when divine lessons are read, as
carefully as men of the world give heed when royal
commands are read. Let the whole mind, thought, and
contemplation dwell on the Lord's precepts. Fear them with
care. "Cursed be they who avoid your commands" (Psalm
118.21). And whoever does not keep one or the least one of
God's commandments "shall be called the least in the
kingdom of heaven" (Matthew 5.19). Carry this out: "The
meditation of my heart is always in your sight. In my heart
I have hidden your words so that I may not sin against you"
(Psalm 18.15; 118.11).

And because God has deigned to choose you, ladies most
beloved to me, in hereditary succession to him, render thanks
to him, bless him in every season. Abstain from all vice, from
all sin, because "who sins is a slave to sin" (John 8.34). Love
and fear the Lord, because "the eyes of the Lord are on those
who fear him, and his ears turn to their prayers" (Psalm
32.18). Let a pure heart be in you, a pacific heart. Be mild
and humble, patient and obedient. Heed the Lord when he
says: Upon whom shall I rest if not on the humble and the
peaceful? "He has put down the mighty from their seat and
exalted the humble" (Luke 1.52). Granted that you desire to
be holy and good and praiseworthy, living under the Rule,
but there is no teaching greater or better or more precious
or more splendid than the reading of the Evangelists.
Observe this, hold to this: what our lord and master Christ
has taught us in his words and fulfills by his examples — he
who has performed so many miracles in the world that they
may not be counted, and endured so many evils from his
tormentors with a patience that can scarcely be believed. It
is patience that commends us to God.

Hear the Apostle: "If any wish to live a godly life in Christ,
let them patiently endure persecution" (II Timothy 3.12).
Just as God is pleased at your endeavor in taking vows, so

does the devil grieve over it. He has thousands and thousands
of devices for doing harm, and "he desires to take God's food
for himself" (Psalm 103.21). For this reason, pray ceaselessly
that God may act against him. "Act manfully and let your
heart be comforted" (Psalm 30.25). Heed the Scripture that
says, "My son, go to the service of God, stand in
righteousness and awe, and strengthen your soul against
temptation" (Sirach 2.1).

If you had been men, you would be going out, strongly and
manfully, to fight your enemies so that your body might not
be injured. Fight the devil just as strongly and manfully, so
that he cannot slay your souls with his counsels and
exceedingly evil stratagems. Cry continually to God, "God,
incline to my aid! Be my help! Do not abandon me and I will
be safe!"

When you recite the Psalms, be attentive and diligent to
what it says there and what it teaches you. Sing the Psalms
wisely, just as the Lord remains on the cross for you. Since
he stayed on the cross, you too stay — as if crucified — with
the work of God! Do not do otherwise! Do not dare to speak
or do anything! Be peacemakers in all things, because his
dwelling-place [the Church] has been built in peace. "Blessed
are the peacemakers, since they shall be called the children
of God" (Matthew 5.9). "Let not the sun go down on your
wrath" (Ephesians 4.26). "Great peace have they who love
thy name, Lord, and it is not an offense to them" (Psalm
118.165). For the virginity of the flesh means nothing where
wrath of heart dwells. And elsewhere Scripture says: God
has commanded you to be peaceful and harmonious
"together in his house" (Psalm 67.7).

I greet you with the humility and love that I owe — more
than it can possibly be said — even though I am very
insignificant and undiscerning. I pray God that he may deign
to rule, protect, and preserve you, and that he who deigned
to give you your novitiate may also deign to bring it to
perfection. For it is not the one who begins, but the one "who
perseveres to the end that will be saved" (Matthew 24.13).
Just as our humility rejoices and delights in God,
concerning your undertaking, so God and his angels are
happy about your profession of vows and your achievement of

perfection. You have assets, I also know, since you have inherited resources in abundance.

Give as much as you can to the poor. "Store up treasures for yourself in heaven" (Matthew 6.20) so that this Scripture may be fulfilled in you: "He distributed, he gave to the poor. His righteousness endures forever" (Psalm 111.9). Just as it is written — as water quenches fire so do alms wipe out all sin (cf. Tobit 4.11). Let your hope be in God, because it is written, "Cursed be the man that trusts in man" (Jeremiah 17.5).

Let there be no woman from among those entering who does not study letters. Let them be bound to know all the Psalms by memory. And as I have already said, be zealous to fulfill in all things what you read in the Evangelists. I have sent a copy of the Rule which our lord and bishop Caesarius of holy and blessed memory has made for us. See well to yourselves how you safeguard it!

Let your sisterhood be firm under my authority, because if you live according to it you will take your place among the wise virgins, and the Lord will lead you into his kingdom. You will perceive that "neither has the eye seen nor the ear heard, nor has it entered into the heart of man what the Lord has prepared for those who love him" (I Corinthians 2.9) in the land of the living where the saints rejoice in glory. There you will say, rejoicing and exulting in the Lord: "For he that is mighty has done great things for us, and holy is his name" (Luke 1.49). And "he has raised up his people in exaltation and his chosen ones in happiness" (Psalm 104.43). May God, who reigns forever, see to it that your stainless women arrive there. Amen.

It has come to me that you are fasting to excess. Do all things reasonably if you care for me and are at all times able. For if — because of that excess — you begin to fall sick, afterwards those things will be necessary for you which God did not intend. You will require and need to consume dainty foods out of the proper season, and you will not be able to rule over those blessed women. Heed what the Lord says in the gospel: "Not that which enters the mouth defiles man" (Matthew 15.11). And the Apostle: "Let your service be reasonable" (Romans 12.1). Do everything, lady, in such a way — according to what you possess in the Rule you requested — that God may be blessed and praised by your good profession of vows. May you be a model for the faithful. "For whosoever shall do and teach, the same shall be called great in the kingdom of heaven" (Matthew 5.19).

Praise, therefore, and rejoice in the Lord, revered sisters in Christ, and give thanks continually that he has deigned to call you from this world's darkened way of life to the gate of tranquility and religious rule. Be continually mindful of where you have been and to what reward you have come. Faithfully you have given up the world's darkness, and you have undertaken blissfully to see the light of Christ. You have disdained the firebrand of lust, and have attained to the cool refreshment of chastity. And because life's combat to the death is not wanting in you, be as careful about the future as you have been safeguarded from the past; for indeed all manner of sin and crime quickly returns to us if they are not fought against each day. Heed the apostle Peter when he says, "Be sober and watchful because your adversary the devil circles around like a roaring lion seeking whom he may devour" (I Peter 5.8).

As long as we are living in this body let us fight against the devil, day and night, with Christ the Lord as our assistant and commander. There are some undiscerning women who suppose that it is enough for them to change their clothing. For indeed to put aside worldly dress and to assume religious garb — we can do this in the moment of an hour. We must truly work continually to uphold the practices of good persons, as long as we live, with Christ as our help. Let every soul that desires to preserve the religious Rule so strive to avoid gluttony, sexual desire, and drunkenness, that she cannot be weakened by excessive abstinence or provoked to luxury by an abundance of delicacies.

Continually read or listen to the divine lessons, because these are the ornaments of the soul. Out of them, hang precious pearls from your ears; out of them derive your rings and bracelets. As long as you constantly perform good works you will be adorned with these jewels. Let the woman who truly longs to safeguard the religious Rule in a stainless heart — so that she may walk unstained in God's sight — not go out in public, or else, let it be made difficult.

By all means, use male protection as infrequently as you can if you wish to guard your chastity. Nor let it be said by anyone, "My own conscience is good enough for me. Let anyone say what they like about me!" That kind of defense is wretched and fully odious to God. Look to it — you are secure in your own scruples; can you see into the scruples of the person you are speaking to? Know this most certainly — that a woman who doesn't avoid the protection of men will destroy either herself or another. Against the other vices it is useful for us to struggle employing every virtue; but you will not be able to combat lust unless you flee from living communally with men!

If you are of noble birth, be more humble in your religious life, rather than delighting in your worldly rank. "If anyone will leave everything and follow me, he shall receive an hundred-fold and life everlasting" (Matthew 19.29). If any poor woman embraces holy living, let her give thanks to God, who will grant salvation to the poor and who will free those women from the world's shackles. "The rich will lack life's necessities and will suffer hunger, while those who seek God shall not want for all good things" (Psalm 33.11). Love one another if you wish God to dwell in your hearts, for it is written, "Whoever hates a brother or a sister is in darkness, and walks in darkness and doesn't know where he goes because the shadows blind his eyes" (I John 2.11).

There are perhaps women who have left their inherited fortunes to their families and are from that point forth disinherited. Let them heed the Lord when he said, "Sell all you own and give alms, for behold, all the world will be yours" (Luke 12.33). "He has distributed, he has given to the poor, and his righteousness endures forever" (Psalm 111.9).

Run the race faithfully, so that you may blissfully arrive and stand delighting and exulting in the sight of the Lord our God, who has deigned to choose you among the sheep of his flock; and in his kingdom just as in his earthly ministry, he will be ready to bestow thrones in heaven — he who reigns forever. Amen.

Baudonivia of Poitiers

Some twenty years after Radegund's death, a nun in her community named Baudonivia was asked by her abbess Dedimia to write a life of the saint. This was meant to supplement the more famous one of Venantius Fortunatus. Baudonivia probably wrote between 605 and 610, since Queen Brunhild (d. 614) was said to be still on the throne. Baudonivia protests her ineptitude for the task in an ornate style that reflects the monastery's taste for classical letters and rhetorical study. She says she knew Radegund as a child at Sainte-Croix, but also must rely on the accounts of people who remembered her well.

Baudonivia borrows some terms from Fortunatus's *Life of St. Hilary* and other hagiographical sources. In her account of how Radegund procured the Holy Cross, Baudonivia includes details that are missing from Gregory of Tours and differs from him in certain respects. The manuscript of Baudonivia's *Life of St. Radegund* was kept at Sainte-Croix monastery until the seventeenth century, when the Jesuits acquired it. While the original was lost, several manuscript copies exist. The illuminations are from the eleventh century. Selected chapters from Baudonivia's biography of Radegund are translated here.

4. The Life of St. Radegund

To the holy ladies adorned with the grace of worthiness, to the abbess Dedimia, and all the glorious congregation of the Lady Radegund, from Baudonivia, the most humble of all.

This task you have assigned me of writing the life of the Lady St. Radegund is like attempting to touch heaven with a fingertip. It is our duty to say the best possible things of her. But it is a task that ought to be given to those who have within them a fount of eloquence. For when such a thing is enjoined upon those eloquent persons, they are able to expound with fluency and refreshing song. On the contrary, those limited in their ideas and lacking the articulate flow can neither provide refreshment for others nor relieve their own dryness. Such persons would never attempt to write of their own accord, and if asked to write are exceedingly fearful.

I recognize myself to be this kind of person, humble of spirit and possessing few expressive ideas. It is as important for the unlearned to keep silent as it is for the learned to speak out. Those who are well taught can discourse eloquently upon a modest theme, whereas those lacking in education cannot produce even a modest discourse upon a great theme. For this reason, there are some who eagerly seek out an undertaking, while others shun and fear it.

Although I myself am the most humble of all the humble, yet it was she, the Lady Radegund, who reared me from childhood as her own menial household attendant and servant. And so I am able to discourse briefly, not fully, but at least incorporating some part of the immeasurable benefits I received from her illustrious example. To this end, as long as I continue publicly to commend her glorious life to the ears of her flock, I am ready to obey your most benevolent will, with an eloquence that is as devoted as it is unworthy. Full of devotion, though lacking in erudition, I beg you for your prayers.

Let us not repeat those things which the apostolic man, the bishop Fortunatus, wrote in his Life of the blessed lady, but those things which he in his comprehensiveness passed over. He enunciated it just so in his book when he said, "Let brevity suffice in the matter of the saint's virtues. Neither let an overly long account prove tedious, nor let the tale be too briefly told. Rather let the sense of the whole emerge from a few details."

Therefore, I have been inspired by the same divine Power that the blessed Radegund was so zealous to placate in this world, and with whom may she reign in the next. With simple rather than polished words do we strive to tackle the deeds she performed, and to embrace in brief space the great part of her miracles.

The Prologue ends.

Chapter 1. The family and high rank of Radegund and King Clothar

The first book of the life of the blessed Radegund contains an account of her royal origin and rank. There is no one who is unaware of what her conduct was when she was converted by her king and earthly consort, the lofty King Clothar. A noble sprig, she sprang from a royal race; what she inherited from her lineage she further ornamented with her faith. The noble queen, married to an earthly prince, was herself more heavenly than earthly. In that same short time of her marriage, while a bride and in the guise of a wife, she conducted herself so as to serve Christ with greater devotion. It grew clear among the laity that she acted as if she desired them to imitate her example. For while she was living in the world, even before her conversion, she was being formed by the religion of her soul as a model of the religious life. She was in no way shackled with the clogs of this world, but had girded herself with the obedience of a servant of God. She was diligent in the redemption of captives, lavish in spending for the needy, and whatever she gave to the poor she believed was for her own benefit.

Chapter 2. The temple built by the Franks

Although Radegund had been living until now with the king in a worldly manner, her mind was intent on Christ. I speak with God as my witness, for it is to God that the heart confesses even though the mouth is silent. From him the heart hides nothing even though the tongue does not speak. We tell what we have heard, and give an eye-witness account of what we have seen.

When Radegund was invited to dine with the matron Ausfrida, she set out on the journey accompanied by a solemn procession of retainers. Traveling the length and breadth of the countryside, she came upon a place between a stretch of country and a path approaching a temple which the Franks had built. The temple was nearly a milestone's distance from the blessed queen's route. When she heard that the Franks had constructed a temple there, she ordered it to be burned down by her servants, for she judged it wicked to scorn the heavenly God and to venerate the devil's devices.

When the Franks heard about this, they rushed to the place in a mob, attempting to defend the temple with swords and cudgels, and bellowing like devils. The holy queen remained persistent and unmoved, for she bore Christ in her heart. She did not bestir her horse but sat mounted all the while until the temple had been burned to the ground. As she prayed, the people made peace among themselves. Once this was over, all of them marveled at the queen's strength and self-possession, and they blessed God.

Chapter 3. The vision she saw of a ship in the form of a man

Later, through the working of divine influence, she left the earthly king, since her vows demanded it while she was living on the country estate at Saix which the king had given her. In the first year of her conversion, she had a vision of a ship in the form of a man, with men seated on all his limbs. She herself was seated on his knee. The man said to her, "Now you are sitting on my knee, but in time you shall have your place to sit in my heart." The grace she was to enjoy was shown her.

She reported this vision quite secretly to her faithful followers, calling them as witnesses, since no one would know these things unless they were present. How discreet she was in conversation, how pious in every deed! In prosperity, in adversity, in joy, in sorrow, she was always even-tempered. Neither did she lose heart in adversity, nor grow proud in prosperity.

Chapter 4. How the king wanted to have her back again; lord John the recluse

While she was living at that same country estate, word came that the king wanted her back. He was grieving over the loss he suffered as a result of having permitted such a queen to leave his side. Unless he could get her back he scarcely wanted to go on living. When the blessed lady heard this, she was so extremely terrified that she gave herself over to even greater mortifications. She fitted a garment of harsh goat's hair to her tender body, she made it known that she would undergo additional torments of fasting, and she lay awake in nocturnal vigils. She threw herself wholly into her prayers. She scorned the throne of the country, she vanquished the blandishments of her spouse, she shut out the love of the world, and chose to make an exile of herself lest she wander away from Christ. With her she still had her decorated felt cloak encrusted with gold and fashioned with gems and pearls. It was worth a thousand coins of gold. She ordered a nun who was close to her, named Fridovigia, along with several of her faithful followers, to send it to a reverend man, John, who was a recluse in Chinon castle. She asked him to pray for her so that she would not have to return to the world again, and asked him to send her a coarse garment of goat hair so that she might sully her body with it. He sent her the rough cloth, from which she made both undergarments and outergarments for herself. She also asked him to keep her informed if there were any cause for fear. For if the king insisted on having her back, she would rather end her life than have to return to be joined again to this earthly king, she who had already wedded the king of heaven. This man of God then spent the night in wakefulness and prayers, inspired as he was by the heavenly power. The next day he notified her that although this might be the king's will it was not to be permitted by God. The king would be punished by God before he could take her back in marriage.

Chapter 5. How the sainted queen built a monastery in the city of Poitiers by the order of the king Clothar; spurning the world, she entered joyfully

After this pronouncement, the same Lady Radegund, her mind intent upon Christ, and inspired and aided by God, built herself a monastery at Poitiers by the order of the most high king Clothar. The apostolic man, Bishop Pientius, and the lord Astrapius quickly ordered this building to be placed under her authority. The holy queen joyfully entered this monastery, casting off the world's false allurements. There she gathered the ornaments of perfection and joined a great congregation of young girls to Christ, the immortal Bridegroom. Agnes was elected abbess, and it was agreed that Radegund would give her all of her personal goods, and she handed over her own abdicated authority. By her own jurisdiction she retained nothing for herself so that she might run unshackled, a light-armed footsoldier, in the footsteps of Christ. She enhanced herself in heaven to the great degree that she disburdened herself in the world. Soon her holy profession of vows began to burn with the practice of

humility, the fruitfulness of charity, the light of chastity, and
the luxuriance of fasting. So completely did she surrender
herself to the love of the heavenly Bridegroom that by
embracing God in her pure heart she was able to feel Christ
dwelling within her.

*Chapter 6. How the above-mentioned king went to Tours so
that he might reach Poitiers and get back his queen*

But that malicious enemy of human happiness, whose will
she loathed doing as long as she was in the world, did not
cease to pursue her. She learned from messengers about the
very thing she feared — namely, the arrival of the most high
king together with his son, the eminent Sigibert of Tours.[5] The
king was coming to Poitiers, supposedly for pious reasons,
but really so that he could take back his queen.

*Chapter 7. How the Lady Radegund sent a letter to the Bishop
lord Germanus, and how the king sent the bishop to St.
Radegund to ask her forgiveness; how he did this*

When she realized this, the blessed Lady Radegund had
a solemn letter composed in the presence of a sacred witness,
and sent it to the apostolic man Germanus[6], Bishop of the city
of Paris, who was with the king at the time. She had the letter
sent secretly by her agent Proculus, with a gift and an official
seal. When this man, who was filled with God, read it, he
threw himself weeping at the king's feet before the tomb of
St. Martin, in the presence of a sacred witness. He begged
the king to abide by the message of the letter and not to go to

---

[5]Clothar's youngest son Sigibert was King of Austrasia, the
ancient Frankish lands on both sides of the Rhine. Brunhild was his
queen. Radegund enjoyed a cordial relationship with Sigibert, who
helped her to bring the true Cross to Poitiers.

[6]Germanus became Bishop of Paris in about 556. He was buried
in the church of the monastery he founded there; the church later
became known as St.-Germain-des-Près.

the city of Poitiers. In sorrow, the king repented fully, understanding that this was the blessed queen's petition. He reconsidered the advice of his evil counselors. He judged himself unworthy, realizing that for a long time he had not deserved such a queen.

On the threshold of St. Martin's he prostrated himself at the feet of the apostolic man Germanus, and asked him to seek Queen Radegund's mercy on his behalf. He begged that she might forgive him for having sinned against her because of his evil counselors. As a result, divine vengeance punished those who were present — in the same way that Arrius, when he disputed the Catholic faith, sent his household members off to their deaths. So it was with those who had acted against the queen. Then the king, fearing God's judgment — since the queen had been more obedient to God's will than to the king's when she had lived with him — asked Germanus to go quickly to her.

So the apostolic man, on arriving in Poitiers, went to the monastery. In the oratory dedicated to the name of the Lady Mary, he threw himself at the feet of the holy queen, begging her mercy on the king's behalf. Filled with joy that she had been snatched from the jaws of the world, she generously forgave him and prepared herself for the service of God. Wherever she went she was now unencumbered and free to follow Christ, whom she loved, and she hastened after him with a devout spirit. Deeply intent upon such things, therefore, she kept additional vigils and made herself the jailer of her own body so as to keep awake at night. And although she was merciful to others, she made herself her own judge; devoted to others, she was harsh in her own abstemiousness; generous to all, she was stingy with herself. For her it was not enough to be drenched in fasting unless she could conquer her own body.

Chapter 12. Her servant, Vinoperga, who dared to sit on her throne

In addition to her miracles in praise of Christ, she performed others that frightened her followers. Vinoperga was one of her servants who — out of rash boldness — presumed to sit on the blessed queen's cushioned chair after

she had died. When she did this, the girl was struck a blow
by God's judgment and burned so fiercely that everyone saw
smoke pouring from her body and rising upward.

The girl cried out in the presence of all the people,
confessing that she had sinned. She was on fire because she
had sat in the blessed queen's chair. For three days and three
nights together she suffered the heat, and screaming aloud,
she cried, "Lady Radegund, I have sinned. I have done
wrong. Please cool my limbs that are burnt with harsh
torment. Be generously merciful; you who are renowned for
your good works, you who are compassionate to all, be
compassionate to me!"

Seeing her in such anguish, all the people prayed for her
just as if Radegund were present, saying that whenever she
was called on in good faith she was there. "Benevolent lady,
spare her so that she may not be abandoned to such miserable
torment!" The most blessed lady yielded to the prayers of
all of them, and curbed the raging flame. She sent the girl
home uninjured. And so the girl's punishment made everyone
wary and respectful.

*Chapter 14. The relic of the lord Mammes, which Lady
Radegund desired*

From the time she entered the monastery, the East bore
witness, and the North, South, and West proclaimed how
great a number of holy relics she collected with the most
faithful prayers. From every quarter she sought out those
precious jewels which are hoarded in heaven and which
Paradise possesses, and this devout woman succeeded in
obtaining them for herself by means of gifts and prayers.
Through these means, in continual meditation, she gave
herself over to the chanting of Psalms and hymns.

Word came to her at length about the lord Mammes,[7] the

---

[7]Both St. Basil and St. Gregory of Nazianzus wrote about this
eastern saint, a shepherd youth who died under Aurelian in 274, but
whose remains were buried at Caesarea. Perhaps some relics were
translated to Jerusalem.

martyr whose sainted limbs reposed at Jerusalem. When she heard about this, she drank the news in avidly and thirstily. Like a person afflicted with hydropsy, who — however much she drinks from a fountain — grows increasingly thirsty, Radegund burned with the need to be drenched with God's dew. She sent the venerable priest Reovalis,[8] who was then still a layman and who to this day survives her in body, to the patriarch of Jerusalem to beg for a relic of St. Mammes. The man of God benevolently undertook to fulfill this request. He made Radegund's prayers known to his people in order to discover God's will.

On the third day, after he had celebrated the mass, he went with all the people to the blessed martyr's tomb. In a loud voice full of solemnity he publicly declared in this manner, saying, "I beg you, confessor and martyr of Christ, if the blessed Radegund is a true handmaid of Christ, let your power be revealed among the people. Allow her faithful soul to receive some relic of yours that she desires." When the prayer was ended and all the people responded "Amen," he went into the holy sepulchre, continually announcing the blessed lady's faith. He touched the saint's members to ascertain which of these the most blessed saint would authorize to be granted to fulfill the Lady Radegund's request. He touched each finger of the right hand; when he came to the little finger, it detached itself at the pleasant touch of his hand so that it might satisfy the blessed queen's desire to fulfill her wish. The apostolic man sent the finger to the blessed Radegund with due ceremony. From Jerusalem to Poitiers the praise of God resounded continually in her honor.

Can you imagine with what fervent spirit, with what faithful devotion Radegund, awaiting the prize of such a relic, gave herself over to fasting? But while the blessed queen was

---

[8]Reovalis was a physician of Poitiers who had also studied medicine in Constantinople. Later he became a priest. His name comes up again in Gregory of Tours (*History of the Franks,* X, 15) because he had removed the testicles of a boy who was Radegund's servant, a medical procedure he learned in Constantinople.

rejoicing with complete enthusiasm at receiving this
heavenly gift, she — together with her entire community —
busied herself for a whole week in keeping vigils with the
singing of Psalms, and in fasting and blessing God that she
had deserved to receive such a gift. So God does not refuse
his faithful who ask for a thing.

Often Radegund would gently say, as if it were an oblique
manner of speaking that no one would understand: "Whoever
has the care of souls must greatly fear the praise of all." But
despite this, however much she wished to avoid it, the
Bestower of virtue was increasingly bent on revealing to
everyone that she was faithful to him. And so, whenever there
was a sick person, afflicted with any illness whatever, that
person could call upon her and be restored to health.

*Chapter 16. How she sent to the Emperor for a relic of the
wood of the Holy Cross*

Now that she had gathered together relics of the saints,
she would have wished for God himself to come down from
his throne of majesty to dwell among us, if only that were
possible. Even though she was unable to see him with her
bodily eye, her spiritual understanding eagerly contemplated
him with zealous prayers. But the Lord "will not deny good
things to those who walk in innocence" (Psalm 83.13) and
seek him out with their whole heart, soul, and mind. Such
were the achievements of this sainted woman that divine
benevolence showed itself favorable to her, and sent her an
inspiration. Both day and night the thought reposed in her
heart that she might do as the blessed Helen had done.[9]

Helen, inspired with wisdom, full of the fear of God, and
renowned for her good works, had made a diligent search for
the beneficent wood on which the world's Treasure had been
suspended and weighed in order to save us from the devil's

---

[9]Although St. Helen (3rd century), the mother of the emperor
Constantine, built churches at Jerusalem and Bethlehem, the legend
that she secured the true Cross circulated only after her time.
Neither Eusebius nor Egeria, contemporaries of hers, mention it.

might. When the Cross arrived and was raised up, Helen ascertained that it was the same divine Cross on which God had been stretched to death.[10] She clapped her two hands together and, falling to the ground on bended knee, she adored God saying, "In truth you are Christ, the son of God, who came into the world and redeemed your own captives whom you created!"

What Helen accomplished in the East, blessed Radegund brought about in Gaul. Since she wanted in no way to act without consultation as long as she was living in the world, she sent a letter to the most excellent lord King Sigibert, under whose sovereignty the country was ruled. She asked his permission, for the sake of the whole country's well-being and the stability of his realm, to try to obtain the wood of God's Cross from the Emperor Justin.[11] The king very graciously gave his approval to the holy queen's request.

Full of devotion, and kindled with ardent longing, Radegund did not send any gifts to the emperor, since she needed moneys to serve God's poor. Instead she occupied herself with prayer in the company of the saints, whose relics she called on continually, and she dispatched messengers to the emperor. She obtained what she prayed for — the holy wood of God's Cross, ornamented with gold and jewels,[12] in addition to the many saints' relics that had been preserved in the East. Now they would reside together in one place, and she gloried very much in this.

---

[10]Doubt that the Cross might not be Christ's but one of the thieves' was dispelled when a sick woman was said to be healed by touching the wood.

[11]Justin II, Byzantine Emperor of Constantinople, with whom Sigibert was seeking an alliance at the time. Sigibert included Radegund's petition with his own negotiations.

[12]Justin had five fragments of the wood set in a cross-shaped plaque of blue enamel, decorated with a leafy scroll design. The plaque measured 57 centimeters in width and 60 centimeters in length.

In reply to the sainted woman's request the emperor also sent his ambassadors with an evangeliary encrusted with gold and gems. With the arrival in the city of Poitiers of the wood on which the world's salvation had hung, together with the company of the saints, the Bishop,[13] enemy of mankind, was working through his satellites, so that they rejected the world's Treasure. They were unwilling to receive it in the city, despite all the tribulations the blessed Radegund had undergone. Each one refused it for different reasons, as if joining ranks with the Jews. But it is not our place to discuss this. They would see — God knows his own people.

With blazing spirit and beating heart, Radegund sent a message to the most blessed king that the town was unwilling to receive its salvation. While her messengers were on their way back from the lord king, she entrusted for safekeeping the Cross of God and the relics of the saints to the male monastery she had founded at Tours. This was done amidst the singing of Psalms.

Because of jealousy, the sacred Cross suffered no less than God himself, who, for the sake of his faithful followers, is continually being called and recalled before rulers and judges. He has endured all kinds of contempt so that his creatures shall not perish.

How much torment Radegund imposed upon herself through fasts, vigils, and the copious shedding of tears! Her entire congregation wept and lamented throughout these days until God looked down on the abjectness of his handmaid and put it into the king's heart that he must bring judgment and justice to the populace. So the devout king dispatched his loyal man, the distinguished Count Justin, to the city of Tours. There the apostolic man of God, the Bishop lord Euphronius, was told to place the Cross of God and the saintly relics in Lady Radegund's monastery in high honor.

The blessed lady reveled joyously, and all the members of her house with her, once this advantageous gift from heaven had been bestowed upon her congregation. She

---

[13]Maroveus, Bishop of Poitiers, refused to be present and galloped off to his country estate, according to Gregory of Tours.

gathered them together to celebrate the service of God, for she sensed in her mind that after the transfer of this possession they might have too little cause for gladness.[14] Nevertheless, she exulted with the King of Heaven, from whom this heavenly gift had been permitted to descend, this noble nurturer, this beneficent guide that would never under any circumstances abandon her flock, the world's ransom from Christ's relic which she had sought from a faraway country for the honor of the house and the salvation of the people, and left to her monastery.

There, with the help of God's goodness and the power of heaven assisting, the eyes of the blind received light, the ears of the deaf were opened, the tongues of the mute regained their function, the lame walked, and demons were put to flight. What else is there to say? Each person, handicapped with whatever infirmity, came out of faith and regained health through the virtue of the Cross. Who can say how great a gift this sainted lady had brought to the city? Whoever lives by faith God blesses in his name. The most excellent lord king and the most serene lady Queen Brunhild, whom Radegund loved with deep affection, praised her monastery before divine witness.

Chapter 20. The year before her death she saw in a vision the place prepared for her

The year before she died she saw in a vision the place that was prepared for her. There came to her a very beautiful and richly dressed man who seemed youthful in age. As he addressed her he touched her sweetly and spoke caressing words to her, but she, zealous about her virtue, sought to repulse his blandishments. He said to her, "Why then are you inflamed with desire for me, and why do you seek me with tears, petition me with groans, beg me with lavish prayers? Why have you suffered so many torments for my sake — for me, who am always with you? You, precious jewel, you know

---

[14]A reference to the strife between Sigibert and his brothers and the resulting turmoil besetting the country.

that you are the foremost jewel in the diadem on my head.'' There is no doubt that he himself visited her, and that she surrendered herself to him with total devotion, even while she was still alive in body, and that he showed her the glory which she was to enjoy, but this vision she very secretly confided to two quite faithful followers, adjuring them not to reveal it to anyone as long as she was still alive.

Further Reading on Radegund and Baudonivia

Texts:
Venantius Fortunatus. *Monumenta Germaniae Historica: Auctorum Antiquissimorum,* Vol. 4, pt. 1. Berlin, 1881.
———. "Vita Sanctae Radegundis," Liber I. *Monumenta Germaniae Historica: Scriptores Rerum Merovingicarum,* Vol. 2, pp. 358-377. Hanover, 1888.
Baudonivia. "Vita Sanctae Radegundis," Liber II. *Monumenta Germaniae Historica: Scriptores Rerum Merovingicarum,* Vol. 2, pp. 377-395. Hanover, 1888.

René Aigrain. *Sainte Radegonde.* Rev. ed. Paris, 1952.
F. Brittain. *Saint Radegund.* Cambridge, 1928.
Martin Conway. "St. Radegund's Reliquary at Poitiers." *The Antiquaries Journal* 3 (January 1923), 1-12.
Etudes mérovingiennes: Actes des journées de Poitiers, 1-3 mai 1952. Paris, 1953.
Jo Ann McNamara. "A Legacy of Miracles: Hagiography and Nunneries in Merovingian Gaul." *Women of the Medieval World: Essays in Honor of John H. Mundy.* Julius Kirshner and Suzanne F. Wemple, eds. New York, 1985.

Further Reading on Caesaria

Text: *Patrologia Latina. Supplementum,* Vol. 4, cols. 1404-1408. Paris, 1967; and *Monumenta Germaniae Historica: Epistolae,* Vol. 3, pp. 450-453. Berlin, 1892.

M.C. McCarthy, tr. *The Rule for Nuns.* Washington, 1933.

4   A Learned Woman
Writes a Letter

Anonymous (Sixth Century)

Because a fragment of Baudonivia's *Prologue to the Life of Radegund* precedes this letter in the manuscript, the suggestion has been made that a nun of Radegund's convent could have written it. Affectionate friendship and the respect for erudition inspire the writer. Like Baudonivia she extravagantly protests her unworthiness. Her uses of Scripture are imaginative, in fact, wildly so, and she feels the need to explain them. Surprising metaphors abound. The throat is a candleholder whose wick can go dry; the speaker's lack of eloquent "oil" must refer to the plea of the Foolish Virgins to the Wise. Learning forms a headdress whose gold fringes flow, like words, on both sides of the face; learning is a brilliantly colored robe, or a spindle made by Jesus, the carpenter's son, for weaving history in bright wools. These figures of speech reflect feminine concerns, as do the writer's allusions to concubinage, wifehood, fertility, conception, pregnancy, childbirth, and maternity to express the life of the mind and spirit. Although the letter-writer is a religious woman addressing another pious woman of higher rank and learning, she takes the same delight in fanciful language as do the secular writers of this time, notably Eucheria, whose lyric follows in the next section.

Letter to a Friend

If you were not judging my silence as an offense to you — you who are of so lofty a lineage — I would have thought that the prophet's epigram applied to me when he declared,

57

"If you have something to say, speak at once; if not, let your hand cover your mouth" (Sirach 5.12). For what could I respond, where could I venture to find the words to utter, when you embrace the entire substance of all the writings of the Bible in your letter so that you have left me nothing to say![1]

Until now, the treasure chest of the Testament has remained hidden from me, that is, the bookbinding clasps of your heart, in which a library of all the books is gathered. It certainly deserves to be gilded both inside and outside by princely gold, because it is such a faithful guardian of the words which God's finger has written.

That spouse in the mystery of Christ who satisfied the thirsting servant of Abraham with the liquid in her water jar, which she lowered down from her shoulder, has merited the testimony of the prophets (Genesis 24).[2] But you, no less than she, deserve to be given honorary monuments and to be consecrated by the testimonials of witnesses. You have satisfied us — the servants of Abraham (because all who sin are his servants) — with the water jar of your heart. You have satisfied us, that is, from the treasure of an earthenware vessel.[3] I have surely drunk from this letter you have written, and have given water to my camels. That is, I have acknowledged all my vices, because I have discovered nothing of those good things that you judge to be within me. But it is perfectly clear that you have counterbalanced my unworthiness and ignorance by your good work. Whatever care your daily labor has heaped upon you, you have put this

---

[1]In a roundabout way, the author says, "If you weren't asking me to write, noble lady, I wouldn't dare, since I have nothing left to say after you have said it all so eloquently."

[2]Like many virtuous wives of the prophets in the Old Testament, Rebecca at the well prefigures the Church and so is a bride "in the mystery of Christ."

[3]The addressee is merely human, not a *figura ecclesiae* like Rebecca.

care totally in the service of vindicating me. I ought to be whatever you feel me to be, because all things are possible for the believer. But since it does not come close to me to desire it, it is impossible for me to be completely perfect.

But in you, truly, both the desire to be perfect and the achievement of perfection exist, and both bear fruit. I have recognized the worth of what the prophet has said: "Behold a virgin shall conceive in her womb and bear a son" (Isaiah 7.14). You can freely say: "We have conceived in our womb the spirit of salvation that you, Lord, have wrought on earth, and we have given birth!" You breed the word of God, you are in labor with his sayings, and thus you give birth to the knowledge of God for our sake in such a way that you are always replete and pregnant.

Let people who doubt understand the manner in which a virgin might conceive and how she could give birth. Let them read your writings, for here is the immaculate fertility of virginal fruit. Obviously, your case is the same as Sara's (Tobit 3.7-17). There were seven husbands dead — that is, the spirits of the world. But when the angel led Sara to the bridal chamber and she espoused Christ, the enemy lay dead.[4] As for me, unworthy as I am, I must beg my father to let me weep for my virgin garlands before I can fulfill the vow of my father's lips, because I have not shown before now any visible fruit of my virginity (Judges 11.26ff.). My father slew the Moabites and the Ammonites — that is, he has annihilated in me the tribe of insobriety and fornication.[5] But what good is that to me if I do not have the word of God in my womb, that is to say, in my heart? And I know that virginity without learning walks in the shadow and knows not the light. The name of virginity only, which does not possess the substance,

---

[4]Tobit's son Tobias marries Sara, seven of whose betrothed lovers have been successively carried off by an evil spirit, Asmodeus. At length the angel drives away Asmodeus and binds him in Egypt.

[5]The writer compares herself to Jephtha's daughter, whom her father vowed to sacrifice once he had defeated his enemies.

cannot in any way cross the threshold of the Bridegroom's canopy.

I carry a candelabrum, which is my throat; but I am empty because of the dryness of my wick — that is, the lightness of hollow words — since the rich oil of learning does not touch it. In this respect I know I am unworthy; at least let me implore you, you who have an abundance of oil, to explain to me from whom I ought to acquire it.

But now I shall sometimes say what Job said to the Lord: "What can I utter when I hear such words, and what shall I respond, since I am nothing? Having spoken once, I will add nothing" (Job 40.4). I have recognized that I am earth and ashes, because I see such achievement in others. Because of this I myself feel that there is nothing in me. But it appears that the angel — the spirit, that is — speaks in you as in the example of the blessed Mary, because you are so learned in speaking.

I have guarded, I have surely guarded — I address you not as sister but as one who should be called Lady — what the sanctuary of your heart has conceived and the fruit of your belly has brought forth. You carry around and display as a sacred object "your son in Egypt" (Hosea 11.1; Matthew 2.15), that is, you offer the fruit of your teaching to us who are living in the world's darkness. I shall say without hesitation that you are one of the four prophesying virgins whom the writer of the Acts of the Apostles has described (Acts 21.8). You are without a doubt she of whom the singers of the holy Psalms have sung. You are arrayed in a garment of many colors, bearing fringes of gold (Psalm 45. 13-14). For how may I interpret the gold fringes if not as the beautiful and faithful sense of your words, which flow and hang down from the two sides of your face? In them is a beautiful, brilliant-hued diversity, because out of law, the prophets and the evangelists, you have dyed the wording of your letter with the various colors of their testimonies.

It is clearly evident that you do not eat your bread in idleness, because your husband — he who used to be called the carpenter's son (Matthew 13.55) — has fashioned for you a spindle of the wood of learning. With it you spin, out of the splendid wool of history, threads of the spirit's words.

I confess to you, revered sister, I did not understand the

prophet's words when he said, "Wheat is sweet to young men, and wine is sweet to maidens" (Zechariah 9.17) until I perceived it from the power of your words. For it is you who have the sweet wine, out of the fruits of Christ, that is, who is the true vine. You are fruitful with the joy of spiritual learning, which quickens the innermost part of your vitals with the juice of its sweetness and power. You surely rival that Shunammite virgin who was found to minister to and care for the body of King David (I Kings 1.1-4). For performing this service you have already won the reward of receiving his keys, with which you open what no one can lock and you lock what no one opens (Isaiah 22.22; Revelations 3.7). There is in you the son of Bathsheba — that is, Wisdom — which is ardently adored, so that a false brother neither lusts for you nor touches you.[6]

What your Holiness writes should surely be revered by me, since I have hidden the linen cloth which covered my loins in a hollow of the rock above the River Euphrates (Jeremiah 13. 1-7). I know this — that beside the worldly precipice, the hardness of my heart, the husks of my virtue are rotten, and now, stripped of wisdom's covering, I do not recognize myself despoiled of the "old man."[7]

But because the lack of my heart's skill and the sorrow of motherly anguish have hindered my speech, and the sadness of my heart scarcely allows this little thing to be spoken, I beg that you will frequently sprinkle the dry roots of my understanding with a basket of fertilizing dung — that is, the fecundity of your words (Luke 13.8) — so that when you come to visit me in your customary manner, you will find in me some of the fruit of your good work.

---

[6]Bathsheba's son by David was Solomon. The "false brother" may refer to one of David's older sons laying claim to the throne.

[7]After being told by the Lord to bury his linen girdle in the hole of a rock by the Euphrates, the prophet dug it up days later to find it ruined. The Lord then told him he would destroy the pride of Judah and Jerusalem in the same way. The sense is that the writer has buried her own pride and will not consider the stripping away of her old self to be a loss.

Further Reading on this letter

Text: *Monumenta Germaniae Historica: Epistolae,* Vol. 3, pp. 716-718. Berlin, 1892; and C. P. Caspari, ed. *Briefe, Abhandlungen und Predigten aus den zwei letzten Jahrhunderten des Mittelalters,* pp. 178-182, 398-404. Christiana, 1890.

Pierre Riché. *Education et culture dans l'occident barbare,* p. 339 and note. Paris, 1973.

5 From a Literary Circle in Provence

Eucheria of Marseilles (Sixth Century)

A patrician group of poets clustered around Dynamius of Marseilles, a sixth-century governor of Provence under Childeric and notable man of letters. Very little of their work has survived. Extant, however, is an agreeably malicious epigram, attributed by Venantius Fortunatus to Dynamius's wife, Eucheria. Fortunatus had personally met Dynamius, with whom he also exchanged lyrics and letters.

Eucheria's epigram against a lowborn suitor bears the traits for which her husband's literary circle was known — refinement, intricacy, and the wittily ornate use of metaphor. A match with the oafish suitor, says the poem, would be comparable to a series of grotesque incongruities in both art and nature, which Eucheria develops in an outrageous array of *impossibilia* — conditions that violate the natural order. A bracketed last line, appearing in only one of the five manuscripts, may or may not be Eucheria's.

Satirical Verses Against a Wooer

I would twine together golden threads, glittering like metal, with heaps of bristling horsehair. I am thinking of matching a Chinese silken coverlet and the gem-encrusted weavings of Sparta to a goat hide. Let noble purple be stitched to a coarse and loathsome wool.

Let the gleaming jewel be fixed in a heavy leaden setting. Let the pearl, its lustre now entrapped, shine dully when enclosed in steel. And in the same way let the emerald be locked in the bronze of Gaul. Let the amethyst now be paired with flint, the jasper with crags and boulders. Let even the moon now choose the chaos of Hell!

We shall also now command the lily to be joined to stinging nettles, and let the crimson rose be choked by deadly hemlock.

Now at the same time do we wish the great seething ocean to scorn its delicacies and instead prefer coarse fish. Let the rock-dwelling toad love the gilded serpent. Similarly let the trout seek out the snail for herself. Let the lofty lioness be joined with the foul fox, the ape take the keen-sighted lynx. Let the doe be joined to the donkey, the tiger to the wild ass. Marry the fleet gazelle to the plodding ox.

Let foul stinkweed now spoil the rosy nectar, let honeyed mead be mixed with bitter fruit. Let us mingle crystalline water with bodily filth, the refreshing fountain with the privy's excrement!

Let the winged swallow sport with the deadly vulture, the nightingale sing with the hateful horned-owl. Let the sullen night-owl stay with the clear-eyed partridge. Let the pretty dove lie down with the crow.

Let these monstrous couplings overturn for themselves the decrees of the dark fates — since a churlish farmhand hankers for Eucheria!

[The stag, the boar, the snake will not escape — by flight, tooth, or poisoned fang — your stings, Maiorianus!]

Further reading on Eucheria

Text: Helene Homeyer, ed. and tr. *Dichterinnen des Altertums und des frühen Mittelalters,* pp. 185-187. Paderborn, 1979; and M. Cabaret-Dupaty, ed. and tr. *Poetae Minores,* pp. 408-416. Paris, 1842.

Pauly-Wissowa. "Eucheria." *Realencyclopädie der classischen Altertumswissenschaft*, Vol. 6. Stuttgart, 1909.

6   A Carolingian Mother
Dhuoda (fl. 824-843)

A Carolingian woman named Dhuoda, living in Uzès, a town in southern France near Nîmes in Septimania, has left us a remarkable document in the form of a letter to her son William. Dhuoda shows herself to have been extremely well-read in Scripture, in the fathers of the Church, and in Christian poets like Prudentius and Venantius Fortunatus. She was acquainted with the grammarian Donatus, and displayed a fervor for the kind of etymology and numerology that she would have found in the writings of Isidore of Seville. Her "Handbook," the *Liber manualis,* is not only a guide to moral, spiritual and feudal conduct; it is more touchingly an autobiographical work. In addition to details about her own life, she describes her anxiety and love for her children, particularly sixteen-year-old William, then being held hostage through his father's wishes at the court of Charles the Bald, a monarch just two years older than William.

In those tempestuous days when the Carolingian Empire was breaking up, Charles — half-brother to Charlemagne's older grandsons, Lothar, Pepin, and Louis "the German" — fought bitterly to retain his hold on the crown. His mother, the Empress Judith, had been accused of witchcraft and adultery, common enough slanders leveled against women considered political threats. In fact, one of her alleged lovers

65

was Dhuoda's husband, Bernard of Septimania.[1] Whether or not this was so, Bernard, an energetic defender of the Spanish border, comes through as an embattled and cordially hated warrior in Charles's retinue. He had a way of shifting his allegiances, but after the crucial battle of Fontenay-en-Puisaye on June 22, 841, he quickly reconfirmed his homage to young Charles. To make this convincing, he sent his own son William, then nearly fifteen, as a hostage. He ordered William to swear allegiance to the seventeen-year-old Charles.

By this means Bernard hoped to ingratiate himself with his new overlord, and to get back certain of the honors and lands of which he had been stripped. When as the governor of Septimania he had been accused of disloyalty with the Empress Judith, second wife of Louis the Pious, he had in 832 been deprived of this title. Bernard had already been punished through his sister Gerberga, a nun in a convent of Châlons-sur-Saône. Lothar accused her of sorcery, had her thrust into a wine cask and thrown into the Saône to drown.

It is against these barbarous realities of her time that Dhuoda's learned treatise has to be seen. When she exhorts her son to revere his superiors and his father, we sense a piety motivated by fear, self-preservation, and maternal concern as much as by a love of books. Bernard's treatment of his wife would certainly have intensified her wish to placate him. Married to Bernard at the imperial palace of Louis at Aix-la-Chapelle in June 824, Dhuoda was whisked away to the little southern town where she was compelled to live out her days. Bernard visited her infrequently enough to father two sons, William (b. November 29, 826) and Bernard (b. March 22, 841). Bernard took both sons from her — William when he was fourteen, and the infant Bernard before he was baptized. Parted from her children, and an outsider to the events at court, Dhuoda must have sought comfort in writing this

---

[1]Godson and kinsman to Charlemagne, Bernard was the son of Count William of Toulouse, later known as St. Guilhem du Désert, when he established the monastery in Gellone to which he retired. He also earned literary fame as Guillaume d'Orange of the epics.

treatise, speaking of herself in more than simply conventional commonplaces.

She mentions her marriage, the birth of her children, a woman who is her companion, and her anxiety that her illness will prevent her from writing another such book for her younger son. She tells how she has had to borrow money in order to pay for the defense of the Spanish march. Her iconography is vivid: the dogs of the Church, and Christ the Tree. It is noteworthy that Dhuoda continually emphasizes to this child of hers, caught up in the violence of the masculine world, her motherly role and authority. Intriguingly, she weaves her own name and William's in the Latin text, thus conspicuously inscribing her presence.

We should recall what the state of the language was when Dhuoda wrote (she began her book on November 30, 841, and finished it on February 2, 843). In the military camps of the North a pact was being hammered out by Charlemagne's grandsons in speech plain enough for soldiers to grasp. The earliest French document, in the *romana lingua*, was the Oaths of Strasbourg, February 14, 842. And yet to her soldier son, Dhuoda writes in the language of the Fathers, reflecting the allusive style and the word play of her models. The text is spun out of Scripture, much of it from the Psalms, as well as Genesis, Job, and the Wisdom books, the New Testament, notably Paul, the Fathers of the Church — Jerome, Gregory, Augustine, Alcuin, and the Christian poets. She calls her method "contextus," woven together from many sources.

Dhuoda also schools William in the noble, military and Christian virtues of justice and courage, the protection of widows and orphans, charity to the poor, reverence for the Church and its priesthood, respect for feudal authority, and instruction in the vices and virtues. Perhaps more striking is her repeated insistence on the importance of the reading habit, and the energy it entails. One wonders if William had time to read as much as she advised, and yet the exhortation "Lege!" is everywhere in the book in various forms. Initially Dhuoda points to the physical connection between author and reader. She elaborates the tangibility of the book as a preliminary to reading, repeating Augustine's definition of enchiridion, a little guidebook "that can be clasped in the hand." When she writes that her Rule issues from her, the mother, and takes its shape in the son, her language concretizes the bond between author and reader, making it as physical as giving birth.

Indeed, Dhuoda gives the laborious effort of her authorship a word of her own invention: *agonizatio* (I.1.13; I.3.20), based on *agon,* which she uses elsewhere to refer to her husband's military combat. She exhorts her reader/son to reciprocate her authorial struggle by striving with equal effort to read and understand. Throughout the treatise, Dhuoda writes of the reading act. She uses *legere* (to read), *volvere* (to turn over, or unroll, even though the book was by now a block of leaves — a *codex libelli*), *perscrutare* (search through, investigate, literally, to sift down to the rags and shreds), as well as offering advice on how to read an acrostic or study paragraph headings to learn what follows. Reading also provides diversion, she points out, like a game of backgammon. Dhuoda's imagery about reading is particularly delightful: "Taste this book like a nourishing brew of honey"; "Read as doves do who sip the pure clear water, while being on the lookout for rapacious hawks."

Dhuoda's reference to her book as a mirror in which William may read his salvation, *and* perceive his mother's image is surely astonishing. To the patristic reading of the text as a mirror of the firmament and of God's truth, Dhuoda adds her own variation. Dhuoda herself passes into the book's mirror surface as an image of piety and authority. Hers is the image that gazes back at the reader. The child will find the mother in the text. Her acrostically entwining her name with his simply reaffirms this point, by braiding even more intimately the mother/child, author/reader connections. The opening acrostic spells: *Dhuoda dilecto filio UUilhelmo salutem lege,* or "Dhuoda greets her dear son William. Read!" In the epitaph the acrostic spells: *Dhuodane,* "by (or about) Dhuoda."

1. Dhuoda's Handbook. The text begins

This little book has been arranged in three parts. Read all of them and you will better be able to understand the whole. I wish the three parts to be labeled in a comparable way so that they will follow the most useful sequence: the

Rule of Conduct; the Form it assumes; and the Handbook. The Rule of Conduct comes from me; the Form it assumes is within you; the Handbook is as much from me as it is for you, composed by me, and established within you.

Now the "Hand" in "Handbook," or *Manualis,* can be understood in many senses: sometimes it means God's power, sometimes the Son's power, and sometimes it means the Son himself. The power of God is as the Apostle says: "Humble yourself beneath the power of God's hand" (I Peter 5.6). The power of the Son is as Daniel says: "His power is an eternal power" (Daniel 7.14). When it means the Son himself, it is as the Psalmist says: "Send your hand from on high," in other words, "Send your Son from heaven's heights" (Psalm 143.7).

All these and similar passages can be understood as Divine Activity and Power. For "Hand" signifies the work completed, as the Scripture says: "The Lord's hand was laid upon me" (Ezekiel 3.22), that is to say, the redemption which has led believers to perfection. Also, "For the Lord's hand was comforting me" (Ezekiel 3.14). And again, "For his hand is with him" (Luke 1.66).

The "-alis" part of *Manualis* has many meanings. I will however explain only three of them here, according to the sayings of the Fathers. In the sense of something "winged," it means *scope,* which is "aim"; *consummation,* which is "achievement"; and *old age,* which is "ending."[2]

Or, indeed, *ales*–"wings"–signifies the herald and messenger of dawn, telling the story of the end of night and singing about the light of the morning hours. What other meaning, then, could this term *Manualis* have but the end of ignorance, and the messenger that foresees the dawn of the future?

It may be said, "The night has gone before, the day is hastening" (Romans 13.12), that is, Christ, who himself has plainly said, "If I am the day and you are the hours, follow

---

[2]Dhuoda's imaginative etymologies are not always clear. Can she be thinking of the Germanic *alt* (old) when she finds "old age" as a meaning for "-alis"?

me" (John 8.12; 9.4-5; 11.9), and so forth.

Furthermore, from the beginning of this little book to the end, both in form and meaning, both in the meters and moving feet of its poetic melody, and the loosened limbs of its prose, everywhere, in every part, know this: that all of it has been written for the well-being of your soul and your body. What I desire is that when this work has been directed from my hand, you will willingly grasp it in your own hand, and holding it, you will fulfill its teachings in most worthwhile actions. For let it be said that this little book in the form of a handbook consists of words from me, and their actualization in you. As a certain one has said: "I have planted the seed, Apollo watered it, and God has made it grow" (I Corinthians 3.6).

What more can I say here, my son, except that on the basis of the good qualities you already have in you, I — with zeal for this undertaking — "I have fought the good fight, and keeping the faith, I have finished the blessed race" (II Timothy 4.7). In whom do these things have value if not in that One who has said, "It is finished" (John 19.30)?

For whatever I have composed in this handbook, beginning with this chapter, whether it follows the Hebrew language, Greek letters, or the Latin tongue, I have completed to the end this task in him who is called God.

2. In the Name of the Holy Trinity. Here begins the book, Dhuoda's Handbook, which she sent to her son William

I have observed that most women in this world take joy in their children. But, O my son William, I see myself, Dhuoda, living separated and far away from you. For this reason I am uneasy, as it were, and eager to be useful to you, and so I address this little book to you, which has been transcribed for me in my own name. It is for you to read as a kind of model. I rejoice that, although I am absent in body, this little book will be present. Once you have read it, it will lead your spirit back to those things that you ought to do, for my sake.

Epigram of the following work:

D ivine Lord, creator of the supreme light, author of the sky
and stars, king of eternal things, Holy One,

H aving begun this work, I pray that you will, with your
mercy, bring it to completion. Although I am ignorant, I
strive for intelligence.

U nderstanding how to please you, and traveling through
present and future time — these things will depend upon
your help.

O ne and threefold, you lavish riches on your people
throughout the ages.

D eserving ones will each have the heavenly rewards you
allot to your servants.

A mple thanks I offer on bended knee to you, the Creator, to
the extent of my ability.

D eign, I beg, to send me aid, raising me up to the skies at
your right hand.

I have faith that your people will find eternal repose in that
kingdom.

L imed in earth's mud, I am frail, an exile, dragged to the
very pit. A faithful woman friend

E ndures a fate like mine, and trusts in your forgiveness for
her sins.

C enter of the universe, who sustains the circling orb of the
heavens, you enclose the sea and the dry land in the palm
of your hand.

T o you I commend William, my son. Allow him always to
thrive and prosper.

O n the course he pursues, at all hours and moments, let him
love you above everything else.

F ar upward to heaven's heights may he ascend with happy
headlong footsteps together with your children!

I n you may his vigilant mind find guidance! May he live
blessed forever!

L et him not become wrathful if he should be hurt; let him
not stray far from you.

I n joy may he pursue a happy course, so that, shining with
virtue, he will ascend above.

O f your will let him be mindful. You who give without pomp, bestow intelligence upon him.

U nderstanding in faith and love, and the ability to praise you with redoubled gratitude — Holy One grant him these.
U nto him let your bounteous grace be given, with peace and safety of body and mind.
I n this world may he and his offspring flourish, possessing these good things here in such a way that he shall not lack the blessings of Heaven.
L et him read this volume and turn to it again at appropriate times, heeding the sayings of the saints and obeying them in his thoughts.
H elp him to reflect, with the intelligence he receives from you, how, when, and to whom he should offer his support.
E ndlessly, for your sake, may he pursue the four virtues, so that, keeping to them, he may accomplish anything.
L et him be generous, wise, dutiful and brave, never straying from self-control.
M other am I to him. He will never have anyone like me, unworthy as I am.
O n him have mercy, I resolutely pray to you at every moment and hour.

S orrows and cares assail me while I strive on his behalf with my frail efforts.
A nd to you — Giver of all good things — I entrust him with gratitude.
L ands are in turmoil, kingdoms torn apart by discord. You alone remain immutable.
U pon your divine will all things depend, whether or not good people seek the proper solutions.
T o you belong the royalty, the power, the fullness of the earth extending through the world.
E verything serves you alone, you who reign forever. Have mercy on my children.
M y two sons, who were brought into the world — I pray that they may live and always love you.

L etters at the beginning of each verse will spell the meaning. Reader, diligently examine these to know the formula.
E ventually you will be able to understand — with swift pace — what I have written.

G rant to me, mother of two male children, that you will pray
to the life-giving Creator, to
E levate the father of these children to heaven, and unite me
to them in his Kingdom.

Begin your reading with the letter D. With M all is ended.
The verses are finished. With Christ's help I will embark on
the work I have begun for my children.

3. Here Begins the Prologue

Many things are clear to many people, and yet these
things are not clear to me. Those who are like me have
darkened minds and are lacking in understanding. If I speak
less, I am more. But he "who opens the mouth of the mute
and makes the tongues of infants eloquent" (Wisdom 10.21)
is always present. I Dhuoda, although I am weak in
understanding, living unworthily among women who are
unworthy, I am your mother nonetheless. It is to you that the
words of my manual are now addressed.

Just as the game of backgammon, among other
pleasurable pursuits, is generally agreed to be an apt pastime
for young people, and just as some women are accustomed
to peer at their own faces in the mirror — so that they may
cleanse away the spots of dirt and show themselves radiant
and, in a worldly way, give pleasure to their husbands — just
in this way, I would like you, in spite of the pressures of your
worldly occupations, to give your devoted attention — for my
sake — to the reading of this little book which I have
addressed to you. Give it that same degree of attention and
zeal that others give to looking in the mirror or to a game
of backgammon!

Even though you own an increasing number of books, may
it please you to read my little work often. May you with the
help of Almighty God be enabled to understand it for your
benefit. You will find in this book in succinct form all that
you want to know. You will also find in it a mirror, in which
you may contemplate the health of your soul. In so doing you
can please not only the world but the God who formed you
from the dust of the earth. This will be necessary from every
point of view, my son William, in order for you to lead a useful

life in the world and be pleasing to God in all things.

My great concerns about you, O my son William, are to send you salutary words. Among these words, my vigilant heart yearns ardently to tell you — with God's help — about your birth. So in this little book, written for you as a result of my desire, these things will follow as planned.

4. Preface

In the eleventh year of the reign of our departed lord Louis, who ruled in splendor by the will of Christ,[3] I was given in lawful marriage on June 29, 824 to my lord Bernard, your father. In the thirteenth year of that reign, with God's help as I believe, your birth issued forth into the world from me, O most desired firstborn son.

In the course of the worsening turmoil of this wretched world, in the midst of much agitation and discord in the realm, the Emperor did not escape the common path of mortality. In fact, his life ended before he had completed the 28th year of his reign. And in the year following his death, on March 22, 841, your brother was born, the second child after you to issue from my womb — through God's mercy — in the town of Uzès. He was still a baby and had not yet received the grace of baptism, when your lord and father to both of you had him taken to Aquitaine by Elefantus, the bishop of that city, and others of his followers.

But now I have remained a long time in this town — by my lord's command — deprived of your presence. While I rejoice in his campaigns, I have undertaken, because of my longing for the both of you, to have this little book copied out and sent to you, insofar as my meager cleverness permits. . . .

I have learned that your father Bernard has entrusted you to the hands of our lord King Charlemagne. I urge you to acquit yourself of your duties with a perfect good will. . . .

---

[3]Louis the Pious, reigning with Charlemagne from 813, actually became emperor in 814. Louis died June 20, 840.

5. Seeking God: The Whelps and Puppies of Holy Church

We must seek God, you and I, my son. In his will we endure, we live, move, and exist. As for me, unworthy as I am and flimsy as a shadow, I seek him as well as I am able, and I ceaselessly ask his help to the extent of my knowledge and understanding. For this is needful in every way.

Now it sometimes happens that a troublesome little puppy among the other whelps under its master's table can seize and devour the crumbs that fall (Mark 7.28; Matthew 15.27). He who has the power to elicit speech from the mouths of dumb animals (Numbers 22.28) can, according to his mercy of old, open the mouth of my spirit (Luke 24.45) and grant me understanding. He who prepares a table in the wilderness for his faithful followers, giving them in time of need a sufficient measure of wheat, can fulfill even my will — that of a handmaid — according to his desire. So I can jump under his table, that is to say, on the lower level of the Holy Church, and gaze from afar at the little whelps — those who are ministering to the sacred altars. Then from among the crumbs of spiritual wisdom I shall be able to gather for myself and for you, O William my beautiful son, some beautiful and luminous words that are worthy and appropriate. For I know that "his mercy has never failed" (Lamentations 3.22).

6. A Reminder: Books and Mirrors

Now I give you a reminder, O my beautiful and lovable son. In the midst of your mundane concerns of this world, do not be slothful in gathering many scrolls of books. From them you ought to discern and learn something greater and better than what is already written here, from the most sacred masters of learned men, concerning God the Creator. Pray to him, cherish and love him. If you do so, he will be your guardian, your guide, your companion, and your fatherland — "the way, the truth, and the life" (John 14.6). He will grant you in abundance the world's prosperity, and he will convert all your enemies to peace. . . .

What more shall I say? Dhuoda is always here to exhort you, my son, but in anticipation of the day when I shall no longer be with you, you shall have here as a memento of me this little book of moral counsels. And you can gaze upon me as on an image in a mirror, and see me reading with my bodily and spiritual eyes, and praying to God concerning those obligations you are to render me. You can fully discover them here. My son, you will have learned doctors who will teach you many more examples, more eminent and of greater usefulness, but they are not of equal status with me, nor do they have a heart more ardent than I, your mother, have for you, O my firstborn son.

These words that I address to you, read them, understand them, and put them to practice. And when your little brother, whose name I do not even know as yet, has received the grace of baptism in Christ, do not be slow to win his affection, to encourage him and love him, to rouse him to go from good to better. When he shall have reached the age of speaking and reading, show him this little volume, this handbook which I have written and in which I have inscribed your name. Watch over his reading, for he is your flesh and your brother. I, Dhuoda, your mother, send reminders to both of you as if you were already — in the midst of the mundane cares of this world — about to "Lift up your heart! Look to him who reigns in the heavens!"

May the Almighty, of whom — despite my unworthiness — I speak so often, render you, together with your father Bernard, my lord and seigneur, happy and cheerful in the present world! May he give you prosperity in all things! And once the course of this life is ended, may he see to it that you joyously enter the heavenly sky with the saints! Amen.

7. The Tree of Mercy

It has, in short, been written, "In whatever place the tree has fallen, there he will be" (Ecclesiastes 11.3). By the tree is meant each man. Whether he is good or bad, by his fruit shall he actually be known (Matthew 7.17-20). A beautiful and noble tree produces noble leaves and brings forth suitable fruit. This is indicated by a great and very faithful man. The cultivated man deserves to be filled with the Holy Spirit and to burgeon with leaves and fruit. He is distinguished by his sweet fragrance. For his leaves are his words, his fruit is his judgment, or indeed, his leaves are his intellect, his fruit his good deeds. The good tree flourishes, but the wicked tree will be delivered to the flames. It is written, "Every tree that does not bear good fruit shall be cut down and thrown into the fire" (Matthew 3.10; 7.19).

The true tree, together with the vine that is in concord with it, is our Lord Christ. That is, the Lord Jesus from whom all chosen trees arise and vineshoots burgeon, has deigned to choose the worthy branches that will bring forth beautiful fruit. He himself says, "I am the true vine and you are the vineshoots." And again, "I have chosen you from the world so that you may go and bear fruit and that your fruit shall remain. Who remains with me and I in him, will bear much fruit" (John 15.5,16), and so forth.

It is to such a tree, therefore, that I urge you to graft yourself, my son, so that you may cleave to him without fail, and — since fruit means good deeds — you will be able to bring forth much fruit. Those who behold him and have sure trust in him are compared to this saintly tree which is transplanted beside the flowing water (Psalm 1.3). Those trees which have deeply and profoundly fixed their roots in the moisture will not grow dry in the summer season (Jeremiah 17.8). Their leaves will always be green and abundant and they will never fail to produce fruit.

Why this, my son? Because, as the Apostle says, "Rooted and grounded in charity" (Ephesians 3.17), with the coming of the Holy Spirit's grace, they will never fail in any season to weigh their fruit for those who are nearby.

And so that you may know which trees are worthy of yielding their fruits in abundance, hear the Apostle when he says, "The fruits of the spirit are charity, joy, peace, forbearance, kindness, gentleness, patience, chastity, self-control, modesty, sobriety, vigilance, and wisdom" (Galatians 5.22-23),⁴ and other virtues like these. Since those who practice such virtues will deserve to attain quite readily to the kingdom of God, graft those fruits in your mind and body, my son, and bring them forth and meditate upon them

---

⁴Dhuoda has added a few qualities to the list.

continually. In this way, with the fruit and perseverance of good works, you will deserve on the day of tribulation and adversity to be sheltered and supported by the True Tree.

8. The Epitaph for my tomb, which I ask you to inscribe

When I have finished my days, be sure that you have my name inscribed among the dead. What I wish, and ask you most emphatically to do — as if it were the present — is to have the following inscription permanently carved on the stone that marks the tomb in which my body will be buried. In this way the passer-by who see this epitaph may worthily pray to God for me, unworthy woman that I am.

And for those who will some day read this Handbook that you are reading, let them also meditate on what follows, and pray to God to forgive me, as if I were already enclosed in the tomb.

Read here, Reader, the little verses of this epitaph:

$$+ D + M +^5$$

D huoda's body, formed of earth, lies buried in this tomb. Infinite King, receive her.

H er frail filth, formed of earth, has been enclosed in the depths of this tomb.
Benevolent King, grant her mercy.

U lcerous and wet is her body. There is nothing more left for her but the grave's deep shadows.
O King, absolve her from her faults!

O travellers of whatever age and sex who come and go this way, I beg you to utter these words:
"Great holy God, unbind her chains!"

D riven down into the cave with her horrible wounds, hedged round with bitter gall, she has reached the end of her filthy life. O King, pardon her sins!

A nd lest the dark serpent seize her soul, utter this prayer:

---

[5]These letters stand for *Dis manibus* — in God's hands — as seen on other funerary monuments.

"Merciful God, help her!"
N o traveller shall pass this way without having read this.
I adjure all that they pray, saying, "Grant her repose,
Cherishing God."
E ternal light shall be bestowed upon her in the company of
the saints. Command this, Benign God, that the Amen[6] shall
receive her after her funeral rites.

Further reading on Dhuoda

Text: Pierre Riché, ed. *Manuel pour mon fils.* Sources
chrétiennes, pp. 66-87; 98-100; 114-116; 268-270; 356-358.
Paris, 1887.

Eleanor Shipley Duckett. "Dhuoda and Bernard of
Septimania." In *Medieval Portraits from East and West,*
pp. 197-218. Ann Arbor, 1972.

---

[6]Christ is called the Amen in Revelations 3.14.

7   A Convent in Saxony

Hrotswitha of Gandersheim (ca. 935-1001)

The tenth-century noblewoman and canoness Hrotswitha, of the Benedictine monastery of Gandersheim in Saxony, is best known for her plays and saints' lives,[1] on which critical attention has been justly lavished. On completing her six dramas, inspired by the Latin poet Terence, as well as the eight structurally related saints' legends, Hrotswitha turned in 967 to the composition of two Latin epics to glorify the Ottonian dynasty. These epics are of considerable interest and appeal for their emphasis on women's roles.

Both are historical family epics, connected in theme. The *Gesta Ottonis* or *Carmen de Gestis Odonis I Imperatoris* celebrates the deeds of emperor Otto the Great, under whose protection Hrotswitha's powerful monastery thrived and a Christian humanist revival took place.

The reign of the Ottonian house — from 919 to 1024 — became a period of immense cultural and political ferment. Imperial prestige had weakened among Charlemagne's descendants; now an imperial renaissance occurred, with its heart in the wild remoteness of Saxony. With the victories of the Saxon duke

---

[1]The plays are *Gallicanus, Drusiana and Calimachus, Mary the Niece of Abraham, The Conversion of Thais, The Martyrdom of the Holy Virgins Agape, Chiona, and Hirene,* and *The Martyrdom of the Holy Maidens Faith, Hope, and Charity.* The legends are *Mary, Ascension, Gongolf, Pelagius, Theophilus, Basilius, Dionysius,* and *Agnes.*

Henry "the Fowler" on the battlefield, driving out the Huns for instance, the *imperium* of divine election was revived and granted to Henry by his men. Henry's son Otto I brought back the Roman gala of the Carolingian coronation banquet when he had himself crowned and anointed at Aachen, with the dukes of Franconia, Swabia, Bavaria and Lorraine waiting on him.

Otto's court developed thereafter as a cosmopolitan center of Roman Christian splendor and creativity to the glory of God and empire, building churches and libraries, and fostering the collecting, production and ornamentation of books, as well as painting and the decorative arts. Scholars, artists, and other foreign personages gathered there; the authors Liutprand, Widukind, Ekkehard, and Rather were part of the court circle. Otto's learned and widely connected brother Bruno, chancellor and later archbishop of Cologne, was responsible for much of the cultural life at the imperial court; he also kept close touch with Gandersheim. Under the beneficial effects of this cultural rebirth, and invested with complete autonomy by Otto, Gandersheim with its wealth, courts, mints, and army was its own small principality.

Hrotswitha's other great epic, the *Primordia Coenobii Gandeshemensis,* commemorates the founding of the convent of Gandersheim and traces its history to the death of the abbess Christina in 919. This was her last work, finished before 973. Although the *Primordia* follows the *Gesta* in sequence, it actually records the ancestral doings of Otto's house, for the monastery had been established in 852, long before Otto's birth. The *Primordia* therefore gains a precedence, a primacy of divine authority.

Two kinds of narrative are discernible in the *Gesta Ottonis,* after an invocation by Hrotswitha to Gerberga II, Otto's niece, as her abbess, mentor and muse. The work begins with Otto's family, his first marriage to Edith of England and her death, his own accession to the throne, and the troubles of his realm — the intrigues, and rebellions, and the Italian campaigns, in which he successfully prevailed. Two-thirds of the way through, the account takes a different turn, shifting from Otto to the beautiful, accomplished Adelheid of Italy, formerly a Burgundian princess (whose

later life was also written by Odilo of Cluny) who would be
Otto's second wife.

Adelheid, then living with her small daughter Emma in
Pavia in Lombardy, was the widow of Lothar, and herself
a capable claimant to the Italian crown. In this portion of the
narrative Hrotswitha gives us one of the most attractive and
heroic episodes of the epic. A powerful member of Adelheid's
household, Berengar of Ivrea — previously a margrave at
Otto's court — seized the throne and tried to consolidate his
own claims to the crown by forcing Adelheid to marry his son.
Meeting her resistance, Berengar locked her in a cell and
seized the crown with its treasures. With her maid's help, as
Hrotswitha tells it, Adelheid actually dug her way out of her
prison, escaping by means of an earth tunnel. She ran under
cover of night; by day she hid in caves, woods, and ploughed
furrows. Berengar followed her with his soldiers to a
cornfield, where he slashed right and left with his spear, but
Adelheid managed to elude him by hiding under the shelter
of leaves of grain. On hearing about this woman's trials and
her courage, Otto invaded Italy, determined to make her his
wife, the worthy consort of his reign. With Adelheid's
coronation as empress, Hrotswitha finishes her epic, simply
sketching swiftly in the last 34 lines the subsequent warlike
events about which she will refrain from writing, modestly
kept back as she is by her womanly nature. Effectively, the
placement in the *Gesta* of Adelheid's heroic feats, partly
modeled on the adventures of Hildegund in the *Waltharius,*
gives a climactic importance to the empress. So the great
deeds of Otto are framed by two significant female references
— the invocation to Gerberga and Adelheid's coronation.

As a companion piece to the *Gesta,* Hrotswitha's
Primordia also pays tribute to Otto, whose family founded
Gandersheim. But the *Primordia* especially honors Otto's
female relatives and the women in charge of the convent
thereafter. In this way Hrotwsitha shifts much of the family
glory to a female succession of patrons, visionaries, saints,
and workers. Virgilian epic had as its theme the founding of
a nation, whereas Hrotswitha employs epic conventions to
describe the establishing of a female community whose right
of power surpasses that of any earthly authority, even that
of the imperial family who originated that power.

Instead of conquering alien peoples and territories, the founders cause the fauns and woodland creatures to be expulsed from the forests; they order the woods cut down and the rocks quarried. Hrotswitha emphasizes the women's involvement while glossing over the role of the bishops. In the course of events, husbands and overbearing suitors are conveniently struck down or simply die so that wealth and available time may freely be employed by the women to the glory of Gandersheim convent. Aeda, Oda and her three daughters, the first three abbesses in succession — Hathumoda, Gerberga I, and Christina — are responsible for the inspiration, the work and financing of the monastery. Gerberga, though betrothed to a nobleman and forced to meet him in her courtly gown of rich gold, had nonetheless secretly dedicated herself to Christ. The disappointed fiancé furiously swore by her white throat and his sword that he would return from his military campaigns and force her to break her sacred vow. He was, however, killed in battle, in heavenly retribution. Oda herself lived to a great age. Hrotswitha delicately suggests that divine power may have allowed Oda to become a widow. "Perhaps," she writes of this first founder, "God took Liudulf from this world when he had hardly reached the fever of middle life, in order that the mind of the illustrious lady Oda, his wife, might remain concentrated on God."

1. The Founding of the Monastery of Gandersheim

Behold! The submissive obedience of my humble purpose bursts forth to tell of the founding of the blessed monastery of Gandersheim. The Saxons' chiefs, powerful in authority, built it with energetic care; the great and illustrious Liudulf and his son Otto completed the work that was begun.

The sequence of these things demands now that the earliest building of the renowned monastery of Gandersheim be sung in a suitable epic. As I have said, it is known that Liudulf, the leader of the Saxons, constructed it with reverence. A child descended from the stock of a very distinguished family, his deeds corresponded to the nobility of his lineage. Outstanding in his behavior and in the practice of his virtue, he grew in excellence among all the Saxons. For he was strong, very handsome in body, wise in his speech, and circumspect in all his actions. He alone was the hope and honor of his entire nation. Almost from his earliest years he served in the army of the great Louis, King of the Franks, who raised him to the highest honors.

2. Aeda's Vision of John the Baptist

The wife of Liudulf was the very celebrated Oda, illustrious offspring of the race of the powerful Franks. Her father was Billung, a benevolent prince; her mother was Aeda of good and noble reputation.

Aeda was many a time in the habit of delivering herself and her whole life over to praying to her Lord. Persisting very often in her pious acts, this diligent queen, who was well-informed about the promises of heaven, earned the right to discover through the message of the blessed Baptist of Christ that her progeny would at some time in future centuries possess the glory of imperial authority.

On one occasion, therefore, when the dawn sheared through the night's shadows with the gleam of its red-glowing light, she lay at full length before the sacred altar that was consecrated in honor of the Baptist, beating with her ceaseless prayers against the inner shrines of heaven. And after she had unloosed her saintly thoughts in these devotions, she perceived — as she lay there face down — the feet of a man who was standing close to her. A little agitated, she greatly wondered in her mind who he might be that dared to disturb her solitude in this hour so fittingly associated with prayer. She turned a little with her forehead raised up from the ground, and gazed at a young man who glittered amazingly with light. He was clothed in a garment of tapestry as golden-haired as if it had been woven from the fleece of a hump-backed camel. On his beautiful and shining face, he had a little fringe of beard, the same black as the hair of his head, which formed a crown of gleaming splendor.

The married lady, upon seeing him, did not believe he was mortal. She was stunned in her mind in the way of women, and, constrained as she was by a great fear, she fell forward.

But he spoke to her sweetly to soothe her agitation, and said, "Do not tremble or be frightened or deeply disturbed, but — once you have driven away the terror of your strong fear — know who I am. I have come to bring you great solace. For I am John, who merited to touch Christ with the clear water. Because you have often honored me, I bring you tidings that your illustrious descendant shall found a cloister for saintly virgins and a triumphant peace for the kingdom, provided that his religious spirit stands firm. Your progeny will henceforth, at some time in future ages, attain to such a height of powerful sovereignty that no potentate among the kings of earth at that time will be able to rival it in authority."

He had spoken, and turning away suddenly, he entered the upper air, leaving the benevolent married lady a sweet consolation. The august promise of this lofty honor pointed specifically to the illustrious offspring of the lady Oda: her son, the noble ruler Otto, became the father of Henry, so capable of reigning.

[Hrotswitha traces the family lineage down to the present Otto, her patron, the Holy Roman Emperor. She then returns to Oda, wife of Liudulf and daughter of the same lady Aeda who had seen John the Baptist in a vision. Oda follows her mother's counsels to build the convent. Its first location is on the banks of the Gand on a mountain not far from a small church. Permission has to be obtained from Pope Sergius, who sends relics of popes Anastasius and Innocent.]

3. The designation of the site

According to the well-founded opinion of many knowledgeable people, there was near our monastery a little wood surrounded by shaded hills — the same that surround us today. In that wood there was a little farm where the men who herded Liudulf's pigs would take shelter in the paddock belonging to a certain man. There they would settle their weary bodies to rest in the quiet of the night, while the pigs in their charge ran to pasture.

Here, once upon a time, two days before the venerable feast of All Saints was to be celebrated, these same swineherds saw many luminous lamps burning in the forest in the dark of night. When they saw these, all the swineherds were dazed with stupefaction. They wondered what this could mean, this strange vision of brilliant light, shearing through the night's shadow with astonishing brightness.

Shaken, they reported this to the householder of the farm, gesturing to show him the place that was bathed with light. He was avid to test with his own clear gaze what he had heard about, and left the protection of his house to remain outdoors in their company. He remained awake with them the following night, never closing his heavy-lidded eyes despite the inducements of sleep, until they could again see the enkindled lamps glowing redly. They saw the lamps now increased in number, outdoing those of the previous night. They were indeed in the same place, but came at an earlier hour than before.

As soon as Phoebus scattered his first rays from the sky, this glad sign of a blessed omen became known when joyful tidings proclaimed it to all. Nor could it remain hidden from noble Liudulf, but it struck his ears more quickly than can be told. On the holy eve of the All Saints feast to come, Liudulf himself — observing carefully whether the vision would again reveal any heavenly sign — kept watch throughout the night with a throng of people in that same forest.

Before very long, when murky night had covered the earth with its cloud, everywhere within the circle of the wooded valley where the very celebrated temple was to be founded, a great many lights were seen arranged neatly in a row. And they sheared through the tree-shadows and the thick dark of night at the same time, with the bright dawn of their potent radiance. At once those who were present, giving praise to the Lord, affirmed that the place should be sanctified and dedicated to the divine service of him who had filled it with light.

Now the Duke Liudulf, joyful over heaven's beneficence and in harmonious agreement with his dear wife Oda, ordered that the trees and brambles should be cut and pruned, so that the valley should be completely cleared. He saw to it that this wooded place, filled with fauns and sprites, should be purified and made suitable for divine worship. As soon as he had first acquired for them the moneys that the work demanded, he immediately built there the walls of the beautiful church which the splendor of the redly glowing light had designated. And so in this circumstance the founding of our monastery was begun under the favorable auspices of God.

4. How a supply of building stones was found

Meanwhile, appropriate stones for the structure could not be found in those areas. For this reason the completion of the temple suffered a delay. But the abbess Hathumoda, confident that those who believed in the Lord could prayerfully secure all things by faith, continually wore herself out with excessive toil, day and night ministering to God with sacred fervor. And with many of her subordinates acting in consort with her, she begged that the solace of heavenly aid might be conferred so that the work so well begun should not remain unfinished. Before very long, she sensed that the heavenly beneficence she was seeking would quickly take pity on her prayers.

For one day when she was fasting and allowing herself to be unoccupied, she lay prostrate before the altar. She was urged to go, through the counsels of a gentle voice, and follow a bird which she saw as she went forth. The bird had come to rest on the summit of a great rock. She embraced these urgings with a prompt spirit and set forth, trusting in her heart the words of the One commanding her. She took experienced stone-masons with her, and went quickly in the direction where the Holy Spirit was guiding her, until she came to the place where the stately temple had been begun. There she beheld the white dove settle on the highest summit of the designated stone.

Then spreading its wings and soaring, it went ahead and moderated its flight — different from its usual way — so that the dear little maiden of Christ together with her companions might follow its airborne track in a direct route. And when the dove in its flight arrived at that place which we know now is not bereft of great rocks, it alighted and with its beak it struck against the earth beneath which a great many stones lay hidden. Convinced by what she saw, the most meritorious virgin of Christ commanded her companions to clear the land, and by delving to cut through the heap of earth. When they had done so, through the kindly beneficence of God, an immense quantity of great rocks was unearthed. From this quarry could be dragged all the raw material needed for the monastery walls and the church that had been begun. After this, the builders of the temple to be consecrated to the glory of the Lord labored more and more, both night and day devoting themselves to the new undertaking.

Further Reading on Hroswitha

Text: Helene Homeyer, ed. *Hrotsvithae Opera,* pp. 450; 451-453; 457-460. Paderborn, 1970.

Mary Bernardine Bergman, tr. *Hroswithae Liber Tertius.* Covington, Kentucky, 1943.

Anne L. Haight. *Hrotsvitha of Gandersheim.* New York, 1965.

Dennis M. Kratz. "The Nun's Epic: Hroswitha on Christian Heroism." In D.C. Reichel, ed. *Wege der Worte: Festschrift für Wolfgang Fleishhauer,* pp. 132-142. Cologne and Vienna, 1978.

Katharina M. Wilson, tr. *The Dramas of Hrotsvit of Gandersheim. Matrologia Latina.* Saskatoon, Saskatchewan, 1985.

8   A Byzantine Historian of the First Crusade

Anna Comnena (December 2, 1083-1153)

At the age of 55, Anna Comnena began writing the *Alexiad,* a prose epic which remains one of the foremost histories of the First Crusade, as well as of the Comnenus family and the Byzantine state, providing for us a mirror of Byzantine politics and society during her lifetime. For the previous twenty years Anna had been effectively retired or exiled from court, living in the monastery of Kecharitomene overlooking the Golden Horn. This religious house of retreat for imperial women and nuns had been founded by her mother, Irene Ducas, author of the *Typikon,* the charter and rule of the order.[1] Anna, known for her wit and learning, had gathered savants and philosophers around her at Kecharitomene, a coterie devoted to reviving Aristotelian studies. But this proud, strong woman had once believed herself cut out by birth and talent for a very different sort of life.

Born in the purple chamber — "porphyrogenite" — she was the daughter of Alexius Comnenus, ruler of the Eastern Empire at Constantinople when it stretched from Italy to Armenia. Anna had been given a crown as a child and had fully expected that at her father's death she would become the Basilissa of the Eastern Empire. The birth of her brother John dashed these hopes. At the age of nine, Anna heard her brother proclaimed Basileus. Her parents married Anna when she was fourteen to Nicephorus Bryennius, a

---

[1] *Typikon,* PG 127, cols. 985-1120. See also Charles Diehl, *Byzantine Empresses,* tr. Harold Bell and Theresa de Kerpely (New York, 1963), pp. 198-225.

court official and historian to whom she bore four children.

Anna never gave up trying to persuade her father to accept her as his successor. When she was 35, and Alexius lay dying, Anna and her mother strove fruitlessly to persuade him to leave the crown to Anna and her husband. With her mother's (though not her husband's) support, Anna then led a conspiracy to kill her brother. The plot was discovered, and Anna was sent to Kecharitomene, where she devoted herself to literature and authorship.

Her purpose was, as she writes, to glorify her father Alexius and his reign, so that future generations should not be deprived of a knowledge of him. History is a dam, she notes, erected against the moving river of time, which otherwise would carry everything to oblivion. The Comneni were a powerful, wealthy military family that had come to prominence in the middle of the eleventh century. Isaac Comnenus, Alexius's grandfather, had reigned as emperor; the succession shifted to the Ducas family when Isaac's brother refused the throne. Then in a *coup d'état* two years before Anna's birth, her father had himself crowned emperor.

An energetic warrior and gifted administrator, Alexius dealt ably with the pressing problems of the empire, consolidating it against three encroaching invaders in the main: the Scythians (also called Patzinaks) in the North, the Moslems from the East, and the European crusaders from the West. These last he kept at bay with the aid of the Venetians. He also had to deal with internal dissensions and pressures from the clergy and the bureaucratic nobility in his capital, and the great feudal families from the provinces. Despite his mother's opposition, Alexius married a Ducas princess, for he hoped thus to neutralize the rivalry between the two families.

Anna's work is only nominally and partly about Alexius, however, for it is a monumental history in fifteen books, modelled on Homer with christianized Byzantine variations. Her learning was considerable: she was thoroughly versed in classical literature, including Homer, Plato, and Aristotle, in Scripture and sacred writings, in rhetoric, philosophy, and the sciences, notably medicine. She was acquainted with heresy. Her sources for the *Alexiad* were documents, treaties, letters, and an unfinished manuscript left by her husband at his death. The *Alexiad* contains Anna's personal memoirs and viewpoints. Interestingly, the *Alexiad* expresses only love and praise for Anna's father, despite any ambivalence she may have harbored toward him for denying her hopes of the throne. Her brother she passes over in silence.

Anna provides many eyewitness accounts, along with her own and other people's conversations, whether remembered or invented. Her chronology is sometimes confused, and yet she preserves material not available in other sources. There are details of court intrigues and military battles, stratagems and disguises, gougings, maimings, and public burnings. Stylistically flamboyant, Anna's writing is charged with the imagery of strife and disintegration: smashing, splintering, foundering. Events are in a state of dynamic change; things threaten continually to fall apart. A recurrent metaphor, a favorite with Byzantine writers and incidentally with Boethius, is that of the tempest. Whirlwinds and crashing waves buffet the ship of state. Against this sea of troubles, however, and in all weathers, emerges a heroic personality who manages to rise larger than life to quell the churning disorder.

Often this personality is Alexius himself, laboring tirelessly to stem the destructive tides, but there are others. Indeed Anna bases her view of history on a theory of personality, for at crucial junctures in the action strong figures decide the outcome. Anna's portraits, which include Saladin, Richard the Lionhearted, and Godfrey of Bouillon, are vivid. The result is a theatrical effect, a spectacle in which historic personages, like the two whose portraits are given below, are the players engaged in dramatic exchanges and confrontations.

Passionate, self-willed, incandescent Anna stirred the imagination of writers long after her death. Sir Walter Scott mocked her learning in his medieval novel, *Count Robert of Paris,* and hinted at her secret infatuation for Bohemund the Norman, who figures so conspicuously throughout the *Alexiad.* In a sympathetic lyric, the modern Greek poet Constantine Cavafy attributes Anna's frequent tearful outbursts to her jealousy of her brother and her disappointed imperial hopes. A portrait of Anna was left by a contemporary, Georgios Tornikes, who wrote her funeral oration:

> Her large eyes . . . radiating a restrained joy
> . . . were endowed with a lively and easy
> movement when glancing around her, but most
> often were steady and calm. Her eyebrows
> were like a rainbow; her nose was slightly
> curved towards the lips edged like a rose
> blossom. The whiteness of her skin was tinged
> with a rosiness which gave color to her cheeks
> up to her old age. Her face was a perfectly
> chiseled circle. . . . Her shoulders, even . . .
> her limbs were agile and beautiful. . . . Her
> body was like a lyre or like a well-harmonized
> guitar, a fine instrument for a fine soul.[3]

Anna's own portraits of women in the *Alexiad* show them as strong and influential. Anna Dalassena (1025-1105), Anna's paternal grandmother, is the capable female ruler who appears in the epic's opening pages. Anna's description of her grandmother dwells on the matriarch's exemplary piety and habitual prayer in the beautiful Church of St. Thecla — which the Emperor Isaac had built. But Anna goes beyond religious idealization. She gives an admiring account of a gifted administrator, a woman as desirous of reigning as Anna herself was.

Anna Dalassena had been fiercely disappointed when her husband, John Comnenus, had refused the crown from his abdicating brother Isaac. Resentful of the Ducases, who succeeded instead, Anna Dalassena intrigued, cultivated alliances, and nourished her sons' ambitions from 1059 to 1081, until at last with her constant urging Alexius mounted the throne. By then she was a widow with eight children. At 75, after an energetic public life, Anna Dalassena entered the convent of Pantepoptes.

According to Anna Comnena, Alexius really wanted his mother to reign in his stead, having claimed that the survival of the Empire depended entirely on her judgment. When he left to fight the Norman Robert Guiscard, Alexius issued his

---

[2]Cited in Rae Dalven, *Anna Comnena*, pp. 67-68.

first chrysobull, a document inscribed in imperial purple ink
and pressed with a gold seal that conferred authority upon
his mother and any of her written decrees. Anna Comnena's
lavish praise of her grandmother in her several lengthy
tributes in the *Alexiad* serves as a reminder that her father
had not at that time hesitated to entrust the state to a woman,
and implies a protest against her being denied the same right.

The second portrait here is that of the Norman Bohemund
of Taranto, Prince of Antioch (ca. 1050-March 7, 1111). After
the siege of Durazzo, in which Alexius defeats his lifelong
enemy Bohemund, and which Anna also records, Bohemund
stands at last before the emperor.

Hard-pressed by the Moslems to the East — Turkomen and
Seljuks — Alexius appealed to Pope Urban II to recruit
mercenaries to help him retake the Holy Land. Urban's
somewhat delayed response, on seeing an opportunity to assert
power in the East, was to preach his famous sermon at
Clermont in November 1095. Its result was initially to draw
independent adventurers from among the land-hungry French
baronetage. Then it unloosed in successive waves from western
Europe five great migrations toward Asia Minor.

The Normans, long eager to expand their holdings
eastward from France and Italy, responded with alacrity to
the call. Anna distinguishes two types of crusaders — those
with pious motives and those intent upon conquest. To the
latter class belonged the Hauteville men who, soon after other
Normans had taken England, carved up Sicily and moved
then into Italy. One of the Hauteville descendants was Marc,
nicknamed Bohemund, who was called the most important
leader of the First Crusade. Anna's description of this
captivating "barbarian" (to Anna all of Europe was
considered barbarian), marked by odium and admiration,
accurately assesses his cunning, brutality, charm, and great
military acumen.

Anna first saw Bohemund at court when she was a
princess of thirteen. In May 1097, when Bohemund did
homage to Alexius, Emperor of Constantinople, Anna notes
the mutual distrust of these two. Bohemund refused to eat
the cooked food provided by the emperor, though he accepted
his rich gifts. Anna often writes of Bohemund's greed and
treachery, while he continued to reassure Alexius of his

friendly motives. Although many of the Normans — there were perhaps 30,000 of them — looted and raided for supplies, Bohemund restrained his own men.

From Constantinople, Bohemund proceeded to Antioch [Antakya in modern Turkey] where he was able to establish his kingdom, and enlarge his territories. Imprisoned by the Turks and ransomed, he returned to Europe to raise money and he was received as a conquering hero, even as "Christ himself." He married Constance of France, using the royal wedding at Chartres as an occasion for troop recruitment, climbing to the organ-loft to address the crowds in the spring of 1106.

Now with papal approval, Bohemund organized a fresh crusade against Constantinople, envisioning for himself an entire eastern empire. He spent a year building a fleet at Brindisi and collecting the army that flocked to him. But at Durazzo, the modern city of Durres in Albania, a seaport city on the Adriatic coast considered the gateway to Constantinople, Bohemund met his defeat. Instead of doing hard battle with Bohemund, Alexius let the besieged city of Durazzo wait it out. He tired the Normans by starving them, and blocked the mountain passes to prevent them from getting supplies. Soldiers deserted; famine and disease followed. By 1108 Bohemund had finally to sue for peace at Deabolis, an outlying district of Durazzo. Anna was twenty-five at the time; her husband, court official Nicephorus Bryennius, arranged the preliminaries of the surrender.

Anna has documented in full detail the treaty and terms of Bohemund's surrender, as well as Bohemund's arrogant outbursts, his insistence on standing at the head of the emperor's couch, his refusal to bend his neck. The following passages describe the first part of the losing siege of Durazzo, giving a lively account of medieval warfare. The siege occupies a climactic place, near the close of the *Alexiad,* as a major victory of Alexius against the west. Following the battle is Anna's striking portrait of Bohemund, a powerful and Satanic figure standing boldly in defeat. In Anna's dramatic vision of history, Bohemund symbolizes the terrible Norman power that the Emperor was able to quell.

1. Anna Dalassena

It may cause some surprise that my father the Emperor had raised his mother to such a position of honor, and that he had handed complete power over to her. Yielding up the reins of government, one might say, he ran alongside her as she drove the imperial chariot, and contented himself with the title only of Basileus. . . .

My father reserved for himself the waging of wars against the barbarians, and all the strains and hazards that these involved, while he entrusted to his mother the administration of state affairs, the choosing of civil servants, and the fiscal management of the empire's revenues and expenses. One might perhaps, in reading this, blame my father's decision to entrust the imperial government to the gyneceum.[3] But once you understood the ability of this woman, her excellence, her good sense, and her remarkable capacity for hard work, you would turn from criticism to admiration.

For my grandmother really had the gift of conducting the affairs of state. She knew so well how to organize and administer that she was capable of governing not only the Roman Empire but also every other kingdom under the sun. Indeed she had a considerable experience: she understood the nature of all sorts of affairs of state; she knew how each matter began and how it would finish, and which things would destroy an enterprise and which, on the other hand, would strengthen it. She was very shrewd in seizing on whatever was called for, and clever in carrying it out with certitude. Not only did she have an outstanding intelligence, but her powers of speech matched it. She was a truly persuasive orator, in no way wordy or long-winded. Nor did she run out of the breath of inspiration after a short time: she would begin speaking with purpose and she would end on a note of even greater resolution.

She was ripe in years when she ascended the imperial throne, at the moment when her mental powers were at their

---

[3] Anna says elsewhere that the women's quarters, the gyneceum, were separated only by a curtain.

most vigorous, and her understanding at its keenest, while her experience in affairs of state was also at its richest — all qualities which give strength to government.

Formerly, when Anna Dalassena was still a younger woman, it was really wonderful to see her display the wisdom of old age in the flower of her youth. Her eyes alone revealed the Basilissa's courage and level-headedness to anyone who wished to take notice. . . .

The gyneceum of the imperial palace had been completely addicted to vice since the notorious Constantine Monomachos[4] had seized the imperial power and had been reputed — right up to my father's reign — for his foolish love affairs. But Anna Dalassena reformed the women's quarters, and restored them to a wonderful propriety, while in the palace a marvelous orderliness prevailed. For she established specific hours for sacred hymns, she fixed the times for meals and for the choosing of civil servants; she herself became a model for others to emulate, so much so that the palace seemed rather to be a holy monastery as a result of this truly extraordinary and holy woman. For she surpassed the famous women of antiquity, who are so celebrated, as much as the sun outdazzles the stars.

As for her compassion toward the poor and the lavishness of her hand toward the destitute, how can words describe these things? Her house was a shelter for her needy relatives, and it was no less a haven for strangers. She venerated priests and monks in particular; she invited them to share her meals. One never saw her at the table without there being monks present. Her expression, which revealed her true character, demanded the worship of the angels but struck terror among demons. To licentious people — those carried away by their passions — her look alone was unendurable. Yet to those who were concerned about improving their ways, she seemed amiable and kind.

So well did she understand the right degree of control and seriousness that she herself betrayed neither a harsh, cruel restraint, nor a lax, soft carelessness. And this, I think, is the

---

[4]Constantine IX (1042-1054).

definition of decorum: to balance bounty with moral seriousness.

Anna Dalassena's nature was conducive to reflectiveness. She was continually making fresh plans which, far from hurting the public good (as some people were whispering), were intended to restore the empire — which had already become corrupt — to its original vigor, and to raise up as much as possible the fallen condition of the people. Although she was involved in the administration of the government, she did not neglect a single one of the duties of the monastic life she embraced. She devoted the better part of the night to sacred hymns, and fatigued herself with continual prayers and vigils. And yet at dawn, at the second cock-crow, she set about attending to affairs of state.

2. The Siege of Durazzo

Bohemund, their leader, as we have said, had crossed over from Italy into our territory with his formidable fleet, and had unleashed the entire Frankish army to attack our province. Next he marched in battle formation against Epidamnus[1] in the hopes of taking it in the first onslaught. Failing in this, he decided to level the city by using siege engines and catapults for hurling rocks. This was his aim. He pitched his camp facing the eastern gate, over which there is a bronze horseman, and after having reconnoitered all the areas he began to lay siege to the city.

Throughout the entire winter he made plans and marked out all the places where Durazzo was vulnerable. When spring began to smile, and he had brought over all his troops, he set fire to the ships that had transported his supplies, horses, and men. This was a calculated move to prevent his army from looking back toward the sea. He was moreover driven to this because of the presence of the Roman[2] fleet.

---

[1]Epidamnus was the ancient name for Durazzo, which the Romans called Dyrrachium, and which is today Durres in Albania.

[2]By Romans Anna means her father's army, since Alexius still considered himself to be reigning over the Roman Empire

Bohemund now concerned himself with the siege alone.

To begin with he surrounded the city with his barbarian forces, and sent out detachments of the Frankish army to create skirmishes. But the Roman archers responded by shooting at them, both from the towers of Durazzo or from afar. In short, there were attacks and counterattacks. Bohemund seized Petroula and a place called Mylos, located on the farther side of the Deabolis River. Other places like these that lay outside Durazzo fell into his hands, through the luck of combat. While his military ability in general brought about these victories, his skill as an inventor impelled him at the same time to build battle engines, and to prepare tortoise-like structures. Some of these tortoises[3] bore towers and battering rams, while others had covered roofs to protect the men who were miners and sappers digging under the city walls.

Bohemund worked throughout the whole winter and the summer, terrorizing the citizens both by his threats and his actions. But he did not manage to shake the might of the Romans. Food supplies, moreover, were causing him problems. Everything he had collected by pillaging the country around Durazzo had been consumed, and the places from which he had hoped to procure additional provisions were cut off by the Roman army, which from the first had occupied the valleys and the defiles, and even guarded the sea. The result was a terrible famine which killed Bohemund's men and horses alike, the horses getting no fodder and the men no food. Dysentery also raged throughout the barbarian army, apparently because of the inadequate diet consisting of millet cereal. In reality, divine wrath struck down these innumerable and invincible forces, and slaughtered the men one after another.

However, these trials seemed slight to this man,

---

[3]The military word (in Latin *testudo*) used for shelters or sheds. Originally men held their overlapping shields above their heads to provide such a plated, tortoise-like carapace of shelter.

Bohemund, who had the spirit of a commander, and who was threatening to destroy an entire land. Despite his reverses, he continued to try all kinds of stratagems, and like a wounded wild animal he turned inward upon himself and fixed his gaze only on the siege. First he constructed a "tortoise" with a "ram," an indescribable monster, and had it brought up to the east wall of the city. You had only to look at it — it was a terrifying sight. It was built in the following way; a small rectangular "tortoise" was made under which wheels were placed. It was then covered on every surface, above and on the sides, by ox hides stitched together, so that, as Homer said, the roof and walls of this engine were made of "the hides of seven oxen."[4] Then the "rams" were hung on the inside.

Once this engine was finished, it was brought to the ramparts by a team of thousands of men armed with pikes, who pushed it forward from the inside and led it right up to the walls of Durazzo. When it was brought to within the desired distance, just close enough, they took away the wheels and fastened the engine solidly to the earth with wooden stakes, so that the violent jolting within would not cause the roof to collapse. After this, several very sturdy men positioned themselves to the right and left of the battering ram, with which they drove violently against the bulwarks with a regular rhythmic pounding force. They thus drove the ram powerfully for the first time; this first time it struck the wall, bore into it, then rebounded. They thrust at it a second time, and continued to breach the wall.

This procedure was repeated many times, while the instrument came and went ceaselessly in a way that was intended to burst through the bulwark. Undoubtedly the inventors of antiquity who devised this engine near Gadeira [Cadiz] called it a "ram," borrowing a metaphor from our actual rams who engage in butting into each other.

But the city's inhabitants, who were laughing at this goat-like attack and these futile attempts to besiege the city, actually threw open their gates and invited the soldiers to

---

[4]*Iliad* 7.545.

come in that way — making fun of the blows delivered by the ram. "This ram," they said, "with its thrusts against the ramparts, will never make a hole as big as the entrance the gate provides!"

[Anna goes on to describe other military weaponry deployed by Bohemund and his men. But while using sappers to mine under the great towers, the Normans met the Greeks, who, tunneling toward them in the opposite direction, sprayed them with fire. Their final effort to construct immense towers overtopping the city walls, equipped with drawbridges for running over the city roofs, also failed. The roofs of Durazzo had been provided with loose planks which would not support the invaders. Alexius's men threw "Greek fire"[5] down on Bohemund's towers, as they did upon the the tortoise and battering ram described above, reducing these to ashes, to the utter dismay of the Norman armies.]

3. Bohemund

In short there had never been seen anywhere in the Roman world a man like him, whether Greek or barbarian. The sight of him inspired awe; his reputation caused terror. To give a detailed description of this barbarian: he was so great of stature that he was taller than other men by nearly a foot and a half. He was slim, without any excess of weight, broad-shouldered and big-chested, with muscular arms. His body overall was neither thin nor corpulent, but perfectly proportioned, in conformity, one could say, with standards of Polycletus.[6] He had strong hands, and stood firmly planted

---

[5]Greek fire was an inflammable mixture, which might consist of pitch, sulfur, and burning charcoal. Tallow, saltpeter, quicklime, bitumen, naptha were other possible ingredients. This incendiary technique was used in medieval warfare by the Byzantine Greeks especially.

[6]A Greek sculptor of Argos, Polycletus was perhaps a younger contemporary of Phidias, living in the second half of the 5th century

on his feet, stalwart and well-built across the neck and shoulders. To a close observer he seemed slightly bent, though this was not due to any weakness of the spinal bones, since he apparently had this slight curvature from birth.

He had very white skin, but in his facial coloring, both fair and ruddy mingled. His hair was tawny, and did not tumble over his shoulders as did the locks of the other barbarians; in fact, this man did not have a mania for long hair. Instead he kept it clipped short around the ears. Was his beard russet or some other color? I couldn't say, since the razor had shorn it and left the skin as smooth as marble; still, it seemed that it might have been russet. His blue eyes revealed both force and dignity. His nose and his nostrils breathed the air freely, his chest being proportioned to his nostrils and his nostrils to his chest. Through the nostrils, indeed, nature gives free passage to the breath that surges from the lungs.

A certain charm emanated from this warrior, but it was lessened a little by the terrifying quality that issued from his being. The man as a whole was tough and brutal, both in his stance and in his look, it seemed to me, and even his way of laughing — which in another person would have been a snorting shudder — made the court circle tremble. Body and soul he was so constituted that both violence and desire strove within him, and both of them drove him to combat. He had a spirit that was subtle, sly, and full of subterfuges for every occasion. His utterances were in fact calculated and his replies always double-edged. This man, so superior in all these ways, could be defeated by no other than my father the Emperor, who surpassed him with respect to fortune, eloquence, and the gifts of nature.

Further Reading on Anna Comnena

Text: Bernard Leib, ed. *Anne Comnène, l'Alexiade*. Texte établi et traduit. 3 vols. Paris, 1937-1945.

B.C. His great reputation, during his lifetime and afterwards, was based in part on his Olympic *Victors*.

Georgina Buckler. *Anna Comnena: A Study.* Rpt. London, 1968.

Rae Dalven. *Anna Comnena.* New York, 1972.

Elizabeth Dawes. *The Alexiad of Princess Anna Comnena.* Rpt. New York, 1967.

E.R.A. Sewter, tr. *The Alexiad of Anna Comnena.* Rpt. New York, 1979.

Basile Skoulatos. *Les Personnages Byzantins de l'Alexiade.* Louvain, 1980.

Benedictine Visionaries
in the Rhineland
Hildegard of Bingen (1098-1179)
Elisabeth of Schönau (1129-1165)

Two cloistered women in the Rhineland, both of different Benedictine monasteries, earned widespread reputations for their piety and their gifts of vision and prophecy. Hildegard of Bingen led the way with her astonishing revelations and writings. The more frail Elisabeth, thirty-one years her junior and deeply influenced by Hildegard, produced a body of visionary writing that bears the stamp of her own individuality and had important repercussions in hagiography and art.

Hildegard of Bingen

The woman who would be known as the "Sibyl of the Rhine" was born into a noble family at Bermersheim near Alzey. Her writings reveal a prodigious talent and energy, their variety unparalleled among medieval women writers: she produced works of drama and lyric, music, mysticism, prophecy, cosmology, the lore of animals and gems, medicine, and three books of dazzling allegorical visions.

Much of what Hildegard wrote contains autobiographical information. She carried on a voluminous correspondence with notable people of her day, among them Eleanor of Aquitaine and Henry II of England, Bernard of Clairvaux, popes Eugenius III, Anastasius IV, Adrian IV, and Alexander III, the emperors Conrad III and Frederick Barbarossa, and the mystic Elisabeth of Schönau. An important letter to a man who served as her secretary, Guibert of Gembloux, vividly describes the workings of Hildegard's visions, and the appearance in them of a mirroring "shadow of the Living Light." Further sources on her life are the two contemporary biographies by the monks Godefrid and Theodoric, for which Hildegard herself wrote a dozen passages. A later inquiry into her life and miracles, conducted in the thirteenth century for Pope Gregory IX, adds to her *Vita*.

Hildegard recalls that her visions of great light began when she was five. From the age of eight, she lived at the convent at Disibodenberg, where her parents Hildebert and Mechthild had placed her, their tenth and last child, under the tutelage of the anchoress Jutta of Sponheim. The Benedictine house of Disibodenberg emphasized prayer and study, the reading of Scripture and Psalms, together with physical labor. Despite her protestations of ignorance, Hildegard must have studied Latin, although she could not have had the same kind of classical education — in Ovid, Horace, Terence, and Virgil — as Hrotswitha in the Ottonian renaissance of the tenth century.

Hildegard reluctantly succeeded her beloved Jutta as *magistra* of the community in 1136. Five years later when she was nearly forty-three, she experienced a vision of stunning radiance in which a heavenly voice commanded her to write what she saw. She resisted, however, until sickness compelled her to record the succession of visions she experienced over the next ten years. These visions formed the beginning of her first book, *Scivias,* or, "Know the Ways." Parts of the *Scivias* were read by Pope Eugenius before the Synod of Trier. He also examined Hildegard, ascertaining the authenticity of her visions. She answered his interrogations with truth and simplicity. She began to be famous.

When in 1148 Hildegard wished to found her own convent, she was refused permission by Kuno, abbot of Disibodenberg. Her further debilitating sickness persuaded Kuno that divinity had a hand in Hildegard's affairs, and she was allowed to begin building the independent convent of Rupertsberg near Bingen on the Rhine. She moved with eighteen nuns, all noblewomen, to the new site in 1150; in the same period she was completing the *Scivias* with the aid of the monk Volmar and her secretary-companion Rikkardis von Stade, to whom she was intensely devoted. When Rikkardis transferred to a position of authority in another convent, Hildegard suffered.

She began her second book of visions, the *Liber vitae meritorum* ("The Book of Life's Rewards"), and wrote during 1158-1163 while traveling and preaching throughout towns and cities in Germany. Though chronically ill she made four preaching journeys from the ages of sixty to seventy-two, not shrinking from contact with large numbers of people. She visited Cologne on three occasions, very taken with the St. Ursula legend, then at its height with the discovery of what appeared to be bones belonging to the saint and her companions. Hildegard composed thirteen lyrics honoring the saint, while Elisabeth of Schönau recorded her own visions, translated below, of Ursula's band, refashioning the legend in what would be its most influential form.

Hildegard wrote her third and final book of visions, the *Liber divinorum operum* ("The Book of Divine Works") between 1163 and 1173. In it she suggests a human microcosm, mapping the interconnections between humanity and the cosmos; between the human and divine Christ; between the physical body with its humors, and the soul with its emotions and capacity for salvation. An indwelling fiery force, the *ignea vis,* unites all aspects of the universe in a way that is serene, rational, and harmonious — in contrast to the swirling commotion of the *Scivias.*

In the last year of her life — she was over eighty — Hildegard became involved in a controversy when she insisted on burying an excommunicated nobleman at Rupertsberg, and the convent was placed under episcopal interdict. Hildegard refused to yield and the interdict was lifted. On September 17, 1179, according to her biographer, she went to meet her celestial Bridegroom in a blessed death. The sky was said to be illuminated with circles of light and shining red crosses, as if to reveal to her sisters the visions she had experienced.

Hildegard's visions, converted into marvelous, often hallucinating poetry and prose, are characterized by scintillating lights, fires, colors, stenches, oval and circular shapes, and personages, often larger than life, who speak out of fogs, clouds, and winds. A light will pour over some central scene, such as a mountain, a river, an abyss, a human presence, a beast, or an architectural structure. Greenness and greening — *viriditas* — have a peculiar meaning for her, associated with the divinely energetic life-force pulsing through all being.

Hildegard's visions, startling in their brilliance, have attracted the notice of modern pathologists, who trace their source in her lifelong illnesses.[1] And yet, the effective power of her visions — like those of seers from Elisabeth of Schönau to Joan of Arc — remains undiminished by scientific diagnosis.

Passages 1-4, translated here from Hildegard's works, are her "Solemn Declaration" (*Protestificatio*) and selections from the first three visions in Book I of the *Scivias*. The *Scivias* comprises 26 visions. The six visions of Book I trace the history of God, humankind, and the world from the Creation and Fall, and the promise of a Savior. In seven visions, Book II describes the redemption through Christ, as the Sun, and his mystic marriage with the Church at the foot of the Cross. Book III, in thirteen visions, represents through architectural imagery the rebuilding of salvation by divine powers, or virtues; the last days of the world; the last struggle against Satan; and the Church's entrance into the apocalypse of Eternity.

From the *Liber vitae meritorum* are taken passages 5-7. The "Book of Life's Rewards" is a vast cosmic psychomachia of verbal battles. Vices and Virtues, represented as universal forces, confront one another, using words as weapons. These battles culminate in the triumphs of human goodness, with the Church's coming into eternal glory. The book opens with a central figure of God. Hildegard's dazzled eyes behold him as a powerful, perfect, and transcendent Man, who reaches

---

[1]Oliver Sacks, *Migraine: Understanding a Common Disorder* (Berkeley, 1985); John F. Benton, "Consciousness of Self and Perceptions of Individuality," pp. 267-268, in *Renaissance and Renewal in the Twelfth Century,* ed. Robert L. Benson and Giles Constable, with Carol D. Lanham (Cambridge, Mass., 1982).

from the clouds to the depths of the abyss. He is the principle of all being, who guides human salvation on its course. Hildegard observes his cloud-shaped trumpet that blasts forth three winds. Above these hover three clouds — one fiery, one turbulent, and one luminous. These trumpeted winds of God's blowing invite comparison to Chaucer's windy, smoky trumpets in *The House of Fame*. Now Hildegard's verbal psychomachia unfolds. The book also dramatizes eternity's punishments and rewards: the last selection tells of the heavenly virgins, ecstatic companions — like the 144,000 maidens in Middle English *Pearl* — of the Lamb.

Some of Hildegard's lore on gems appears in passages 8 and 9, from the book commonly known as *Physica,* or *Liber simplicis medicinae* ("The Book of Simple Medicine"). This work, together with her *Causae et curae,* or *Liber compositae medicinae* ("The Book of Advanced and Applied Medicine") belongs to Hildegard's great work on the natural sciences, the *Liber subtilitatum diversarum naturarum creaturarum.* The *Physica* lists in nine sections the basic and curative properties of plants, the elements, trees, stones, fish, birds, animals, reptiles, and metals. In the fourth book of the *Physica,* called *De lapidibus,* Hildegard composed 26 short chapters on precious stones: emerald, jacinth, onyx, beryl, sardonyx, sapphire, sard, topaz, chrysolite, jasper, prase, chalcedony, chrysoprase, carbuncle, amethyst, agate, diamond, magnet, ligurius, crystal, pearl — both true and false — carnelian, alabaster, chalk, and a category of "other gems."

Section 10 includes seven lyrics from the *Symphonia harmoniae caelestium revelationum* ("Symphony of the Harmony of Celestial Revelations"). The first two honor the Blessed Virgin Mary, the third celebrates St. Maximinus, and the fourth consisits of an antiphon and responsory to St. Ursula. There is a love song chanted to Christ by his virgin brides, and the last two are hymns to the green life force, that *viriditas* which is one of Hildegard's pervasive presences.

In addition to these works, the letters, and the three visionary books mentioned above, Hildegard's opus includes her drama, the *Ordo virtutum,* two books on her secret language, the *Lingua ignota* and the *Litterae ignotae,* a book of exegesis on the Psalms, the *Expositio Evangeliorum,* and two works of hagiography honoring St. Rupert and St. Disibode.

*1. A Solemn Declaration Concerning the True Vision Flowing
   from God:*
   Scivias. Protestificatio

Lo! In the forty-third year of my temporal course, when I clung to a celestial vision with great fear and tremulous effort, I saw a great splendor. In it came a voice from heaven, saying:

"O frail mortal, both ash of ashes, and rottenness of rottenness, speak and write down what you see and hear. But because you are fearful of speaking, simple at expounding, and unlearned in writing — speak and write — not according to the speech of man or according to intelligence of human invention, or following the aim of human composition, but according to what you see and hear from the heavens above in the wonders of God! Offer explanations of them, just as one who hears and understands the words of an instructor willingly makes them public, revealing and teaching them according to the sense of the instructor's discourse. You, therefore, O mortal, speak also the things you see and hear. Write them, not according to yourself or to some other person, but according to the will of the Knower, Seer, and Ordainer of all things in the secrets of their mysteries."

And again I heard the voice from heaven saying to me: "Speak these wonders and write the things taught in this manner — and speak!"

It happened in the year 1141 of the Incarnation of the Son of God, Jesus Christ, when I was forty-two years and seven months old, that a fiery light of the greatest radiance coming from the open heavens flooded through my entire brain. It kindled my whole breast like a flame that does not scorch but warms in the same way the sun warms anything on which it sheds its rays.

Suddenly I understood the meaning of books, that is, the Psalms and the Gospels; and I knew other catholic books of the Old as well as the New Testaments — not the significance of the words of the text, or the division of the syllables, nor did I consider an examination of the cases and tenses.

Indeed, from the age of girlhood, from the time that I was fifteen until the present, I had perceived in myself, just as until this moment, a power of mysterious, secret, and marvelous visions of a miraculous sort. However, I revealed these things to no one, except to a few religious persons who were living under the same vows as I was. But meanwhile, until this time when God in his grace has willed these things to be revealed, I have repressed them in quiet silence.

But I have not perceived these visions in dreams, or asleep, or in a delirium, or with my bodily eyes, or with my external mortal ears, nor in secreted places, but I received them awake and looking attentively about me with an unclouded mind, in open places, according to God's will. However this may be, it is difficult for carnal man to fathom.

Once the term of my girlhood was completed, and I had arrived at the age of perfect strength which I mentioned, I heard a voice from heaven saying:

"I am the Living Light who illuminates the darkness. I have, according to my pleasure, wondrously shaken with great marvels this mortal whom I desired, and I have placed her beyond the limit reached by men of ancient times who saw in me many secret things. But I have leveled her to the ground, so that she may not raise herself up with any pride in her own mind. The world, moreover, has not had any joy of her, or sport, or practice in those things belonging to the world. I have freed her from obstinate boldness; she is fearful and anxious in her endeavors. She has suffered pain in her very marrow and in all the veins of her body; her spirit has been fettered; she has felt and endured many bodily illnesses. No pervading freedom from care has dwelt within her, but she considers herself culpable in all her undertakings.

"I have hedged round the clefts of her heart, so that her mind will not elevate itself through pride or praise, but so that she will feel more fear and pain in these things than joy or wantonness.

"For the sake of my love, therefore, she has searched in her own mind as to where she might find someone who would run in the path of salvation. And when she found one and loved him,[2] she recognized that he was a faithful man, one similar to herself in some part of that work which pertains to me. Keeping him with her, she strove at the same time with him in all these divine studies, so that my hidden wonders might be revealed. And the same man did not place himself above her. But in an ascent to humility, and with the exertion of good will when he came to her, he yielded to her with many sighs.

"You, therefore, O mortal, who receive these things — not in the turmoil of deception but in the clarity of simplicity for the purpose of making hidden things plain — write what you see and hear!"

But although I was seeing and hearing these things, I nevertheless refused to write for a very long time because of doubt and wrong thinking — on account of the various judgments of men — not out of boldness but out of the duty of my humility.

Finally, I fell to my sickbed, quelled by the whip of God. Racked by many infirmities, and with a young girl[3] of noble blood and good character as witness — as well as a man I had secretly sought out and discovered, as I have already said — I put my hand to writing.

While I was doing this, I sensed the profound depth of the narration of these books, as I have said. And despite the strength I experienced when I was raised up from my sickness, I carried out that work with difficulty to the end, completing it after ten years. These visions and these words took place during the days of Heinrich, Archbishop of Mainz,[4] Conrad, Emperor of the Romans,[5] and Kuno, abbot of Mount

---

[2] The monk Volmar of Disibodenberg, Hildegard's secretary.

[3] Rikkardis von Stade, a spiritual daughter of Hildegard's toward whom she felt deep affection.

[4] Heinrich I of Wartburg, archbishop between 1142 and 1153.

[5] Conrad II, 1138-1152, who died on crusade in the Holy Land.

St. Disibodenberg,[6] under Pope Eugenius.[7]

I have spoken and written this, not according to the invention of my heart, or of any man, but as I saw these things in the heavens and heard and perceived them through God's sacred mysteries. And again I heard a voice from the sky saying to me, "Shout, therefore, and write this way!"

2. The Iron-Colored Mountain and the Radiant One: Scivias. Book I, Vision I

I saw what seemed to be a huge mountain having the color of iron. On its height was sitting One[8] of such great radiance that it stunned my vision. On both sides of him extended a gentle shadow like a wing of marvelous width and length.[9] And in front of him at the foot of the same mountain stood a figure full of eyes everywhere.[10] Because of

---

[6]Fl. ca. 1136-1155

[7]Eugenius III (1145-1153). Through his permission and encouragement Hildegard continued to write her books, a stroke of inspiration or good fortune during a time when it was possible for popes and councils to condemn and burn such books.

[8]Notes 8 through 14 represent in abbreviated form the explanations Hildegard receives from the One sitting on the mountain.

The iron-colored mountain signifies the strength and immutability of God's eternal realm. The One who has stunned Hildegard's vision is the same One who, reigning over all the spheres of earth and heavenly divinity in unwavering brightness, is incomprehensible to the human mind.

[9]The shadow is the sweet, gentle protection of the blessed Defense. It both admonishes and chastises, justly and affectionately, showing the way to righteousness with true equity.

[10]This figure is Fear of the Lord (*Timor Domini*). Armored by the keen-sightedness of good and just intentions, he inspires in

those eyes, I was not able to distinguish any human form.

In front of this figure there was another figure, whose age was that of a boy, and he was clothed in a pale tunic and white shoes.[11] I was not able to look at his face, because above his head so much radiance descended from the One sitting on the mountain.[12] From the One sitting on the mountain a great many living sparks cascaded, which flew around those figures with great sweetness.[13] In this same mountain, moreover, there seemed to be a number of little windows, in which men's heads appeared, some pale and some white.[14]

And see! The One sitting on the mountain shouted in an extremely loud, strong voice, saying: "O frail mortal, you who are of the dust of the earth's dust, and ash of ash, cry out and speak of the way into incorruptible salvation! Do this in order that those people may be taught who see the inner-most meaning of Scripture, but who do not wish to tell it or

---

human beings his own zeal and steadfastness. His acute vigilance drives away that forgetfulness of God's justice that often afflicts mortals.

[11]The boy-like figure in white shoes is the poor in spirit. In pale submission to God, he puts on a white tunic and faithfully follows the gleaming white footsteps of the Son of God.

[12]The radiance descending from the One on the mountain is the shining visitation from that One who governs all creatures, pouring down the power and strength of his blessedness.

[13]The living sparks cascading down from the One on the mountain are the many potent virtues that emanate from him. These virtues ardently embrace and soothe those who truly fear God and love poverty of spirit, enfolding them with their aid and protection.

[14]The men's heads, some pale and some white, appearing in the little windows, show that human actions cannot be hidden. The pale, dull-colored ones indicate those who are lukewarm and sluggish in their deeds, and therefore dishonorable. The white and shining ones are those who are vigilant.

preach it because they are lukewarm and dull in preserving God's justice. Unlock for them the mystical barriers. For they, being timid, are hiding themselves in a remote and barren field. You, therefore, pour yourself forth in a fountain of abundance! Flow with mystical learning, so that those who want you to be scorned because of the guilt of Eve may be inundated by the flood of your refreshment!

"For you do not receive this keenness of insight from man, but from the supernal and awesome judge on high. There, amidst brilliant light, this radiance will brightly shine forth among the luminous ones. Arise, therefore, and shout and speak! These things are revealed to you through the strongest power of divine aid. For he who potently and benignly rules his creatures imbues with the radiance of heavenly enlightenment all those who fear him and serve him with sweet love in a spirit of humility. And he leads those who persevere in the path of justice to the joys of everlasting vision!"

3. The Fall of Lucifer, the Formation of Hell, and the Fall of Adam and Eve:
   Scivias. Book I, Vision 2

Then I saw what seemed to be a great number of living torches, full of brilliance. Catching a fiery gleam, they received a most radiant splendor from it. And see! A lake appeared here, of great length and depth, with a mouth like a well, breathing forth a stinking, fiery smoke. From the mouth of the lake a loathsome fog also arose until it touched a thing like a blood-vessel, that had a deceptive appearance.

And in a certain region of brightness, the fog blew through the blood-vessel to a pure white cloud, which emerged from the beautiful form of a man, and the cloud contained within itself many, many stars. Then the loathsome fog blew and drove the cloud and the man's form out of the region of brightness.

Once this had happened, the most luminous splendor encircled that region. The elements of the world, which previously had held firmly together in great tranquility, now turned into great turmoil and displayed fearful terrors.

[Hildegard hears a voice explaining the meaning of what she

has seen. The style suggests a sermon]:

The "great number of living torches, full of brilliance" refers to the numerous army of heavenly spirits blazing forth in their life of blessedness. They dwell with much honor and adornment, for they have been created by God. These did not grasp at proudly exalting themselves, but persisted steadfastly in divine love.

"Catching a fiery gleam, they received a most radiant splendor from it" means that when Lucifer and his followers tried to rebel against the heavenly Creator, and fell, those others who kept a zealous love of God came to a common agreement, and clothed themselves in the vigilance of divine love.

But Lucifer and his followers had embraced the sluggardly ignorance of those who do not wish to know God. What happened? When the devil fell, a great praise arose from those angelic spirits who had persisted in righteousness with God. For they recognized with the keenest vision that God remained unshaken, without any mutable change in his power, and that he will not be overthrown by any warrior. And so they burned fiercely in their love for him, and persevering in righteousness, they scorned all the dust of injustice.

Now "that lake of great length and depth" which appeared to you is Hell. In its length are contained vices, and in its deep abyss is damnation, as you see. Also, "it has a mouth like a well, breathing forth a stinking, fiery smoke," which means that drowning souls are swallowed in its voracious greed. For although the lake shows them sweetness and delights, it leads them, through perverse deceit, to a perdition of torments. There the heat of the fire breathes forth with an outpouring of the most loathsome smoke, and with a boiling, death-dealing stench. For these abominable torments were prepared for the devil and his followers, who turned away from the highest good, which they wanted neither to know nor to understand. For this reason they were cast down from every good thing, not because they did not know them but because they were contemptuous of them in their lofty pride.

"From that same lake a most loathsome fog arose, until

it touched a thing like a blood-vessel that had a deceptive appearance." This means that the diabolical deceit emanating from deepest perdition entered the poisonous serpent. The serpent contained within itself the crime of fraudulent intention to deceive man. How? When the devil saw man in Paradise , he cried out in great agitation, saying, "O who is this that approaches me in the mansion of true blessedness?" He knew himself that the malice he had within him had not yet filled other creatures. But seeing Adam and Eve walking in childlike innocence in the garden of delights, he — in his great stupefaction — set out to deceive them through the serpent.

Why? Because he perceived that the serpent was more like him than was any other animal, and that by striving craftily he could bring about covertly what he could not openly accomplish in his own shape. When, therefore, he saw Adam and Eve turn away, both in body and mind, from the tree that was forbidden to them, he realized that they had had a divine command. He realized that through the first act they attempted, he could overthrow them very easily.

The vision "In this same region of brightness he blew on a white cloud which emerged from the beautiful form of a man and the cloud contained within itself many, many stars" means this: In this place of delight, the devil, by means of the serpent's seductions, attacked Eve and brought about her downfall. Eve had an innocent soul. She had been taken from the side of innocent Adam, bearing within her body the luminous multitude of the human race, as God had preordained it.

Why did the devil attack her? Because he knew that the woman's softness would be more easily conquered than the man's strength, seeing, indeed, that Adam burned so fiercely with love for Eve that if the devil himself could conquer Eve, Adam would do anything she told him. Therefore the devil "cast her and that same form of a man out of the region." This meant that the ancient seducer, by driving Eve and Adam from the abode of blessedness through his deceit, sent them into darkness and ruin.

4. The Cosmic Egg:
Scivias. Book I, Vision 3

After this I saw a huge creation, rounded and shaded and shaped like an egg.[15] It was narrow at the top, wide in the middle, and compact below. The outer part was surrounded by a brilliant fire[16] that had a kind of shadowy membrane beneath it. Within that fire was an orb of glittering red flame,[17] of such great size that the whole creation was illumined by it. Above it were aligned in a row three little torches[18] that steadied the orb with their fires so that it would not fall.

Sometimes the orb reared itself upwards, and many fires rushed to meet it, so that it then further lengthened its own flames.[19] At other times it sank downwards and a great cold obstructed it, and the glittering red orb quickly retracted its

---

[15]Notes 15 through 32 represent in abbreviated form Hildegard's allegorizations of what she sees. The firmament is Almighty God, incomprehensible in his majesty and unfathomable in his mysteries, the hope of all the faithful.

[16]In this fiery circumference, God consumes those who are outside the true faith with the fire of his vengeance, but those remaining within the Catholic faith he purifies with the fire of his consolation.

[17]The Sun, explained allegorically as the solar Christ, or the Sun of Justice, whose fiery love illumines all things.

[18]Mars, Jupiter, and Saturn represent the Trinity, their descending order showing the earthward descent of Christ.

[19]The Sun's lengthened rays signify the fecundating power of the Father, at the same time of Christ's incarnation, by which the heavenly mystery was effected in the Virgin Mary.

own flames.[20]

But from the fire around the circumference of that creation, a wind gusted forth with its tornadoes.[21] And from the membrane that was under the fire another blast boiled up with its whirlwinds, and they spread here and there throughout the creation. In that same membrane there was a dark fire so horrifying that I was not able to look at it.[22] This fire tore through the entire membrane with its force, full of thundering, storms, and the sharpest stones, both large and small. As long as it raised up its thunder, the brilliant fire and the winds and air were thrown into a turmoil,[23] and lightning flashes outdid the thunder. For that brilliant fire was the first to feel the thunder's commotion.[24]

Below that membrane was the purest ether, which had no membrane under it. In the ether I saw an orb of dazzling white fire,[25] very great in size. Two little

---

[20]This sinking indicates Christ's descent to earth to put on wretched human form and physical suffering, after which he ascended again to the Father, as the Scriptures record.

[21]Each of the four speaking winds carries a specific report. The first wind, coming from the South and located in the fiery circumference, is God's word. God the Father reveals his power through the just words of his truth.

[22]The North wind, boiling up from the dark region of fire, is the devil's insane and futile speech.

[23]Cosmic storms are provoked by the sin of murder, which brings on heavenly retribution. These storms pelt creation with thunder, lightning, and hailstorms.

[24]Divine majesty foresees the crime of murder and punishes it.

[25]The Moon, to be understood also as the unconquered Church.

torches[26] were set brightly above it, steadying the white orb so that it would not swerve from its course. And in that ether, many bright spheres[27] were placed everywhere. Into these spheres the dazzling white orb emptied some portion of itself from time to time, sending out its radiance. And so, the white orb, hastening back towards the glittering red orb and renewing its own flames there, breathed forth those flames among the spheres. And from that ether, a wind blasted forth with its tornadoes, and it whirled everywhere through that creation I spoke of.[28]

Below that same ether I saw a watery air that had a white membrane under it. This air, blowing here and there, provided moisture to the entire creation. Now and then it would suddenly gather itself together, and with a great spattering spew forth a sudden torrent. Then it would softly spread itself, and drop a caressing, gently falling rain. But from this place, too, a wind gusted forth[29] with its whirling force, and blew everywhere throughout that creation I spoke of.

In the midst of these elements was a sandy globe[30] of great

------

[26]Venus and Mercury, to be understood also as the Old and New Testaments guarding the Church.

[27]The stars in the ether signify the many splendid works of piety appearing everywhere in the purity of the faith.

[28]The West wind, emanating from the purest ether, spreads the strong and glorious teachings of the faith.

[29]The East wind, blowing from the humid, airy region, brings salvation through true speech and sermons, with the inundation of baptism.

[30]The globe is Earth, surrounded by the elements in commotion. Human beings on earth, though connected to the elements, are meant to rule over them.

size, and the elements enveloped it in such a way that it could slip neither here nor there. But occasionally, when the elements clashed together in alternation with the winds I mentioned, they caused the sandy globe to be moved to some degree by their force.[31]

And I saw between the North and the East what seemed to be a huge mountain. Toward the North it had much darkness, and toward the East it had much light, so that the light was unable to extend to the shadows nor could the shadows extend to the light.[32]

5. The Three Trumpeted Winds of God: Liber Vitae Meritorum. Vision I, Part 1

I saw a man of such height that he touched everything from the summit of heaven's clouds down to the abyss. From his shoulders upwards he was above the clouds in the clearest ether. From his shoulders down to his thighs, he was below the clouds, and in the midst of another white cloud. From his thighs to his knees he was in terrestial air, and from the knees to the calves, in the earth. From his calves downward to the soles of his feet he was in the waters of the abyss, so that he was standing above the abyss. And he turned toward the East so that he was gazing both East and South. His face flashed forth with such brightness that I could not look at him completely.

At his mouth he had a white cloud shaped like a trumpet, which was full of a rapidly ringing din. When he blew the trumpet it blasted three winds. Each of the winds had a cloud

---

[31]These are divine miracles that shake the bodies and minds of mortals.

[32]The mountain is the great fall of man. It stands between diabolical wickedness and divine goodness, between the devil's deceit — that leads toward damnation — and the light of redemption. The peak of the mountain points downward into the earth's green growing particles, or grains; its base is rooted in the white membrane of air.

above it: a fiery cloud, a turbulent cloud, and a luminous
cloud. The winds were holding those clouds up. But the wind
that had the fiery cloud above it remained in front of the
man's face. The other two winds with their clouds descended
to his chest, and there they spread their blasts. The wind
before his face stayed there, and blew from the East to the
South.

In the fiery cloud was a living fiery multitude, who were
all together in one will and one conjoined life. And before
them was spread a tablet full of wings everywhere, which
flew with God's commands. When God's commands lifted
that tablet on which the Wisdom of God had written its
secrets, this multitude zealously examined it together. When
they had examined these writings, the power of God
rewarded them, so that they resonated together in a single
chord of music like that of a mighty trumpet.

The wind that had the turbulent cloud above it blew with
the cloud from the South to the East, so that the length and
breadth of the cloud were like an open city square. Because
of its extent, it could not be grasped by the human intellect.
On that cloud was an enormous crowd of the blessed, who
possessed all the spirit of life, and who were too numerous
to count. Their voices were like the rushing of many waters,
and they said: "We have our dwelling places according to
the pleasure of the One who has brought forth these winds,
and when shall we receive them? For if we were to have our
clouds, we would rejoice more than we do now."

But the crowd that was in the fiery cloud responded to
them in voices full of Psalms: "When the Divinity takes hold
of his trumpet he will breathe forth lightning and thunder and
burning fire toward the earth. And he will touch the fire that
is in the sun, so that all the earth will be moved; and it will
come about that God will make manifest his great sign. And
then in that trumpet all the tribes of earth and all the families
of tongues will shout, as well as all who are inscribed in that
trumpet, and here you will have your dwelling place."

The wind over which the luminous cloud was hovering,
together with that same luminous cloud, spread itself from
East to the North. But very great shadows, thick and horrible,

were coming from the West, and spreading themselves toward the luminous cloud. But the shadows were unable to proceed beyond the luminous cloud.

Within that luminous cloud a Sun [Christ] and a Moon [the Church] appeared. In the Sun there was a lion, and in the Moon a horned goat. The Sun shone above the heavens and in the heavens, and on the earth and beneath the earth, and so it proceeded in its rising and returned to its setting. But as the Sun was moving, the lion advanced with it and in it, plundering and despoiling as it went. When the Sun returned, the lion went back with it and in it, and roared greatly for joy. The Moon, too, in which there was a horned goat, gradually followed the rising and setting of the sun. Then the wind blew and said, "A woman will bear a child, and the horned goat will fight against the North."

In the shadows there was a crowd of lost souls beyond number. When they heard the sound of those singing from the South, they turned away, since they did not wish their society. The leader of these lost souls was called "Deceiver" for they follow all his works and have been smitten by Christ, so that they are powerless. And all of these were crying in sorrowful voices, saying "Woe, woe to the injurious and dreadful deeds that flee from life and travel with us toward death."

Then I saw a cloud coming from the North, which extended itself toward these shadows. This cloud was barren of all joy and happiness, for even the Sun did not touch it or extend to it. It was full of evil spirits, who were drifting here and there on it, and contriving to set traps for me. These spirits began to blush with shame on account of the Man. And I heard the old serpent saying among them, "I will make my strong men ready for the bulwarks, and I will fight with all my strength against my enemies."

Then among the men he spat out of his mouth a foamy froth, full of filth with all the vices, and puffed them up with mockery and said, "Ha! Those who are named suns because of their luminous deeds, I will drive them to the baleful, horrible shadows of night." And he blew out a loathsome fog which covered all the earth like the blackest smoke, and from it I heard a great roaring that thundered forth. It roared, "No

man will worship another God unless he sees and knows him.
What is this, that man cherishes what he does not recognize?"
In that same cloud I saw different kinds of vices, each in its
own image.

6. *Worldly Love and Celestial Love:*
Liber Vitae Meritorum. Vision I, Part 1

The Words of Worldly Love:
   The first figure had the form of a man and the blackness
of an Ethiopian. Standing naked, he wound his arms and legs
around a tree below the branches. From the tree all kinds
of flowers were growing. With his hands he was gathering
those flowers, and he said:
   "I possess all the kingdoms of the world with their flowers
and ornaments. How should I wither when I have all the
greenness? Why should I live in the condition of old age, since
I am blossoming in youth? Why should I lead my beautiful
eyes into blindness? Because if I did this I should be ashamed.
As long as I am able to possess the beauty of this world, I
will gladly hold on to it. I have no knowledge of any other life,
although I hear all sorts of stories about it."
   When he had spoken, that tree I mentioned withered from
the root, and sank into the darkness of which I spoke. And
the figure died along with it.

The Reply of Celestial Love:
   Then from that turbulent cloud of which I spoke I heard
a voice replying to this figure:
   "You exist in great folly, because you want to lead a life
in the cinders of ashes. You do not seek that life which will
never wither in the beauty of youth, and which will never die
in old age. Besides, you lack all light and exist in a black fog.
You are enveloped in human willfulness as if enwrapped with
worms. You are also living as if for the single moment, and
afterwards you will wither like a worthless thing. You will
fall into the lake of perdition, and there you will be
surrounded by all its embracing arms, which you with your
nature call flowers.
   "But I am the column of celestial harmony, and I am

attendant upon all the joys of life. I do not scorn life, but trample underfoot all harmful things, just as I despise you. I am indeed a mirror of all the virtues, in which all faithfulness may clearly contemplate itself. You, however, pursue a path of night, and your hands will wreak death."

7. The Celestial Joys of the Virgins: *Liber Vitae Meritorum. Book VI, Part 6*

In that same brightness I looked, as if through a mirror, upon air having the purity upon purity of the most transparent water, and radiating from itself the splendor upon splendor of the sun. The air held a wind which contained all the green life-force of the plants and flowers of paradise and earth, and which was full of all the scent of this greenness, just as summer has the sweetest scent of plants and flowers.

In that air, which I regarded as if through a mirror, were those beings arrayed in the most gleaming robes, seemingly interwoven with gold; they had long sashes encrusted with the most precious stones, that hung from the breast to the foot. From them, moreover, breathed forth the intensest fragrance like that of spices. And they were girded round with belts ornamented with what seemed to be gold, gems, and pearls beyond human understanding.

Encircling their heads they wore crowns of gold intertwined with roses and lilies and stems studded with the most precious stones. When the Lamb of God called to them, the sweetest breath of wind, coming from the mysteries of Divinity, touched those stems so that every kind of lyre song, and lyre and organ music, rang out from them, together with the voice of the Lamb. No one else sang except for those wearing the crowns. Indeed the others were listening to it and rejoicing in it, just as one rejoices in beholding the splendor of a sun not seen before.

And their slippers were so transparent, so bathed in light that they seemed to be shod with a living fountain. Sometimes they stepped forth as if walking on wheels of gold, and then they were carrying their lyres in their hands and playing the lyres. Then they understood and knew and spoke a strange

tongue that no one else knew or could speak. I was not able
to see the rest of their ornaments, of which there were more.

For while they had lived in the world in their bodies, they
had acknowledged their faith in the Creator, and had
performed good works. They now, therefore, existed in this
blessed tranquility of bright joy. And since, in the purity of
their minds they had avoided the fleeting vanities of fleshly
delights, and had ascended by the Law's commands into the
love of the true, burning sun above, they possessed the air
having the purity upon purity of the most limpid water, and
the splendor of the sun radiating forth.

Because of their most sweet desires, which they had
proven to God and mortals through the green life-force of
their virginity, and the flower-bloom of their minds and
bodies when they poured forth the good savor of many virtues
— for they had been kindled with ardor by the Holy Spirit —
they felt that breath which contained all the green life-force
of the plants and flowers of paradise and earth, and which
was full of the scent of all greenness, just as summer has the
sweetest scent of plants and flowers.

8. Preface on Precious Gems: Physica

All stones contain fire and moisture. But the devil abhors
precious stones. He hates and despises them, because he
remembers that their beauty shone within him before he fell
from the glory that God had given him, and also because
precious stones are born of fire, and fire is where he receives
his punishment. For he was defeated by God's will and
plummeted into the fire. Just so, he was conquered by the
fire of the Holy Spirit, when humanity was snatched from his
jaws by the Holy Spirit's first breath.

Precious stones and gems arise in the East and in those
regions where the sun is especially hot. For the mountains
which are in those zones contain a very high temperature like
that of fire because of the sun's heat. The rivers in those
regions flow and boil continually because of the sun's
excessive heat. Occasionally a flood gushes forth from those
rivers, and swelling, flows upward toward those burning
mountains. When the same mountains, burning because of

the sun's heat, are touched by those rivers, they hiss wherever the water touches fire or the rivers splash their foam, like a fiery iron or fiery st ne when water is poured on it. In that place the foam sticks like a burdock. In three or four days it hardens into stone.

But after the flood of these waters subsides so that the waters return again to their streambed, the foam which had clung in several places to the mountains becomes thoroughly dry, depending on the various hours of the day and the temperatures of those hours. And, depending on the temperature of those hours, they acquire their colors and their virtues. As they dry they harden into precious stones. Then from various places they loosen like fish scales and fall into the sand.

When the flood of those running streams rises again, the rivers carry off many stones and conduct them to other countries where they are found by men. The mountains I mentioned — on which gems of such quality and number are born in this manner — glitter like the light of day.

So precious stones are engendered by fire and by water, and therefore they contain fire and moisture within themselves. They possess many virtues and great efficacy so that many benefits can be brought about by their means. These are good and worthy effects and useful to mankind — not effects of corruption, fornication, adultery, hatred, murder, and similar things that lead to sin and are inimical to man. For the nature of precious stones procures the worthy and the useful, and wards off the perverse and evil, just as virtues cast down vices and just as the vices cannot operate against the virtues.

There are, however, other gems, that are not born of those mountains or in the manner described. They arise from certain other, harmful things. From these, according to their natures, good or evil can be brought about with God's permission. For God beautified the foremost angel as if with precious stones. He, Lucifer, seeing them glitter in the mirror of divinity, gained knowledge from this. He recognized that God wished to create many wonderful things. Then his spirit grew proud because the beauty of the gems in him shone forth against God. He thought his power was equal to God's, even greater than God's. For that reason his splendor was extinguished.

But just as God saved Adam for a better destiny, so God did not abandon the beauty and virtue of those precious stones, but desired them to remain on earth with honor and praise, and for medical use.

9. The Emerald: Physica

The emerald is formed in the morning of the day and in the sunrise, when the sun is powerfully situated in its sphere and about to set forth on its journey. Then the greenness of the earth and the grasses thrive with the greatest vigor. For the air is still cold and the sun is already warm. The plants suck the green life-force as strongly as a lamb sucks its milk. The heat of the day is just beginning to be adequate for this — to cook and ripen the day's green life-force and nourish the plants so that they will be fertile and able to produce fruit.

It is for this reason that the emerald is powerful against all human weaknesses and infirmities, because the sun engenders it and because all of its matter springs from the green life-force of the air.

Therefore, whoever suffers a malady of the heart, the stomach, or the side, let that person carry an emerald so that the body's flesh may be warmed by it, and the sick one will be healed. But if diseases so overwhelm the patient that their tempest cannot be resisted, then let the patient place an emerald in the mouth so that it may be wetted by the saliva. Let the body frequently absorb the saliva, warmed by the stone, and then spit it out. The sudden attack of those diseases will then in all likelihood cease.

If a person falls down, stricken by epilepsy, place an emerald in the patient's mouth while still lying down, and presently the spirit will revive. After the patient is raised up and the emerald is removed from the mouth, let the patient look attentively and say, "Just as the spirit of the Lord fills up the earthly sphere, so let his mercy fill the house of my body so that it may never again be shaken." Let the patient do this for nine consecutive days, in the morning, and the cure will follow. But the patient should always keep the same emerald and gaze at it daily in the morning, all the while saying these words. And the sick person will be made well.

Anyone who suffers especially from headache should hold the emerald before the mouth and warm it with the breath, so that the breath moistens it. The sufferer should then rub the temples and forehead with the moisture. Let the emerald be placed in the mouth and held there for a little while, and the patient will feel better.

Whoever has much phlegm and saliva should heat up a good wine, and then place a linen cloth over a small vessel and the emerald upon the cloth. Pour the warm wine so that it flows through the cloth. This should be done again and again, as if one were preparing lye. Then consume at frequent intervals a mixture of that wine with bean flour, and drink the same wine prepared this way. It purges the brain so that the phlegm and saliva will be lessened.

And if one is gnawed by worms, place a linen cloth on the sore, and on this the emerald, and tie another strip of cloth over it like a poultice. Do this so that the stone may thus grow warm. Keep it there for three days, and the worms will die.

10. Lyrics:
Symphonia Harmoniae Caelestium Revelationum

O tu, suavissima virga
O you, most delightful branch,
putting forth leaves from the rod of Jesse,
O what a great splendor it is
that Divinity gazed at a most beautiful girl
—just as the eagle fixes his eye on the sun—
when the heavenly Father strove toward
the Virgin's brightness
and he wanted his word to be made flesh in her.

Now when the Virgin's mind was illuminated
by God's mystical mystery,
miraculously a bright flower sprang forth
from that Virgin—
with the celestial!

Glory to the Father and the Son
and to the Holy Spirit,
as it was in the beginning—
with the celestial!

    O splendidissima gemma
O brightest jewel,
and serene splendor of the sun,
the fountain springing from the Father's heart
has poured into you.
His unique Word,
by which he created the primal matter of the world
—thrown into confusion by Eve—
the Father has forged this Word, as humanity,
for you.

Because of this, you are that lucent matter,
through which that same Word
breathed all the virtues—
just as it drew forth all creatures
from primal matter.

    Columba aspexit per cancellos
The dove gazed through the latticed window screen:
before her eyes, the balsam's fragrant moisture
flowed from the luminous Maximinus.

The sun's heat flamed forth
and glittered among the shadows;
from them arose the jewel
of which the purest temple was built
in the virtuous heart.

He stands, a lofty tower made of
the tree of Lebanon, of cypress,
and ornamented with carnelian and jacinth;
he is a city surpassing the arts of all artificers.

He runs, the swift stag, to the fountain
of purest water, flowing

from the most potent stone,
which has refreshed with sweet perfumes.

O makers of unguents and colors, who dwell
in the sweetest greenness
of the gardens of the king,
you rise up to perfect the holy sacrifice
among the rams.

Among you shines this artificer,
this rampart of the temple,
he who desired the wings of an eagle
so that he might kiss Wisdom, his nurse,
in the glorious fecundity of Ecclesia.

O Maximinus, you are the mountain and the valley:
In both you appear, a high edifice,
where the horned goat sprang forth
with the elephant,
and Wisdom dwelled in delight.

You are strong and sweet in sacred ceremonies:
in radiance you ascend the altars
as a smoke of spices
to the pillar's summit of praise.

There you intercede for the people,
who reach to the mirror of light—
to whom there is praise on high.

    Antiphon: O rubor sanguinis
O crimson blush of blood,
you who have streamed from that eminence
bordering on divinity,
you are a flower
which the wintry serpent's blast
has never withered.

    Responsory: Favus distillans
A trickling honeycomb

was the virgin Ursula;
she yearned to clasp the Lamb of God.
Honey and milk beneath her tongue—
for she gathered to herself
a garden yielding fruit, and the flower of flowers
in a throng of virgins.

And so, in the most noble morning light,
be glad, Daughter Zion,
that she gathered to herself
a garden yielding fruit, and the flower of flowers
in a throng of virgins.

Glory be to the Father and the Son
and the Holy Spirit,
for she gathered to herself
a garden yielding fruit, and the flower of flowers
in a throng of virgins.

    O dulcissime amator
O sweetest lover,
O sweetest embracing love,
help us to guard our virginity.

We have been born out of the dust, Ah! Ah!
and in the sin of Adam:
most harsh is it to deny
one's longing for a taste of the apple.
Raise us up, Savior Christ.

Ardently we desire to follow you.
O how difficult it is for us, miserable as we are,
to imitate you, spotless and innocent
king of angels!

Yet we trust you,
for you desire to recover a jewel
from what is rotten.

Now we call on you, our husband and comforter,

who redeemed us on the cross.
We are bound to you through your blood
as the pledge of betrothal.
We have renounced earthly men
and chosen you, the Son of God.

O most beautiful form,
O sweetest fragrance of desirable delights,
we sigh for you always in our sorrowful banishment!
When may we see you and remain with you?

But we dwell in the world,
and you dwell in our mind;
we embrace you in our heart
as if we had you here with us.

You, bravest lion, have burst through the heavens
and are descending to the house of the virgins.
You have destroyed death, and are building life
in the golden city.

Grant us society in that city,
and let us dwell in you,
O sweetest husband,
who has rescued us from the jaws of the devil,
seducer of our first parents!

O viriditas digiti Dei
O green life-force of the finger of God,
through which God sets his planting,
you gleam with sublime radiance
like an upright column.
You are full of glory
in the completion of God's work.

O mountain's height,
you will never be overthrown
because of God's indifference.

Solitary you stand

from ancient times as our defense.
Yet there is no armed might
that can drag you down.
You are full of glory.

Glory be to the Father and the Son
and the Holy Spirit.
You are full of glory!

   O nobilissima viriditas
O noblest green life-force,
you are rooted in the sun
and in pure white serenity.
You illumine in a wheel
what no excellence on earth can encompass.
You are encircled in the embrace
of the divine retinue.

You redden like the morning
and burn like the flame of the sun.

Elisabeth of Schönau

   Elisabeth grew up in a family of the minor nobility in the
diocese of Trier, near Bonn and not far from Cologne. One
of her great-uncles was the Bishop of Münster, and she had
relatives among the nuns of the Augustinian monastery of
St. Andernach. When she was twelve her parents dedicated
her to the double Benedictine monastery of Schönau; six
years later she took the veil. Given to acute depressions and
nervous crises, even a wish for death, Elisabeth would speak
of her "gloom-filled soul." She began in 1152 to experience
a series of ecstatic visions that continued until her death. She
was twenty-three, and in her eleventh year at the convent.
During a trance she could not speak; she felt sensations of
stifling and paralysis, or lost consciousness.
   But sickness was for Elisabeth a fruitful source and
accompaniment of her visionary life, as it was for other
mystics, such as Hildegard and later Julian of Norwich.
Hildegard describes her bodily pains "in all her veins and

flesh to the marrow," declaring that from her birth she was "entangled as it were in a net of suffering." Julian of Norwich asked for her sickness so as to be able to experience what Christ experienced, and to suffer along with the other people who were there at the time. Elizabeth Petroff[33] discusses the connection between illness and ecstasy. Weakness prevented the mystic from performing her usual tasks and served to separate her from others. Sickness might befall the woman who was unwilling to write or dictate her visions; relief came when she finally began to write. Elisabeth describes in her letter to Hildegard how her personal angel lashed her with a whip, so that she had to keep to her bed for three days, a punishment for not revealing her visions.

It was Elisabeth's brother Ekbert (d. 1158), a monk of Schönau at Elisabeth's behest and afterwards an abbot, who wrote down and helped to disseminate Elisabeth's experiences. His prologue to the Visions explains their collaboration, and is explicit about the languages spoken by the angel. Ekbert writes:

"Let all those who are about to read the words of this book know this without a doubt: that some of the discourses of God's angel — which he is said to have delivered to the handmaid of God, Elisabeth — he revealed wholly in the Latin language; some, on the other hand, were wholly in the German language. Some, however, he used to utter partly in Latin and partly in the words of the German tongue." This is how Ekbert dealt with the language problem: "When the angel's words were Latin I left them unchanged, but when they were German I translated them into Latin, as clearly as I was able to do. I did not presume to add anything of my own. I sought neither human approval nor earthly gain. God, to whom all things are naked and revealed, is my witness."

Ekbert describes his sister's trances, which would customarily come on Sundays or other feast days. "A certain

---

[33]*Medieval Women's Visionary Literature* (New York, 1986), pp. 41-44.

malady in the region of the heart came over her and she grew violently agitated. At last she lay as if lifeless, so that at times no breath or vital motion could be felt in her. But after a long period of unconsciousness, when her spirit had gradually revived, suddenly she would utter some exceedingly divine words in the Latin language, which she had not at any time learned from another person, nor could have devised them all by herself, since she was not learned and had no skill — or very little — in spoken Latin."

Elisabeth experienced her first vision during the Feast of Pentecost in 1152; her visions continued until September 23, 1157. It is worth noting that Hildegard's *Scivias* had been completed in 1151. Hildegard's influence over Elisabeth is evident. Elisabeth's *Book of the Ways of God (Liber viarum Dei)* resembles the title of Hildegard's first work, and there is some similarity in content. Like Hildegard, Elisabeth beholds a high mountain at whose summit stands a divine figure bathed in light.

Elisabeth's imagery derives chiefly from popular theology, however, from the liturgy, and the Bible, and differs from the powerful cosmologies and august "Blakean" presences of Hildegard. Characteristically, certain of her trances would carry her, accompanied by her angel, to a mountaintop or pleasant meadow where she would meet maidens, or youths, or venerable men. It is especially interesting that, two centuries before Dante, she beholds the souls of the dead, some damned, some in bliss, who ask her to perform an act on earth on their behalf.

Elisabeth had visions of saints, conversed with the Blessed Virgin, and suffered the taunts of devils, animal shapes, and small boys in the garb of clerics. She also beheld a special angel who visited and befriended her. Instructed by her brothers to ask the angel whether he were real and trustworthy, Elisabeth fearfully did so. The angel became angered, according to her reports, and told her to direct the brothers and sisters of her monastery to offer up masses for him and his brothers. This done, the angel was mollified and agreed to continue to visit Elisabeth.

Elisabeth's visions seized the imagination of people in her neighborhood, making her a celebrity. Her exhortations and apocalyptic warnings drew crowds. Local bishops and divines consulted her on various matters which she was asked to refer to her angel and to the other beings with whom she conversed. As the extraordinary number of manuscripts shows, her popularity spread to the western part of the country, and to France and England.

In the fifteenth year after she became a nun, Elisabeth entered in conversation with the Blessed Virgin concerning the Virgin's Assumption. From these visions, lasting for three years, Elisabeth established the date of the Virgin's Assumption as 40 days after her death. This portion of her visions was translated into Anglo-Norman and Old French as separate poems which named her "Ysabeau."

A large number of bones discovered in 1106 in a Roman necropolis outside Cologne helped to revive the legend of St. Ursula, extant until then in two Latin versions of the 10th and 11th centuries, and hinted at in earlier sources — an inscription, a sermon, a martyrology. Ursula and her troop of 11,000 virgins were said to have sailed in a splendid flotilla of eleven ships, visiting Rome and cities on the Rhine. When they disembarked at Cologne they were slaughtered, possibly by Huns. Geoffrey of Monmouth in 1135 gave some details about the British virgin martyr without naming her. Elisabeth's contemporaries who discovered the bodies at Cologne, and notably the Abbot Gerlach of Deutz, were eager to have them proven to be those of the 11,000 virgins of the legend. A worrisome fact, of course, was that many of the bodies were males. Because of Elisabeth's reputation, three bodies were brought to her, as well as some stones with inscriptions, as a way of inspiring one of her trances.

In a series of self-induced visions, Elisabeth ascertained names for the three: Albina, her sister Emerentiana, and their ten-year-old companion Adrianus, a king's son. Another of the virgin martyrs, St. Verena, showed herself frequently to Elisabeth, informing her that St. Ursula and her companions had singled Elisabeth out for special favor and promising her a place among their blessed number in the next life.

The imaginative Revelations that grew out of this experience call to mind in their dramatic vivacity other literary dream visions of the Middle Ages. They were written down between 1156 and 1157, the first occurring on October 28, the Feast of the Apostles Simon and Jude. The immense popularity of the Revelations of the sacred band of the virgins of Cologne stimulated numerous cycles in pictorial art of the life of St. Ursula, spreading from Germany to Italy and France as well. The expanded legend as composed by Elisabeth became the accepted one, and is the basis of *The Golden Legend* of Jacob de Voragine.

Elisabeth also left 23 letters, two of them addressed to Hildegard. The letter translated here gives an idea of the method of her visions — her custom of keeping a little book by her bed in which to write them down. Following this letter is Elisabeth's vision of the feminine aspect of Jesus, which contributed to the image of the feminized Jesus in later medieval piety. The last translation is that of the Revelations of the virgin martyrs of Cologne.

11. Elisabeth to Hildegard of Bingen

To the Lady Hildegard, revered Superior of the Brides of Christ who are in Bingen, Elisabeth, a lowly nun, sends devout prayers with all love.

May the grace and solace of the Most High fill you with joy! For you have been kind and compassionate toward my distress, as I have understood from the words of my Comforter — whom you have earnestly reminded to console me.

For you have said that things have been disclosed to you about me. I confess that I have recently conceived in my mind a certain cloud of uneasiness because of the absurd talk of people saying many things about me — things that are not true. But I would easily endure the talk of the common people, if it were not for the fact that those who walk about wearing the garb of the religious also deride the grace of God in me, and do not fear to pronounce judgment rashly on those things of which they are ignorant. I hear that some letters, inspired by them, are even being circulated in my name. They have spread the rumor that I have prophesied about the Day of Judgment, a thing which I have certainly never presumed, since its coming eludes the understanding of all mortals.

But I shall reveal to you the circumstance of this rumor, so that you may judge whether I have done or said anything presumptuous in this matter. As you have heard from others, the Lord has magnified his mercy in me beyond what I have deserved or might in any way be capable of deserving — to such an extent that he even has often deigned to reveal certain heavenly mysteries to me. He has also indicated to me many times, through his angel, what kinds of things would befall his people in these times unless they were to do penance for their sins. He commanded me to make this known openly. However, in order to avoid arrogance, and so as not to seem to be the proposer of novelties, I have been zealous to conceal all these things, as much as I have been able.

Therefore, when in my accustomed manner I was in a trance one Sunday, the angel of the Lord appeared by my side, saying, "Why do you hide gold in the mud? This is the word of God which has been sent to earth through your lips, not so that it should be hidden but so that it may be made known to the praise and glory of our Lord and for his people's salvation." And when he had said this, he raised a whip above me, which he lashed most harshly against me five times as if in great anger, so that for three days I was weary in my whole body from that beating. After this, he laid a finger on my lips saying, "You shall be silent until the ninth hour; then you shall reveal these things which God has accomplished in you!"

Accordingly, I remained silent until the ninth hour. Then I signalled to the superior that she should bring me a little book which I had hidden by my bed. It contained a part of these things which the Lord had revealed to me. When I offered it into the hands of the lord abbot who had come to visit me, my tongue was loosened to say these words: "Not to us, Lord, not to us, but to Your Name give the glory!"

After this, when I had also revealed to him certain other things that I had wished to be committed to writing, namely, concerning God's great vengeance which — as I had learned from the angel — would befall the world within a short time, I pleaded with him most earnestly to keep that message hidden within himself. However, he ordered me to exert myself to pray and to ask the Lord that he allow me to

understand whether or not he wanted those things which I
had said to be veiled in silence.

When I had prostrated myself for some time, persevering
in prayer on that account, it was in the season of our Lord's
Advent, on the feast of St. Barbara [December 4] during the
first vigil of the night, that I fell into a trance. And the angel
of the Lord stood by my side, saying, "Cry loudly and say
'Woe!' to all nations, because the whole world has been
returned to darkness. And you shall say, 'Depart! He has
called you, he who has created you out of earth.' And he says
'Repent, because the Kingdom of God is at hand!'"(Matthew
3.2; Luke 21.31).

Stirred by this message, the lord abbot began to spread
the word before the magistrates of the church and religious
men. Several of them received the message with respect. But
certain did not; they spoke perversely of the angel who was
friendly toward me, saying that he was a deceitful spirit who
had been transformed into the shape of an angel of light.
Hence, the abbot bound me in obedience, commanding me
that if the angel should ever appear to me, I should entreat
him to swear in God's name to disclose to me whether or not
he was a true angel of God. But I thought this was
presumptuous, and accepted this command with great fear.

One day, therefore, when I was in my trance, he appeared
to me as he was accustomed to do and stood in my sight.
Trembling, I said to him, "I entreat you to swear by God the
Father, and the Son, and the Holy Spirit, that you tell me
accurately if you are the true angel of God, and if these
visions that I have seen in my trance and the words I have
heard from your lips are true!" He replied and said, "Know
certainly that I am the true angel of God, and that the visions
you have seen are true, and what you have heard from my
lips is true, and will truly come to pass if God is not reunited
in harmony with men. And I am that very one who have
labored long within you."

After this, on the Eve of the Epiphany while I was praying,
my lord again appeared to me. But he stood at a distance and
had his face turned away from me. I, therefore, understanding his displeasure, spoke to him with fear: "My lord,
if I offended to you because I entreated you to swear, do not

attribute it to me, I beg you. Turn your face towards me, I beseech you, and be forgiving toward me. For I acted bound by obedience, and I have not dared to violate the order of my superior.''

When I had shed abundant tears amidst words of this sort, he turned towards me saying, ''You have shown disdain for me and my brothers because you harbored a lack of faith concerning me. Hence you will know with certainty that you will see my face no more, nor will you hear my voice, unless the Lord is placated, as well as we ourselves.'' And I said, ''My lord! How will it be possible for you to be placated?'' And he said, ''You shall tell your abbot that he must solemnly celebrate a divine office in remembrance of me and my brothers.''

When the solemnities of the masses had been celebrated in honor of the holy angels, not once but several times, both by the lord abbot and by the rest of the brothers, and when at the same time the sisters had honored them with readings from the Psalms, my lord appeared to me again with a tranquil mien, and he said to me, ''I know that inasmuch as what you have done has been performed in love and obedience, you have therefore won forgiveness, and from now on I shall visit you more often than I previously have.''

After this, when the lord abbot arranged to go to a certain place — at the request of the clergy residing there — in order to preach the Lord's word of warning among the people (if perhaps they might repent so that God's anger might be turned away from them), he went first to pray to the Lord together with all of us, in order that God might deign to reveal to his handmaid whether the message, already partly revealed, should be spread more widely or not.

And so, when he was celebrating the divine mysteries, and we were praying most fervently, suddenly the joints of my limbs slackened and I grew faint and went into a trance. And lo and behold! The angel of the Lord stood before my eyes, and I said to him, ''My lord, remember what you told me, your handmaid, that the word of God has been sent to earth through my lips, not in order to be hidden but to be revealed for the glory of God and the salvation of his people. And now show me what ought to be done about that word of warning which you have spoken to me. Has it already been sufficiently revealed, or must it still be preached?"

And he, gazing at me with a stern look, said, "Do not tempt God, for those who tempt him will perish. You shall say to the abbot, 'Do not be afraid, but carry through to the end what you have begun.' Those who hear the words of your admonition and preserve them are truly blessed, and will not be scandalized at you. You shall advise him, moreover, that he must change the form of preaching he has used until now. For in this I have been his counselor. Tell him that he must in no way heed the words of those who spitefully express doubt about these things which have been accomplished within you. But let him heed what has been written: 'For nothing is impossible with God'" (Luke 1.37).

Heartened by this message, therefore, the abbot went to the place he had arranged to go to, and exhorted to repentance the people awaiting his arrival. He announced that God's wrath would befall all of them unless they were to strive to prevent it through fruitful penance. He did not, however, recount in any of his preachings — for he had been maligned — what plagues were threatening the world. So it turned out that many of those among whom that sermon was spread very fearfully prostrated theselves in penance throughout the whole season of Lent, and diligently persisted in almsgiving and prayer.

At that time, someone — driven by what zeal I do not know — sent a letter to the city of Cologne in the name of the lord abbot, who himself was unaware of it — God knows! In it certain terrible threats were read within the hearing of all the people. Therefore, although we have been jeered at by some foolish people, the wise ones nevertheless (as we have heard) reverently paid attention to the sermon, and did not disdain to worship God with the fruits of penance.

It happened, in addition, on the fourth holy day before Easter, when I had fallen into a trance after great bodily turmoil, the angel of the Lord appeared to me. I said to him, "Lord, what will become of the message which you uttered to me?" And he answered, "Do not be downcast or troubled if those things which I foretold do not happen on the day I designated to you. For the Lord has been appeased by the atonement of the throng."

After this, on the sixth holy day around the third hour, amidst severe suffering, I went into a trance. And again he stood by my side saying to me, "The Lord has seen his people's distress and has turned the wrath of his outrage away from them." I said to him, "My lord, shall I not be the laughingstock of all those among whom this message was proclaimed?" He said, "You shall patiently and willingly endure all that has befallen you because of this. Earnestly turn to him, who — although he was Creator of the whole world — has endured men's mockery. Now for the first time, the Lord is testing your patience!"

See, my Lady, I have explained the whole sequence of the affair to you, so that you too may be aware both of my innocence and that of our abbot, and so that you may make it clear to others.

I beseech you, moreover, that you both include me in your prayers, and that — insofar as the spirit of the Lord advises you — you requite me with some comforting words.

12. On the Feminine Aspect of Jesus

During the celebration on the eve of our Lord's Nativity, around the hour of the divine sacrifice, I entered a trance and saw something like a sun of marvelous brightness in the heaven, and in the middle of the sun the likeness of a virgin whose appearance was exceedingly beautiful in form and desirable to see. She was seated on a throne. Her hair was loosened over her shoulders, and on her head was a crown of the most splendid gold. In her right hand was a golden chalice. She was emerging from the sun which surrounded her on all sides. From the virgin herself emanated a splendor of great brilliance, which seemed at first to fill the place of our dwelling. Then gradually expanding after some period of time, it seemed to fill the whole earth.

Now next to that same sun there appeared a great cloud, extremely dark and horrible to see. When I gazed at the cloud, it rushed abruptly against the sun, darkened it, and cut off its splendor from the earth for some time. I saw this happen very often, moreover, so that the world was by turns darkened by the cloud and again illuminated by the sun. Whenever it happened that the cloud approached the sun and obstructed its light from the earth, the virgin who was enthroned within the sun seemed to be weeping copiously, as if grieving greatly because of the darkening of the world. I beheld this vision throughout that day without interruption, and all the following night, for I remained ever wakeful in prayer.

On the holy day of Christmas, now, when the solemnities of the masses were being celebrated, I asked the holy angel of God who appeared to me what sort of vision that was and what significance it had. He replied to me concerning that virgin, for I especially desired to know who she was, and he said: "That virgin whom you see is the sacred humanity of the Lord Jesus. The sun in which the virgin is enthroned is the godhead, which wholly contains and illuminates the humanity of the Savior. The dark cloud which by turns keeps the brightness away from the earth is the iniquity that reigns in the world. It is this cloud that obstructs the benevolence of the omnipotent God, which ought to watch over the sons of men through the mediating humanity of the lord Jesus. The cloud brings the darkness of his anger upon the world.

"Now the fact that you see the virgin weeping is similar to what you read, namely, that before the destruction of the first generation, God was inwardly touched by a pain of the heart because of the abundance of human iniquity, and said, 'I regret that I created man.'

"For just as it was at that time, so it is also in these days, that the sins of men have disproportionately grown to the highest magnitude. Men do not realize what great things God has done for them through the Incarnation of his only Son — whom they dishonor with the worst acts, and they basely trample underfoot the benefits of his redemption. Nor do they give fitting thanks to him for all his toils, by which he was worn down on account of all their sins. This is the reason for the bitter accusation against them before the eyes of the terrible God. And now the Son of man has no joy in this generation of men who provoke him, but he has more regret over those who do not show thanks for his kindness.

"This is the lamentation of the virgin who cries out against the cloud. Now the fact that you see the earth at times illuminated by the sun while the cloud departs means this: that God, because of the abundance of his mercy, does not altogether cease to watch over earth from heaven, because of his blessed seed, which is still preserved for him on earth.

"The golden crown which is on the virgin's head is the celestial glory which has been won through Christ's humanity for all those believing in him. The chalice in her right hand is the fountain of living water, which God has offered to the world, teaching and refreshing the hearts of those who turn to him, saying, 'If anyone is thirsty let him come to me, and let him drink, and from his womb shall flow the living waters' " (John 7.37-38).

But on the third day after this, God's chosen, St. John the Evangelist, appeared to me when the office of the mass was being celebrated according to the custom, and together with him appeared the glorious Queen of Heaven. And I questioned him, as I had been advised, and said, "Why, my lord, was the humanity of the Lord the Savior shown to me in the form of a virgin and not in the form of a man?"

And he responded to my questioning saying, "The Lord wished this to be done for this reason — so that the vision could be all the more aptly fitted to signify his blessed mother as well. For she herself, too, is truly a virgin enthroned within the sun, since the majesty of the highest God glorified her wholly, above all who preceded her on earth, and because Divinity descended through her to visit the darkness of the world.

"The golden crown which you have seen on the virgin's head signifies that this illustrious virgin was begotten of the seed of kings in the fleshly sense, and reigns over heaven and earth by her royal power. The drink of the golden chalice is the sweetest and most generous grace of the Holy Spirit, which has come down upon her more abundantly than upon any of God's saints. She herself offers this drink to others, when through her intervention God grants a share of that same grace in his holy church to his faithful.

"Now the virgin's weeping is the constant intercession of that same most compassionate mother, by which she always intercedes with her son for the sins of God's people. These words which I tell you are true, because if she were not to restrain God's anger by her unceasing prayer, all the world would already have fallen into damnation because of its abounding iniquity."

13. The Book of Revelations of the Sacred Band of Virgins of Cologne

To you who entertain pious sentiments toward those things which are sacred, I Elisabeth, maid-servant of the hand-maidens of the Lord who are at Schönau, disclose these things which were revealed to me by the grace of God, concerning the virginal band of St. Ursula, Queen of Britain. In ancient days this band suffered martyrdom in Christ's name, in the suburbs of the city of Cologne.

There are certain men of good repute who do not permit me to be silent about these things. Although I resisted greatly, they compelled me by their prolonged demands to investigate this matter. To be sure, I know that those who are opposed to the grace of God in me are therefore going to take the opportunity to flog me with their tongues. But I shall endure it willingly. For I hope that I shall receive some reward, if the honor of so many martyrs may be increased — as a result of these words the Lord deigns to reveal about them — through my efforts.

When it was pleasing to the Lord to pity his precious martyrs, who had lain for many ages without honor under the feet of men and beasts of burden alongside the walls of Cologne, it happened that certain men dwelling in the same place approached the location of their martyrdom and opened up the many tombs of the saintly bodies. Once these were removed from there, the men transferred them to sacred grounds in the vicinity, as it had been ordained by God. Now that was the year 1156 of the Lord's Incarnation when these things began to be done. The Emperor Frederick held the principate of the Roman Empire, and Arnold II presided in the pontifical Cathedral in Cologne.

It was then that one precious martyr was found in that same place among the others. On her tomb was the following inscription: "St. Verena, virgin and martyr." This virgin martyr was brought from there to our residence by the hand of our reverend abbot Hildelin, after she had been given to him by Gerlach, the lord abbot of Deutz, who was greatly inflamed with pious devotion to gather and to honor the bodies of that sainted company.

While she was being awaited by the convent of our brothers, who were about to receive her near the entrance of the church, I who was living in our chapterhouse — before I had heard anything of her arrival — received from the Lord the following evidence of her holiness: I entered a trance, and I saw on the road along which the sacred bones were being carried something like a flame of the most radiant whiteness, in the shape of a sphere. An angel of extraordinary beauty preceded it. In one hand he carried a smoking censer, while in the other he had a burning candle. Together they moved through the air in a gentle course as far as the interior of the church.

When on the next day the solemnities of the mass were being celebrated in her honor, I was in a trance. The same virgin appeared to me, standing in heavenly radiance, wondrously crowned and gloriously adorned with a palm of victory. I addressed her, therefore, and asked whether her name was exactly as it had been reported to us. In the same way, I inquired about the name of a certain martyr whose body had been brought together with her, but without a definite name. And she responded saying, "My name is such as you have heard. However, through an error it was almost bound to be written differently, but I myself restrained the writer. Caesarius came with me, and when we entered this place, peace entered with us."

Again, on another day when the divine service was being celebrated for that martyr, he himself appeared to me in great glory. When I asked him what his rank had been in his earthly life, and for what reason he had undergone martyrdom with those virgins, he said, "I was a soldier in my earthly life, the son of the aunt of this holy virgin to whom I am now attached. She was very dear to me, so that when she left the country I followed her. Indeed, she gave me the strength to suffer my martyrdom, and as I saw her constancy in pain, I suffered together with her. For a long time our bones were separated from one another, and now we have had our request granted by the Lord that they may be united."

I was led into considerable doubt over this speech, for I supposed, as everyone believes who reads the story of the British virgins, that the blessed sisterhood had journeyed on their pilgrimage without a retinue of men. Above all, I discovered something else to the contrary that moreover disproved this view strongly.

At the same time that the two above-mentioned martyrs were found, many bodies of holy bishops and of other great men were found among the tombs of the virgins. In the tombs of some individuals, stones were deposited with their titles inscribed upon them. From these it was recognized who they had been and where they had come from. The abbot I mentioned from the city of Deutz sent me the distinguished, the most striking of these, hoping that something about them might be revealed to me by God's grace. He wanted to ascertain through me whether or not they should be believed. He had, to be sure, a suspicion about those men who had found the sacred bodies, for fear that they had perhaps fraudulently had those inscriptions written for the sake of profit.

I have taken care, however, throughout various passages in the present discourse, to set before the readers' eyes what sort of inscriptions these were, and what has been revealed to me about them. From this it may be perceived how that sisterhood — which the divine Fatherhood has deigned to honor with the escort of such high-ranking persons — ought to be worthily attended with all honor by Christ's faithful.

I was pondering to myself for some time these things which I have recounted, and I was longing to receive the revelations from the Lord which were being demanded of me. And it happened that the feast of the Blessed Apostles Simon and Jude [October 28, 1156] came up. While the office of the mass was being celebrated for them, a certain affliction of the heart came over me which I was accustomed to suffer when God's mysteries began to be revealed to me for the first time. After being plagued for a considerable period, I came into an ecstasy and so I grew calm. When I gazed in spirit upon heaven, as was my custom, I saw the martyrs I have mentioned. They were proceeding from the place of radiance, in which I am used to seeing visions of the saints, a long way down into the lower air. My faithful guardian angel of the Lord went before them. As I was in a trance I spoke to them, saying, "My lords, it is very kind of you that you deign to visit me now in this way, although I have offered you no service."

To this the blessed Verena responded, "We have sensed that your heart's desire has generously invited us, and for this reason we have come to visit you." So I said, questioning, "My lady, what does it mean that in the grave-plot of your martyrdom the bodies of bishops are also found buried? And should we believe in the inscriptions of the titles which are discovered there on some gems? And who was the inscriber of the stones?"

And she said to me, "God has singled you out a long time ago for this very thing: that he may cause these things to be revealed, through you, which until now were unknown about us. For this reason do not bear it ill that you are being harassed by some people's requests to inquire into these matters. Let it be enjoined upon you, moreover, that through all the span of your life you fast upon bread and water on the eve of our passion each year. Or, if you are unable to carry this out, redeem yourself by the celebration of one mass, so that the Lord may deign to reveal to you what he has arranged to make known about us, and so that you may deserve to be joined one day to our company."

After this she began to speak the following words, saying with great joyfulness of countenance: "When we first began to congregate in our native country, our holy fame became widespread, and many people flocked together from everywhere to see us. It happened through God's ordinance that certain of the bishops of Britain also joined with us. Crossing the sea in our company, they arrived with us as far as Rome. On that journey the blessed Pantalus, Bishop of Basel, also joined us and led us as far as Rome, and became a companion in our suffering. His inscription was as follows: 'St. Pantalus, Bishop of Basel, who led the sacred virgins to Rome, where they were joyfully received. From there he turned back and came to Cologne, where he endured martyrdom with them.'"

After this, I interposed an objection to her words: "In their story we read specifically that when the blessed Ursula was playing at sea with her virgin companions according to her custom, and when the ships which the virgins were steering were driven farther out to sea than usual, a sudden gust of wind swept all the ships away from those seas and they did not return there anymore. According to this account, it is indeed likely that they went on without a retinue of men."

To this she replied as follows: "The blessed Ursula's father, the King of Scottish Britain, a faithful man by the name of Maurus, was aware of his daughter's wishes, and he knew, just as she herself knew, what God had ordained for her. This he disclosed to some men whom he regarded as close friends. Upon their advice, he made cautious arrangements beforehand that his daughter, whom he loved most tenderly, should have on her departure, men in her retinue whose comfort she herself needed as much as did her troop."

One of the noble inscriptions which was the most remarkable went like this: 'St. Cyriac, the Pope of Rome, who received the holy virgins with joy, and upon his return with them to Cologne, endured martyrdom.' Another was found beside it with the following: 'St. Vincent, priestly cardinal.' When I questioned the blessed Verena about these things, she said, "At the time when we entered the city of Rome, a holy man by the name of Cyriac presided over the apostolic see. He had left our borders, and as he was a wise and noble man, and agreeable to all, he had been elevated to apostolic rank, and had already reigned over the Roman church for an entire year and eleven weeks. He was the nineteenth in number among the Roman pontiffs.

"When he heard we had arrived, he was delighted, and all his clergy, and he received us with great honors. To be sure, he had a great many blood relatives among us. But the next night after our arrival it was revealed to him by the Lord that if he relinquished the apostolic throne and set out with us, he would receive the palm of martyrdom together with us. Now he was keeping this revelation to himself, and he gave the benediction of holy baptism to many of our sisters who had not yet been reborn in Christ. When he found the opportune moment he made his wishes known.

"In the presence of the entire church he resigned the rank of his office amidst the protestations of all, especially of the cardinals, who judged it to be madness, so to speak, that he was going astray as if following the foolishness of mere women. The cardinals did not know the divine admonition that was impelling him. He, however, remained firm in his resolution, out of love for our virginity, for he himself had also — since his infancy — guarded a spotless virginity within himself. Consequently, from that time we lost all favor which we had previously enjoyed in the sight of the Roman church, and those who formerly had applauded us became strangers as far as we were concerned. However, our same venerable father, the blessed Cyriac himself, did not leave the city until on his advice another bishop of Rome named Anterus took his place as Pope."

After this, when I had examined the roll of the Roman popes, and nowhere had found there the name of St. Cyriac, I questioned the blessed Verena again when she presented herself to me on a certain day. I asked why he had not been recorded among the other Roman prelates. And she said that this was the result of the clergy's outrage, since he had not been willing to complete his term in the rank of his high office.

Again on another day, when I had asked her about a certain Jacob, whose name was found written in his tomb without any addition, she seemed to me pleased to a certain extent about my question, and she joyfully responded to me, saying, "There was at that time a certain noble father of revered life, the archbishop Jacob, who had set out from our country to go abroad to Antioch. There he rose to the rank of prelate and reigned over that church for seven years. When he heard that the blessed Cyriac, a countryman of his, was elevated at Rome to the apostolic office, he went to visit him. He had already left the city before our arrival. When this was pointed out to us, a messenger was speedily dispatched to summon him back. He was found in a certain castle which was about a two-day's march away from Rome. When he heard of our coming he immediately returned to us, and became a companion of our journey and shared our martyrdom at Cologne. He himself, moreover, had some nieces among our religious order. At the exhortation of the blessed Pope Cyriac, since he was a wise man, he applied great diligence to learn the names of our sisters. These he inscribed to a large degree on the stones after we had been murdered, and he put them over our bodies. But before he was able to finish this, he was caught at the work by wicked men, and was slaughtered in our midst. Hence it is that certain of us are found with inscriptions, but others are not. Moreover, in the very hour of his martyrdom, when he was already about to be struck down, he requested this alone of his murderers — that his martyrdom might be deferred just long enough for him to be able to inscribe his own name on the stone. And this was granted him."

I asked also about the day of his martyrdom, because it was not believable from this account that he himself had also been killed on the same day that the virgins suffered. To this, too, she replied this way, "On the third day after our martyrdom, he suffered his martyrdom at the hands of the same tyrant who slew the blessed Cordula."

She also went on to add the account of a certain martyr whose inscription was 'St. Maurisus, Bishop,' and said, "The blessed Bishop Maurisus was also associated with us when we were still in Rome. This man had been a bishop for two years in Lavicana, though his place of origin was also our country. He was the son of a certain count from a line of great princes. He was the uncle of the two virgins, Babila and Juliana, with whom he was found buried. He was, moreover, a man of the holiest life, and his preaching had great power. His greatest desire was that whatever person outside the faith — whether Jew or Gentile — came to him, that person should not depart from him until he had laved him with the water of holy baptism. And so his name 'of Lavicana' correctly agreed with his office. To us he brought with him the blessed Claudius, a Spoletan, whom he himself had ordained as a deacon, and his brother Focatus, a young layman who had not yet been advanced to military service. These two remained constant to our bishops, they served them diligently, and underwent martyrdom with them."

She said this because I had also questioned her about these men, having seen their inscriptions. She also added of her own accord, "All the bishops who were on the voyage with us had their quarters apart from us, but on Sundays they usually came into our midst, strengthening us with divine discourse and with the communion of the Lord's sacrament."

At one point I longed to inquire about the two bishops whose inscriptions I had received, which were as follows: 'St. Foilanus, Bishop of Lucca, sent from the apostolic see, was struck down in this place and slain by the sword, and was buried with these virgins.' And: 'St. Simplicius, Bishop of Ravenna.' It happened that on a certain day we were celebrating the memory of the blessed Virgin, Our Lady St. Mary, and St. Verena revealed her face to me as it was her benevolent custom. When she had addressed several words to me, I asked her about these bishops and she said, "These two had at that time set out for Cologne; on their return from Cologne they met the sacred band and so joined with the pope and clergy who were there. Returning again with them, they won the palm of martyrdom together with them."

I had been asked to investigate the inscription of a certain venerable tomb which had been inscribed in this manner: 'Here in the earth lies Etherius, who lived twenty-five faithful years. He departed in peace.' Beneath it was written in capital letters: 'REX.' The letter R was large, and so arranged that within it two letters could be distinguished, namely: P and R. The two letters E and X were on the left side of the same figure, while on the right side a capital A had been inscribed.[34] On a certain stone found next to it this inscription was read: 'Demetria the Queen.' I therefore asked the blessed Verena about these things, and at the same time about a certain little girl who was found next to it, with the inscription: 'The maiden Florentina.' And she replied with repect to all these things, saying, "King Etherius was the

---

[34]Tervarent provides an explanation of the actual inscription Elisabeth was attempting to read. A Chi/Rho representing Christus Rex would appear as X over P. Flanking this configuration would appear Alpha and Omega, appearing as A and W. Elisabeth would have had to read the W tipped to give her an E. Some ingenious rearranging yielded the words Rex and Axpara. *La légende de Sainte Ursule dans la littérature et l'art du moyen age*, I, 27.

betrothed spouse of the queen St. Ursula. Now, Demetria was
the mother of Etherius, while Florentina was the same man's
sister."

Of her own accord she added, saying, "I will explain to
you also the meaning of the letter 'A' which has been written
on the king's inscription. Take the same letter 'A' three times
in succession and add to it the three letters 'X' and 'P' and
'R' and you will have AXPARA. This is the name of a certain
duchess who was discovered to have lived in a place in the
vicinity. Now, she was the daughter of an aunt of Etherius,
and she was closely tied to him by the bond of love. This is
what the inscriber wished to signify when he entwined her
name with the king's name. It was not necessary to explain
this more clearly, since it would eventually happen that all
these things would be made clear through you."

While I was marveling to myself about these things,
therefore, and supposing it to be altogether unbelievable
according to the sense of history that the betrothed of St.
Ursula had also undergone this martyrdom, one day the angel
of the Lord, who customarily visited me, presented his
appearance. And I questioned him, saying, "Lord, how did
it happen that the youth who, as we read, had betrothed St.
Ursula, was joined with her in martyrdom although it has
been written that she avoided marriage to him by fleeing?"
And he said, "When the band of holy virgins was coming back
from Rome on the very night on which their six-day journey
was completed, King Etherius, who was remaining in English
Britain, was advised by the Lord in a vision to encourage his
mother Demetria to become a Christian. For his father,
whose name was Agrippinus, had departed from life in the
first year in which he himself had received the grace of
baptism. At the same time it was revealed to him that he was
about to leave his country and meet his betrothed, who was
already returning from Rome, and that he was going to suffer
martyrdom with her and would receive an unwithering crown
from God.

"He assented immediately to the divine admonition and
caused his mother, who agreed to his urging, to be reborn
in Christ. Taking her with his little sister, Florentina, also
a Christian, he hastened to meet his most blessed betrothed.

And he became her companion in martyrdom and in celestial glory."

I further questioned the angel, saying, "Why is it, lord, that this inscription says that he lived twenty-five faithful years? For we learn from history that he had not yet accepted the Christian faith when he began to negotiate his marriage to the blessed Ursula, and that three years before the marriage he was obliged to be instructed in the Catholic faith." And the angel replied, "Although this was so, nonetheless, before he had accepted the Christian faith, he had lived so temperately and so blamelessly in keeping with the circumstance of that life he led at that time, that it seemed to the writer of his inscription that all those years of his could properly be called faithful."

After this, I was instructed through our blessed Lady when she spoke with me one day about a certain holy man whose inscription was 'St. Clemens, bishop and martyr.' She told me that the king I spoke of had brought him with him when he had left his country.

Similarly, when I asked about a certain man whose inscription was 'St. Marculus, Bishop in Greece,' I received this response from the angel:

"There was in the city which is called Constantinople a certain king by the name of Dorotheus, who had originally come from Sicily. His wife's name was Firmindina, and they had an only daughter called Constantia. It happened that both parents died while the daughter was still a virgin and without the solace of a husband. Her nearest relatives had betrothed her, therefore, to a certain youth, the son of another king. But he too was hindered by death before the time of the wedding. Constantia was happy at her reprieve and dedicated the inviolacy of her virginity to God, praying and beseeching that he would never permit her to be fettered to another man.

"Approaching the man of God, St. Marculus, the bishop of the aforementioned city about whom you have inquired, and who was according to the flesh an uncle of hers, Constantia begged his advice as to the protection of her virginity, and most earnestly entreated him to be her helper in this matter. While he was disturbed about this, it was revealed to him one night through a vision from the Lord, that

St. Ursula and her virgins were about to come to Rome very soon. He was told that he should take Queen Constantia and together with her speedily make his way to that place. And he trusted the Lord's revelation. Taking the queen, who for the sake of the Lord spurned her kingdom and all the things of this world, he came to Rome, although the virgins about whom he had received the revelation had not yet arrived there. When they did arrive not long afterwards, the bishop and the queen joined their company. Upon their arrival with them at Cologne, they endured martyrdom for Christ. Moreover, Constantia herself is that woman whom your brother very recently brought to this place."

I asked, "Lord, she who was brought to this place, as they say, had the name 'Firmindina' in her inscription. How can you say that she was named Constantia?" And he said, "Many people in ancient times were accustomed to be called by their parents' names, so that they were designated by even two or three names. So she was given her mother's name of Firmindina. As a result of this it may have turned out that when her inscription was about to be written it was engraved under this name of Firmindina, while her own name which was Constantia was disregarded because the thing was done hastily. This very same thing happened to many others as well — that on that same occasion their names were disregarded and other names were inscribed for them that were not their proper names."

An inscription also of the following sort was sent to me: 'St. Gerasma, who led the holy virgins.' Many requests were made of me to inquire about her for this reason: that she seemed to have been distinguished and worthy of being the leader of so great company. But although I often had the opportunity and the will to ask the question, it was not granted to me, for the question slipped away from my memory so that I marveled over it to myself as to why it should happen this way.

But at length it turned out that the very person who had wanted me to ask questions about her sent to us three dear holy bodies which were from the company of virgins I have spoken of. And after three days of novena, there was the feast of the blessed apostle Andrew, and he himself appeared to me in the silent parts of the mass. With him were one exceedingly glorious martyr and two virgins. And I understood that they were the ones whose bodies had come to us. I therefore questioned the blessed Andre ɾ about their names because they were completely unknown. And he said to me, "Ask them themselves, and they will tell you." When I had done this one virgin replied and said, "I have been called Albina, and she who is with me was called Emerentiana. We were sisters in the flesh, the daughters of a certain count whose name was Aurelianus. This martyr, who came with us, was called Adrianus, and he was a king's son. When he was ten years old he suffered martyrdom for Christ's sake."

And I said, "Lady, how shall we distinguish among your bodies? Which one belongs to which name?" She declared, "Mine is the tallest, while my sister's is the smallest; that of Adrianus, however, is of middle height." And I did not venture to question her further. But God placed in the mouth of the two witnesses this word about the name of the aforesaid martyr — how it was, and what his name was, and that he had been a king's son. This was revealed through a vision during the preceding night to the same brother who had brought the bodies.

After this, as I was pondering over that same martyr and longing to know something more definite about him, it seemed to me one night, in a vision of sleep, as if I were given a book written in golden letters. I read in it a lengthy account about him and his parentage, and how he had left his country with his four sisters, and how he had endured martyrdom with them. The names of those sisters, which I read there, were Babila, Juliana, Aurea, and Victoria. But although it seemed to me that I read all things in that same vision many times over and carefully, I was nevertheless unable to retain in my memory the sequence of the matter exactly as it was.

After a few days, however, the feast of the blessed Nicholas [December 6] approached, and while the office of the mass was being celebrated for him he appeared to me in a manner consistent with his usual kindness. With him again were the three martyrs I have mentioned. I asked him, therefore, to reveal to me something more definite about St. Adrianus, and at the same time it occurred to me that I might inquire about

St. Gerasma, about whom I have spoken. He replied to me
with great kindness and said, "St. Gerasma, about whom you
ask, was a queen of Sicily. She was truly of Aaron's faithful
stock, and abundantly possessed the spirit of the Lord. She
converted her husband King Quintianus. Although he was at
first an extremely cruel ruler, she made of this wolf, as it
were, the tamest lamb. This man had taken her from Britain,
and she was the sister to the bishop St. Maurisus and to Daria,
the mother of the holy Queen Ursula. She had three sons and
six daughters. The smallest among them was the martyr St.
Adrianus, this one of whom you have inquired. Adrianus's
older brother was Dorotheus, King of Greece, who was the
father of St. Constantia, who has been brought to you.

At the same time, however, when the blessed Ursula was
secretly discussing her sacred intention with her father, her
father was feeling great uneasiness about the matter. He sent
a letter to the blessed Gerasma, and revealed to her his
daughter's wish, and disclosed to her the revelations which
they had received from heaven. He desired to hear her
advice, for he knew she was a woman of considerable
wisdom. Now that woman, inspired with divine power, and
knowing that the word had issued from God, set forth on the
journey with her four daughters Babila, Juliana, Victoria,
and Aurea, and with her little son Adrianus. Out of his love
for his sisters he voluntarily flung himself into the
pilgrimage. She left the realm in the hands of one of her sons
and two daughters, and sailed as far as Britain. And so that
entire sacred band of virgins was assembled and organized
by her counsels. She was the leader of all of them on all the
routes of their pilgrimage, through the guidance of her
counsels. At the end she suffered martyrdom with them."

When St. Nicholas had recounted this, he perceived that
I was marveling greatly to myself about this arrangement,
and he said, "You have good cause to be surprised, for all
this business was miraculously arranged by divine
disposition." He added still further, saying, "The martyrs
whom God has sent you are very precious. For that reason,
show your devotion in rendering them honor and service, for
their coming is the beginning of great grace."

One time when she presented herself to my sight, I asked

St. Verena (as it was suggested to me by a certain brother) who was responsible for the martyrdom of that blessed band. For bearing in mind the story which has been told in the preceding pages about Pope Cyriac, I noted that it was certainly not Attila, King of the Huns, who was as some think responsible for their persecution. The persecution carried out by Attila followed afterwards at an interval of many years. To that query she answered as follows:

"When we were at Rome there were at the time in that very place two unjust princes whose names were Maximus and Affricanus. When they saw that we had a great throng and that many people were flocking to us and allying themselves with us, they became violently opposed to us. They feared that through us the Christian religion would grow very numerous and become strengthened. Therefore, when they had reconnoitered the route along which we were to travel, they speedily sent envoys to a certain relative of theirs named Julius, who was a prince of the nation of the Huns. They incited him to lead out his army and to inflict persecution upon us and to destroy us. He swiftly obeyed their desire, and setting forth with an armed mob, rushed upon us when we reached Cologne, and there shed our blood."

But neither is this to be passed over in silence — what she said when I questioned her about the body of the blessed Ursula: "Her body has never been removed from its original burial place except in these days; truly she is there where her inscription is preserved." And she added to this, saying, "Our prayers have procured this from the Lord, that our bodies have been thus revealed in these days. He no longer desires our groans which we uttered because we had been put away with such disregard and because no worthy praise was being accorded God on our behalf. It will come about, however, before the last day, that our whole troop will be made known."

I received these words of God's revelations, not as acts of justice towards me, but through the merits of the holy virgins and the martyrs of Christ, who obtained them on the various feast days of the saints, as it has pleased God. These writings have been completed within the space of a little more than one year. And it happened that when nearly all these discourses had been completed, the feast day arrived of the martyrdom of those same eleven thousand holy virgins [October 21].

While I was participating in the divine service, after the reading of the gospel lesson I went into a trance, as I was accustomed to do. I saw in a region of light, the sight of which is continually before my mind's eyes, a numerous throng of virgins, remarkable in appearance and crowned as if with the purest gold. In their hands were the likenesses of palms, greatly gleaming. Their garments appeared a radiant white, sparkling in the likeness of snow when it is illumined by the sun's splendors. And on their foreheads was the redness of blood, in testimony of the fresh blood they shed in their holy confession. With them, moreover, there also appeared a great many illustrious men with these same tokens.

Now I had a desire still to ask something of them. But because there was such a large number of them I did not know which one of them I could address. Immediately two of them, strikingly distinguished in appearance, stepped forth from the company of the others. They stood apart in front of the rest and gazed directly at me. And I understood that this had been done because of me, and I addressed them saying, "I pray, my ladies, that you may deign to tell me who you are and what your names are."

Now one of them said, "I am Ursula, and she who stands with me is my sister Verena, the daughter of one of my uncles, the great prince." And I spoke to her who was conversing with me, saying, "I beseech you, most holy lady, that you now deign to finish the history, and that you may be willing to clear up for me the manner of your burial. For so many things about you have been revealed to me, an unworthy sinner, through God's grace. Who were those men who at the time of such great persecution so attentively laid your sainted bones to rest and provided you with such honorable burials?" To that she replied to me in this way:

"There was at that time in Cologne a certain sacred bishop filled with the holy spirit named Aquilinus, who was the fourth after the blessed Maternus to guide the church there. When we were about to return from Rome, and were already preparing ourselves for that return, this man saw our entire throng (since it was revealed to him by God), and he became aware of the whole course of the martyrdom which we were about to endure. He also heard a voice saying to him that he should be prepared to bury our bodies, and that he should procure with haste all the things that would be necessary for our interment. Now while he was distressed about these things, two bishops came to him, of whom you have already heard something, that is to say, from Lucca and Ravenna. They recounted to him how it had been revealed to them by God through a vision, that they were as yet uncertain as to the manner and under what circumstances this would come about. However, he about whom it was said on his inscription that he had been sent by the apostolic see received instruction about his journey from the leader of the apostolic see before we arrived. When, moreover, they themselves also had heard from the aforementioned bishop of Cologne about the vision which he had seen concerning us, they returned again upon the route by which they had come, and met us, and so remained constantly in our company until the end."

When she had said these things, I interposed a remark of this sort, saying, "I would like to know, my lady, what specific charge your adversaries made against you so as to put you to death. In particular I desire to know about you yourself. By what manner of death did you end your life?"

And she replied, saying, "The unjust tyrant who was responsible for our death demanded this of us, both with threats and cajolery — that we renounce our spouse in heaven, the Lord Jesus Christ, and that we submit to his embraces and those of his men. But we had not come there for such a purpose, and we steadfastly refused to comply with his injurious desire. We chose rather to die than to be separated from our spouse. For this reason they vented their rage upon us. I myself was struck down by the shot of an arrow to my heart.

"When, therefore, all of us were lying in our blood, that venerable prelate carried out the deed of great piety towards us as he had been instructed, and fulfilled the duty of our burial with great attentiveness and dignity. The majesty of the Lord was present with him and those who labored with him, and God's angels directed them, and the work of our burial was swiftly completed. We, however, did not delay asking the Lord that he might grant him a reward for his toil. And it happened that soon after this he was removed from this life, and God gave him a unique reward for those honors which he paid us. After several days our burial was completed. There came a respectable man, Clematius, and he carried certain bodies which until that time had remained in a certain place. He buried them with great honor, just as he himself had been advised beforehand by the majesty of the Lord."

I immediately submitted a question, saying, "Was it he, lady, Clematius who is said to have built your church?" And she answered, "Not at all; the truth is, that man came a long time afterwards." And when she had finished these explanations she added at the end, saying, "May God grant a reward of his handiwork to that person who has revived the memory of our martyrdom!"

And now, may God reveal those hidden things to the one who is the witness of hidden things, and to those to whom he desires to reveal them, neither favoring the position of the great nor despising the humility of the small. To the benevolent and merciful God, let there be honor and glory and thanksgiving forever and ever. Amen.

Further Reading on Hildegard

Texts:

Pudentiana Barth, M. Immaculata Ritscher, and Joseph Schmidt-Görg, eds. *Lieder: Nach den Handschriften herausgegeben*, pp. 226-28, 218, 294-96, 264-66, 258-60, 244. Salzburg, 1969.

Adelgundis Führkotter, ed. and tr. *Briefwechsel: Nach den ältesten Handschriften übersezt und nach den Quellen erläutert*. Salzburg, 1965.

———— and Angela Carlevaris, eds. *Scivias.* Corpus Christianorum, Continuatio Mediaevalis 43. 2 vols. I, 3-6, 9-11, 13, 16, 18-19, 40-50. Turnhout, 1978.

J.B. Pitra. *Analecta Sacra, 8. Sanctae Hildigardis Opera. Liber vitae meritorum*, pp. 8-11, 236. Monte Cassino, 1882.

Patrologia latina 197: *Hildigardis abbatissae opera omnia. De lapidibus*, cols. 1247-50.

Anton Brück, ed. *Hildegard von Bingen 1179-1979: Festschrift zum 800. Todestag der Heiligen*. Mainz, 1979.
Peter Dronke. *Poetic Individuality in the Middle Ages*. Oxford, 1970.
————. "Tradition and Innovation in Medieval Western Colour-Imagery." *Eranos Jahrbuch* 1972.
Barbara L. Grant. "An Interview with Sybil of the Rhine: Hildegard von Bingen (1098-1179)." *Heresies* 10 (1980), 6-10.
Kent Thomas Kraft. *The Eye Sees More than the Heart Knows: The Visionary Cosmology of Hildegard of Bingen*. University of Wisconsin Dissertation, 1977.
Werner Lauter. *Hildegard-Bibliographie*. Alzey, 1970.
Barbara J. Newman. *Sister of Wisdom: St. Hildegard's Theology of the Feminine*. Berkeley, 1987.
Charles J. Singer. *From Magic to Science: Essays on the Scientific Twilight*. Rpt. New York 1958.
Bernhard W. Scholz. "Hildegard von Bingen on the Nature of Woman." *American Benedictine Review* 31 (1980), 361-383.

Further Reading on Elisabeth

Text:
F.W.E. Roth, ed. *Die Visionen von der hl. Elisabeth und die Schriften der Aebte Ekbert und Emecho von Schönau*, pp. 70-74; 60-62; 123-135. Brunn, 1884.

Ruth J. Dean. "Manuscripts of St. Elisabeth of Schönau in England." *Modern Language Review* 32 (1937), 62-67.
————. "Elisabeth, Abbess of Schönau, and Roger of Ford." *Modern Philology* 41 (1944), 209-220.
Schönauer Elisabeth Jubiläum 1965. Festschrift anlässlich des achthundert jährigen Todestages der heiligen Elisabeth von Schönau. Schönau, 1965.
Guy de Tervarent. *La légende de Sainte Ursule dans la littérature et l'art du moyen âge*. 2 vols. Paris, 1931.

10   Queen of the English People

Matilda, Wife of Henry I (1080-1118)

Six daughterly letters have come to us from Edith, renamed Matilda on her marriage, letters written to Anselm, Archbishop of Canterbury. Matilda wrote chiefly in an effort to calm the storms over lay investiture that raged between Anselm and her husband, King Henry I of England. A seventh letter is addressed to Pope Pascal II on Anselm's behalf in the same controversy.

These letters speak out over the centuries with emotional energy, a certain literary flamboyance founded in Matilda's solid Latin training, and a strong political awareness and determination to affect the course of events. Matilda's family background and her position in history — both of which must have given her confidence in her endeavors — deserve mention.

Orphaned at thirteen, the girl who first was called Edith came of English and Scottish forebears rich in saintly and royal blood. Her uncle was Edgar Atheling, descended from Alfred the Great, and heir to the English throne when the Norman conquerers destroyed his hopes. Edith's parents were the English-born St. Margaret of Scotland, and Malcolm Canmore, the Scottish king who regained his crown when Macbeth the usurper was slain. Edith's great grand-uncle, Edward the Confessor, was the object of a developing hagiographical cult which she later as Queen, collaborating with the Westminster monks, helped to further. By marrying Henry I, the only one of the Conqueror's sons born on English soil, Edith both significantly strengthened Henry's otherwise shaky hold on the sceptre[1], and restored her own family's hereditary claim to England.

Henry lost no time in demanding this twenty-year-old Scottish princess as his wife, which meant prying her free from Wilton Monastery. There she had lived for seven years under the tutelage of her aunt Christina, abbess of Romsey and Wilton. It was at Wilton that Edith received her outstanding education. A refuge of well-born English girls during the Conquest and earlier, Wilton boasted a literary tradition. The poet Muriel, whose works have not survived, had been a Wilton nun. Edith showed a talent for letters, but no taste for monastic life. She appealed for her release to the aged Anselm, whom Henry recalled from exile on September 23, 1100; hotly Edith insisted that the veil had been forced on her:

> For, when I was quite a young girl and went
> in fear of the rod of my Aunt Christina,
> whom you knew quite well, she to preserve
> me from the lust of the Normans which was
> rampant and at that time ready to assault
> any woman's honour, used to put a little
> black hood on my head and, when I threw it
> off, she would often make me smart with a
> good slapping and most horrible scolding, as
> well as treating me as being in disgrace.
> That hood I did indeed wear in her presence,
> chafing at it and fearful; but, as soon as I
> was able to escape out of her sight, I tore it
> off and threw it on the ground, trampled on it
> and in that way, although foolishly, I used to
> vent my rage and hatred of it which boiled up
> in me. In that way, and only in that way, I
> was veiled. . . . My father, when by chance
> he saw me veiled, snatched the veil off and

---

[1]Henry's older brother, Robert Curthose, Duke of Normandy, was alive and on crusade. He naturally considered himself the next king. But when William Rufus died in a hunting accident on August 2, 1100, Henry galloped to Westminster to seize the treasury and the throne.

tearing it in pieces invoked the hatred of God upon the person who had put it on me. . . .[2]

Anselm, fearing that the devil had goaded the tempestuous Edith to throw aside the habit in favor of the world, avoided responding directly to her plea. Instead he got together a synod at Lambeth, the Bishop of Rochester's manor, and allowed the matter to be decided by archdeacons and others learned in church and civil law. These men gave permission for the marriage; Edith secured Anselm's blessing, and was both married and crowned Queen at Westminster on November 11, 1100. The crowds at the church door roared their approval. Her gratitude emerges in the letters.

Matilda — her new Norman name, together with Maud and "Mold the gode Quene" — transformed herself from the impetuous girl of Eadmer's report into a ruler with a reputation for saintliness. She was said to be given to kissing lepers' lips and washing their feet, despite the concern of courtiers that her husband might not wish to kiss her thereafter. Better documented is her role as the King's representative in his absence. Matilda issued two writs in her name from the King's bench in the *curia regis*, both involving the tenure of lands and manors. *The Metrical Chronicle of Robert of Gloucester*, filled with her praises, remarks:

Monie were the gode lawes . imad in
engelonde . thoru Mold this gode quene.[3]

Matilda is credited with defusing the anger of the king's brother, Robert Curthose, who planned to march on Westminster to contest the succession. Learning that Matilda was in childbed, he changed his mind and approached London by a different route. She later used her influence to persuade Robert to give up his annual pension of 3,000 silver marks.

---

[2]*Eadmer's History of Recent Events in England. Historia Novorum in Anglia*. Geoffrey Bosanquet, tr., with a foreword by R.W. Southern (London, 1964), pp. 127-128.

[3]Ed. and tr. William Aldis Wright (rpt. New York, 1965), lines 8750-8751.

Of her three children, the first died in infancy in 1101; her son William (b. 1103) died at seventeen in the wreck of the White Ship. Her daughter (b. 1102) was the future Empress Matilda when she married Henry V of the Holy Roman Empire. Widowed, she became through a second, English marriage the mother of Henry II. And so Queen Matilda receives praise in one of the Lives of Edward the Confessor for having revived the "green tree" of English succession.

Matilda's love of learning made her a patron of literature. She commissioned writings in French and Latin; as William of Malmesbury grumbles, she favored foreigners. Among the works she ordered are the poetic version of the *Voyage of St. Brendan* by one Benedeit, and a biography of her mother, St. Margaret, by the scholar Turgot. In his introduction, Turgot acknowledged that the erudite Matilda wished not only to hear about her mother but to read about her.

Matilda's lifelong devotion to Anselm and her concern for the realm involved her in the controversy over investiture, which Anselm had already waged with the previous king, Henry's brother William Rufus. In and out of exile, Anselm continued to clash, though less dramatically, with Henry. The issue was whether those churchmen should be excommunicated who had been invested with their offices by secular princes. During Anselm's exile from 1103 to 1106, Matilda pleaded with him repeatedly to return, and attempted to reconcile his differences with Henry. Matilda's affection for Anselm is evident from the letters, and is also remarked by his biographer Eadmer. There was general rejoicing when Anselm came back to England, but as for the Queen,

> no earthly concerns, no pageantry of this world's glory could keep her from going on before to the different places to which Anselm was coming; and, as the monks and canons went out as usual to meet the Archbishop, she went on ahead and by her careful forethought saw to it that his various lodgings were richly supplied with suitable

furnishings.[4]

The dispute which occupied Henry and Anselm from 1101 to 1106 was resolved in a compromise when Henry relinquished his rights of ring and crozier, but insisted on receiving homage before bishops and abbots were consecrated. He also controlled the right to nominate candidates for ecclesiastical appointments. Matilda's letters show her personal and official involvement in the matter, as well as her concern for Anselm's well-being.

1. To the lord and reverend father, Anselm, Archbishop of the foremost see [of Canterbury], and primate of all the Irish islands of the Northern hemisphere, which are called the Orkneys:

From Matilda, by God's grace, Queen of the English people, his most humble handmaid. May she, once the course of this present life is happily over, arrive at its goal, which is Christ.

There is almost no doubt that you thwart nature in your daily fasting; this is not unknown to me. What I marvel at all the more is that after long fasting you take your customary food, not because nature demands it but because someone or another of your domestic staff persuades you. I have learned this from the frequent reports of many reliable witnesses. I am also aware that you take this food so sparingly that you seem to have assaulted nature by weakening its claims rather than by breaking its law.

For this reason many people — and I especially — fear that the body of so great a priest may waste away. For he is a priest to whose kindness I have been obliged, a priest who is a strong athlete of God and a victor over human nature. The peace of the realm and the dignity of the priesthood have been strengthened and defended through the unfailing energy of this priest, of this steward of God, who is as faithful as he is wise. By his blessing I was consecrated in lawful marriage; through his anointing I was raised to the dignity of earthly

---

[4]*Eadmer's History of Recent Events in England*, p. 196.

rule; through his prayers I shall be crowned in heavenly glory, by God's grace.

It is to be feared that his body may wither, that the windows of his eyesight and hearing and other senses will grow dull, that his spiritually edifying voice will grow hoarse, and that this voice — which formerly used to impart with quiet and gentle discourse those things of song and speech that are sweet to God — may grow much quieter from now on. Then those persons who are at the time farther away from you may be deprived of hearing that voice and may be bereft of its benefit.

Do not, therefore, good and sainted father, give up your bodily strength by such inopportune fasting as this, for fear that you may cease to be an orator. For as Cicero says in the book he has written *On Old Age:* "The orator's gift is not only talent, but also lung power." Once this is gone, your great spiritual renown would quickly be lost, and so would your great memory of the past and your ability to foresee the future. So much art, so much learning, so much invention, so much understanding of human affairs, along with the clear wisdom of the divine, would swiftly be lost.

Consider the abundance of talents that your rich Lord has given you. Consider what he has entrusted to you and what he may require. Reap the profit for the common use, for once this profit has been reaped, it will shine forth more beautifully and may be yielded up to the Lord with manifold interest.[5]

Do not deprive yourself of these two things in turn. Just as spiritual drink and food are necessary to the soul, so are bodily drink and food necessary for the soul. You must, therefore, eat and drink, since by God's grace, the great path of this life remains to you. A great harvest is to be planted, hoed, weighed, and gathered to God's granary, so that no thief can carry it off. You see that there are extremely few day-laborers in this greatest of harvests. You have embarked on this labor on behalf of many people, so that you may bring back wealth to many.

---

[5]The parable of the talents is in Matthew 25.14-28.

Remember, in truth, that you hold the place of John, the apostle and beloved of the Lord, whom the Lord wanted to survive him so that this virgin, cherished and chosen above the others, might take care of [the Lord's] virgin mother. You have undertaken the care that must be assumed of Mother Church, out of whose womb are your brothers and sisters in Christ. They are in daily peril, unless you hasten to their aid with great devotion. Christ himself, who redeemed them with his own blood, entrusted them to you.

O shepherd of so great a God, feed his flock so that it does not fall by the wayside untended! Let the holy priest Martin be an example to you — an indescribable man who, although he foresaw that his heavenly repose was prepared for him, nevertheless said that he would not refuse to labor for the people's needs.

Indeed, I know that you are encouraged and strengthened in your fasting by the examples of many men, and by the many testimonies of Scripture. And yet diligent reading has often shown you how, after fasting, the ravens fed Elijah, the widow fed Elisha, the angel fed Daniel according to Habakkuk, or how Moses, once he had fasted, merited to read the tablets written by the finger of God, and recovered them in the same way when they were broken. Several examples incite you to the frugality of the pagans; for there is no one who does not know that you have read of the sobriety of Pythagoras, Socrates, Antisthenes, and the other philosophers. It would be too long to enumerate them, and so it is not necessary to do so for this little treatise at hand.

We must, accordingly, come to the grace of the New Law. Christ Jesus, who consecrated fasting, also consecrated feasting when he went to the wedding feast where he changed water to wine, and when he attended the banquet of Simon. There, after he drove the seven demons from Mary, he fed her for the first time with spiritual dishes. He did not refuse the meal of Zacchaeus, whom he pulled back from the power of the earthly army and called to the army of heaven.

Heed, father, heed Paul's urging to Timothy to drink wine on account of the pain in his stomach, when he said, "Do not drink water now." Clearly he indicates that he had previously drunk nothing but water. Imitate Gregory, who relieved the weakness and fatigue of his stomach with the comfort of food and drink, while he continued without interruption and in a manly way with his teaching and preaching. Do, therefore, as he did, so that like him you may arrive at Jesus Christ, the fountain of life and the lofty mountain, with whom in immortal glory he has now long rejoiced, and does rejoice, and will rejoice forever and ever.

Let your holiness flourish in the Lord, and with your prayers do not cease to help me, your faithful servant who cherishes you with all the affection of her heart. Deign to receive, read, heed, and obey this letter, which is not framed with art but sent with strong and faithful love, from me to you.

2. *Matilda Queen of the English to Anselm:*

To her most beloved lord and father, Anselm Archbishop of Canterbury, Matilda Queen of the English sends wishes for his continuing good health, with her love and faithful service.

Let the Divine Comforter — the love of God — not fail to recognize that my heart is sorely troubled because of the excessively long and wearisome absence of Your Holiness. The more I am assured by many people of the swift and imminent date of your wished-for return, the more eager I am, in the hope of enjoying your desired presence and conversation.

My soul will in no way rejoice with perfect joy, most reverend lord, and in no true pleasure will it be gladdened until I am happily able to see you before me again, a thing which I desire with all the strength of my mind.

Indeed, I pray the sweet love of Your Benevolence, that during the time I am deprived of the pleasant comfort of your rebuke, you deign to console and gladden me with the sweetness of your letters.

May the almighty and loving God keep you in all things, and may he cheer me soon with your return and your presence. Amen.

3. To her lord and dearest father Archbishop Anselm, Matilda Queen of the English sends greetings for good health:

How much joy and solace was to be given to me in the delight of anticipated elation at your Holiness's promised arrival! And how much more misfortune befalls me, forsaken and sorrowing, now that your illness prevents you!

I come, therefore, weeping and wretched, to prevail upon your fatherly affection, which I know I can count on. If my solicitude is not wholly despicable to you, soothe the anguish of my concern for your health by whatever messenger you wish — as quickly as possible.

For either I will rejoice without delay over your well-being, and indeed my own, or — may God's mercy avert it — I shall endure the blow that strikes indiscriminately against our common fate.

May the most loving omnipotence of God make you completely well. Amen.

4. Matilda Queen of the English, noble in her queenly heart and filled with pious emotions, to Anselm:

Turn my lamentations to rejoicing, blessed lord, merciful father, and encircle me with happiness. See, lord, your humble handmaiden has fallen to her knees before your mercy. Stretching her suppliant hand to you, she pleads for the favor of your accustomed generosity.

Come, lord, come and visit your servant. Come, I say, father, and relieve my sighs, wipe away my tears, soften my sorrows, banish my mourning. Fulfill my longing with a favorable answer to my prayers. But — you will say — "I am forbidden by the law, held by the chains of these certain constraints imposed by my lords, whose decrees I dare not transgress."

What then of the instance, father, of that learned Apostle of the people, the vessel of election, when he was laboring to overturn the Old Law? Did he not offer sacrifice in the temple so as not to offend those among the circumcised who were believers? Can it be said that he himself, although he condemned circumcision, yet circumcised Timothy, so that he might become all men? How then should his disciple — the son of mercy — do amiss, he who offers himself in the face of death to redeem his servants?

See your brothers, your fellow servants, the people of your God, already enduring shipwreck, already slipping down into death. But you do not help, nor do you extend your right hand, nor do you interpose yourself between us and the danger. Was not the Apostle willing to be cursed by Christ on his brother's behalf? Therefore, good lord, pious father, blunt this severity and — pardon what I say — soften the steeliness of your heart! Come and visit your people, your handmaiden among them, who thirsts for you with all the vitality of her being. Find a road on which you can travel ahead of us as our shepherd, without giving offense and without breaking the laws of kingly majesty.

But if both these things should not be possible at the same time, let the father come at all events, let him come to his daughter, to the handmaiden of the Lord, and teach her how she ought to act. Let him come to her before she departs from the world. For if it happens that I should die before I see you, I fear — and I will speak shockingly — that even in that land of the living and the joyful, I may be cut off from the opportunity of all exultation.

You indeed are my joy, my hope, my refuge. Without you my soul is like the earth without water, and it is for this reason that I have opened my hands wide to you so that you may flow through its parched deserts with the oil of exultation, and nourish them with the dew of your inborn sweetness.

If, however, neither my weeping nor my public prayers should move you, I will disregard my queenly dignity, relinquish the insignia of my reign, I will put aside the sceptre, despise the diadem, I will trample the purple linen underfoot, and I will come to you consumed with my grief. I will embrace the ground you have walked on, I will kiss your feet, nor will anything move me from this, even if Giezi should come,[6] unless the sum of my desires is fulfilled. May

---

[6]Gehazi, an official who tried to push away the Shunammite who approached to embrace the feet of Elisha (II Kings, 4.27).

the peace of God which passes all understanding, keep your heart and mind, and cause your innermost feelings to abound with mercy.

5. Matilda, by God's grace Queen of the English, and the lowest handmaid of his Holiness [Anselm] sends perpetual greetings in Christ to the affectionately remembered father and lord worthy of reverence, Archbishop Anselm:
I send innumerable thanks to your unceasing Goodness, which — I am not unmindful — has deigned to offer me the favor of the letter at hand while you are gone. Indeed, now that the clouds in which I was enwrapped have been driven away, the rivulet of your words has purified me like the ray of a new dawn. I hug the little scrap of writing sent from you in your fatherly stead. I cherish it in my heart. I reread with my lips the words flowing from the sweet fountain of your goodness. I go over them in my mind; I reflect upon them in my heart, and after I have done this, I put them away in the heart's own secret hiding place.
Now that all these things have been properly praised, I marvel at this one thing alone, which the excellence of your discretion has introduced concerning your nephew. For in my judgment I cannot deal differently, that is, from my own who are my very own. Certainly, your people are yours by nature, and they are mine by adoption and affection.[7]
Truly, the comfort of your writing strengthens me in all my suffering; it lifts up my hope and sustains it; it raises me when I fall, supports me when I falter, gladdens me when I am sorrowful, lessens my anger, and pacifies my weeping. These things offer me frequent and secret counsels that promise the return of the father to the daughter, the lord to the handmaid, the shepherd to the sheep. Similar promise comes to me from the trust which I have in the prayers of good people, and from the kindness that arises in the heart of my lord [King Henry] — as I infer, after having sagaciously

---

[7]Matilda is refusing to give preferment to Anselm's nephew, for fear of showing favoritism.

made inquiries. For his spirit is better disposed toward you than many people think. With my favorable influence and my prompting him insofar as I can, he will grow more accommodating and more friendly toward you.

Concerning your return — whatever he allows to happen in the present, he will allow to come about in a better way and more fully in the future, once you have made your request as to the circumstances and the time. Yet, even though he may be more tenacious than the just judge, I beg you nonetheless, out of the abundance of your affection, to shut out the rancor of human bitterness — which is not usual in you. Do not turn the sweetness of your love away from him, but rather prove yourself a pious intercessor with God on behalf of him, and me, and our common offspring, and the state of our kingdom. May Your Holiness flourish always.

6. To her lord and father, Anselm Archbishop of Canterbury, both revered and cherished, Matilda, devout handmaiden of his Holiness, sends her greetings in Christ:
As often as you have shared the citadel of holiness with me through the kindness of your letters, just so often have you brightened the clouded darkness of my spirit with the light of renewed joy. For even when you are absent, there is a certain revisiting with you, as it were, the repeated touching of your bits of writing, and the thoroughly joyful and frequent rereading of your letters, committed to memory.

Now, my lord, what is more elegant in style, more bursting with significance than your letters? The seriousness of Fronto, of Cicero, of Fabius, the subtlety of Quintilian are not lacking in them. The wisdom of Paul wells up in them, the diligence of Jerome, the midnight labor of Gregory, the exegesis of Augustine — and what is greater than these — the sweetness of evangelical eloquence that distills from your writing. Because of this grace that pours from your lips, therefore, my heart and my body have exulted with deep affection in your love, and in carrying out your fatherly teaching.

Relying on the support of Your Holiness, therefore, I have entrusted the abbacy of Malmesbury to Eudolph, monk of Winton — formerly known to you, I believe, as the sexton. To you is entirely reserved anew whatever pertains to the investiture and the decree, of course, so that the mandate of the staff as well as of the pastoral care shall be bestowed through the process of your own judgment.[8]

May the power of heavenly grace grant a worthy recompense to the favor of your good will, which has not grown cool toward me. Concerning the rest, may Christ safeguard your office, and may he who blesses you on earth gladden me with your swift return. Amen.

7. To the highest pointiff and universal father, Pope Pascal, Matilda, Queen of the English by the grace of God. May he so administer the authority of the apostolic high office on earth that he shall deserve to be enrolled — together with the hosts of the just — among the apostolic senate in the joys of perpetual peace.

I bring the greatest thanks and praises that I can to Your Sublime Holiness, O apostolic man, for those things which your fatherly kindness has deigned to bestow upon the king, my lord, and me, by way of religious instruction. These dispatches you have both entrusted to the living voices of legates and included with your own writings.

I do not desist and I will not desist from what is proper and what I am able to do with my whole heart, soul, and mind: I will frequent the threshold of the most holy Roman apostolic see, embrace the ground on which my holy father and apostolic pope has walked, and while prostrating myself at the paternal knees, pray with fitting urgency. I will steadfastly remain until I feel I am being heard by you, either because of my submissive humility or rather because of the persistent importuning of my entreaties.

Let Your Excellency not be angered by this boldness of mine and because I dare to speak this way. And let the

---

[8]Matilda's appointment is important in view of the investiture controversy. In this, the only letter of hers from which she omits mention of her queenly rank, Matilda bestows an abbacy and seeks Anselm's approval after the fact.

wisdom of the Roman clergy, the people, and the Senate not be astounded. For under your apostolic high office, Anselm, our Archbishop, was indeed once a protégé of the Holy Spirit. He *was,* I say, for us and for the people of the English — so blessed as we were then — our preacher, the most prudent comforter of the people, and their most devoted father.

What he took in abundance from his Lord's most opulent treasury — whose key-bearer we acknowledged him to be — he distributed among us even more lavishly. As his Lord's loyal minister and wise steward he seasoned each morsel he paid out to us with a generous serving of the condiment of wisdom, softened it with the sweetness of eloquence, and flavored it with the marvelous charm of his speech. And so it happened that the tender lambs did not lack the Lord's abundance of milk, nor did the sheep lack pasturage of the richest fertility, nor did the shepherds lack the most plentiful abundance of provisions. Now that all these things have ceased to be, however, there is nothing left but the shepherd who — hungry for food — weeps with many a groan, the sheep that hungers for its grazing, and the young that longs for its udder.

As long as the greatest shepherd, namely Anselm, is absent, not only is each one deprived of each of these things, but rather all of them are deprived of everything.

In such sorrowful weeping, in such shameful grief, in such disgrace to our realm, in the outrage arising from so great a loss, nothing remains to me — dazed and suffering as I am — but to fly for help to the blessed Peter's apostle and vicar, the apostolic man.

And so I appeal to your generosity, lord, lest we and the people of the English realm should, because of so great an eclipse, sink into an equally great decline. For what use are our life and our lineage, as long as we are descending into error?

Therefore, let your fatherhood think well of it, insofar as it touches us, to deign to open your paternal heart to us within the time period that my lord the king asks of your goodness. Allow us to rejoice in the return of our most beloved father, the Archbishop Anselm, and to preserve our dutiful subjection to the Holy Apostolic

See.[9] Certainly, I have been instructed by your most wholesome and beloved reminders. To the extent that my woman's strength is available to me and the help of good men is provided me, I will strive to the utmost, so that my humility discharges as far as possible what Your Highness advises. May Your Fatherhood blessedly thrive.

Further Reading on Matilda

Texts: *Patrologia Latina,* Vol. 159, cols. 88-90; 239; 240; 131-32; 134-36; 156; and Vol. 163, cols. 466-67.

Derek Baker, ed. *Medieval Women.* "'A nursery of saints': St. Margaret of Scotland reconsidered," pp. 119-141. Oxford, 1978.
Melville Madison Bigelow. *Placita Anglo-Normannica: Law Cases from William I to Richard I,* pp. 137, 100. London, 1879.
Eadmer's History of Recent Events in England. Historia Novorum in Anglia, tr. from the Latin by Geoffrey Bosanquet, with a foreword by R. W. Southern. London, 1964.
M. Dominica Legge. *Anglo-Norman Literature and its Background.* Oxford, 1963.
Kate Norgate. *England under the Angevin Kings.* London, 1887.
R.W. Southern. *St. Anselm and his Biographer: A Study of Monastic Life and Thought: 1059-c. 1130.* Cambridge, 1963.

---

[9]We may read a veiled suggestion of disobedience, together with a plea not to excommunicate Henry, whose precarious claim to the throne needed the prestige of papal support.

11   The Women Troubadours

The Countess of Dia
Almuc de Castelnou and Iseut de Capio
Bieris de Romans
Alaisina, Iselda and Carenza
Anonymous

With the social, economic, legal and cultural renaissance
of the twelfth century, the vernacular began to replace Latin
as an expressive and eloquent medium. The south of France
saw the emergence of a literary language that kept in touch
with the stylistic formality of clerical neo-Latin, yet was also
a hybrid of dialects containing common terms in daily use.
Words about the weather, plants and birds, food and clothing,
curtains and bedding, kissing and "doing it" — *faire-lo,* for
making love — as well as a wittily employed vocabulary
culled from rhetoric, religion, war, feudalism, law and
commerce, with its wages, profits, and damages, entered the
tightly intricate structures of the Provençal or Occitan lyric.
     Twenty-six lyrics, written in the twelfth and early
thirteenth centuries are ascribable to women authors,
twenty-two bearing women's names. These women were said
to be aristocratic and well-educated. They already had rank
— *paratge* — and so did not have to assume the gracefully
groveling pose found among some of the humbler male poets.
When women writers do adopt an air of anxious oppression,
it is because of love, not social difference.
     Many of the women's poems are accompanied by *vidas*
(biographies) and *razos* (commentaries). The *vidas* and
razos are occasionally fanciful, as they are for the male

troubabours, but from them and other sources we may gather that the *trobairitz*, the women troubadours, were relatives, friends, colleagues, and lovers of the male poets.

While there were some 400 male troubadours, the names of 20 women have survived, 18 of them attached to specific lyrics. The *trobairitz* had a choice of the available poetic genres: *canso* (love song), *tenso* (debate), *partimen* or *joc parti* (an intellectual dispute whose question was referred to an authority), *sirventes* (political, abusive, or satirical song), *alba* (exchange between lovers parting at dawn), *pastorela* (amorous exchange between poet/knight and shepherdess), and *planh* (lament, sometimes for the dead). Women's voices do emerge from the *alba* and the *pastorela*. Yet the surviving songs of the *trobairitz* are *cansos* and *tensos*. In general, the lyrics of the *trobairitz* are direct, plaintive or accusatory, argumentative, and problem-oriented.

Precedents for a female lyric voice are found in Spain and Portugal, with the "cantigas de amigo," in which a woman sings tearfully about an absent man. Women's love laments emerge in the Bible, with the voice of the spouse in the *Song of Songs*, and the conversations between the wise and foolish virgins in Matthew 25. In fact the virgins were dramatized in the eleventh-century play *Sponsus*, with the sisters addressing one another in an Occitan dialect. Saints directed love songs to God, as in the eleventh-century Occitan *Chanson de Sainte Foy*, where St. Faith longs to laugh and rejoice with the Lord. Interestingly, the poem claims to be a good *canczon* for dancing, a reminder that women's dance songs, too, incorporated women's voices.

There is also a tradition of fictional letters, stemming from Ovid's *Heroides*, in which deserted heroines of antiquity, such as Sappho and Dido, address a beloved. Love letters in Latin verse survive, and of course, letter-writing of every description had long been a genre available to women, affording a chance for rhetorical ornamentation. The lyrics of the troubadours themselves, both men and women, can be seen as an elegant, playful form of the letter, with their salutation, special pleading, and closing envoy or *tornada*, directed to a messenger.

In only one medieval text do we find the word *trobairitz*,

or "troubaress." It doesn't appear in the lyrics, the *vidas,* or the *razos,* but in the thirteenth-century Occitan romance of *Flamenca.* Flamenca and her women friends have been rearranging the words of a lyric by a colleague, one Peire Rogier, in order to send a message to Flamenca's lover. One of them strings together some of the usual clichés like "Alas, why am I complaining? Because I'm dying! Of what?" and so on. Flamenca exclaims:

> Marguerite, that's very well done!
> You're already a good *trobairitz.*

Marguerite acknowledges the compliment:

> Yes, Madame, the best you've ever seen,
> after you and Alis, of course.

This intriguing repartée suggests that women consciously absorbed and transformed male texts for their own use, and that there was an element of play, community, and competition in the endeavor. *Flamenca* shows women composing for each other's entertainment and approval, even though they may also have been writing for male friends and lovers.

The Countess of Dia

The five poems that have come to us from the Countess of Dia are polished and passionate compositions that seem to court emotional danger, and then deftly evade it. There is no reason to call her "Beatriz." The Countess was said in her *vida* to be married to a Guillaume of Poitou, but not the troubadour Duke Guillaume IX, Count VII of Poitou. She might have been the daughter of Gigue V, dauphin of Viennois in the twelfth century. The *vida* also tells of her love for Raimbaut of Orange, possibly the renowned twelfth-century troubadour, or his grand-nephew Raimbaut VI. If it was the younger Raimbaut, the countess would belong to a later generation of women writers, those affected by wider access to poetic texts whose writing may therefore be rooted more in theory and fantasy than in personal experience. Whatever the conditions under which she wrote, the Countess's poetry is forthright and sensual, investigating a wide variety of moods, while delighting in the play of language.

In the first lyric, *Ab joi et ab joven m'apais,* the singer revels narcissistically in her well-being. She is the *domna* whose own good points give her pleasure. Even while she praises her lover, she parallels his virtues with hers. The poem produces a key word in each line which is mirrored or punned upon in the next, repetitions that link the lovers or reinforce their qualities. In the *tornada* the woman asks the man's protection in feudal terms, as an overlord shields a vassal.

A contrast to the sanguine wittiness of this lyric, the second poem, *A chantar m'er de so q'ieu no volria,* explores an entirely different mood. Resentfully, the singer complains of her lover to a "jury" of hearers. Then still defensive, she turns to accuse him directly. Her wounded anger gives way to pride, however, claiming that she outdoes this valiant lover by being more valiant than he is — in the loving game. Now the poem views love in military terms, as a form of combat in which each vies to face down the other. In *Ab joi et ab joven m'apais,* the singer had invited her lover to be her protective feudal lord; here she chafes against his arrogant sovereignty.

The man's valor, she claims, consists in lording it over her, whereas hers lies in her steadfast loving. She's even better than Seguin, who was valorous in the world of *chanson de geste,* although he was killed for it. The confrontational eye-to-eye aspect of the poem becomes a triangle when the singer introduces the "other woman," thereby adding jealousy to her sufferings. But still undaunted, the singer claims to be stronger than *both* the man and *any* other woman.

The initial impression of the third lyric, *Estat ai en greu cossirier* is one of vulnerable sensuality. Three time frames are evoked: a past in which the singer did not yield sexually to the man even though she says she had the opportunity; a present sense of loss; and a yearning toward future possession, oriented both to sexuality and power. Sensuality is conveyed only through verbs of wishing, however. All is imagined; nothing physical occurs.

The poem deliberately creates rich, teasing doubts through images first of the singer in bed, and then as a possible pillow for her lover. "Fully clad" is echoed by the contrasting word "naked" in the following stanza. The reference to Floris and Blancheflor is a reminder that these lovers from popular romance were discovered in bed together. The literary allusion opens the narrow confines of the lyric's highly cerebral space to the worldly hazards of romance, and keeps before the reader's mind the images of bed and naked lovers. At this point, however, the singer asserts her toughness, her readiness to give up everything, like Blancheflor, including her life.

But the third stanza contains a surprise. No more talk of sacrifice — the singer looks abruptly forward to a time when she can exert her power. Briefly she toys with the dangerous idea of putting the lover in a husband's place, which would make him the master. The ecstatic quality of their clandestine passion would end, and so would her reign as *domna,* powerful lady of the *canso.* Then she makes her final startling and outrageous demand: he must be her servant in everything, husband or no. Yet after all, he remains an *amour lointain,* a faraway, absent love.

In the fourth lyric, *Fin joi me don alegranssa,* the singer flings a gleefully defiant challenge into the faces of malicious gossips.

The final anonymous *tenson* in this group is still sometimes attributed to the Countess of Dia. In it the woman and the man compete once again on the battlefield of love, each one speaking a part. Which should win the prize for greater suffering? Perhaps it is the lady, since her lover finally promises not to think about another woman *again.*

1. *Ab joi et ab joven m'apais*
By joy and youth I'm made content;
Joy and youth nourish me.
My friend is the most gallant of men,
and so I'm gallant and charming.
And since I'm true to him,
he must be true to me.
I've never strayed from loving him,
nor have I a heart that leads me astray.

It pleases me greatly to know he's most worthy —
the man I want most to have me.

And to the one who brought us first together,
I pray God may bring great joy.
If anyone should bear him an evil tale,
let him believe nothing but what I bear to him.
People often gather broom twigs
only to be swept with the same broom.

A lady who delights in true worth
should place her delight
in a worthy, valiant cavalier.
Once she understands his valiance,
let her dare to love him openly.
And when a lady loves openly,
worthy and gracious people
will say only that she is gracious.

I've chosen a daring and noble man
in whom daring itself is enhanced and ennobled.
Generous, skillful, and knowing,
he possesses wit and knowledge;
I beg him to believe in me;
let no one make him believe
I'd ever fail him
unless I found some failing in him.

Floris, your valiance
is known to the valiant and brave.
That is why I ask you now—
if it pleases you — to enfeoff me now
with your love.

    2. *A chantar m'er de so q'ieu no volria*
I must sing about something I would rather not sing—
So much rancor have I against the man whose sweet
    friend I am.
For I love him more than anything.
Pity and courtesy are worth nothing to him.
Neither are my beauty or my merit or my good sense.
I'm as trapped and betrayed
as I might have deserved to be, if I hadn't the least charm.

But this consoles me — that I have committed no
injury against you, dear friend, through any fault
    of mine.
I love you more than Seguin loved valor;
It gives me pleasure to vanquish you in loving —
since you, dearest friend, are the most valiant of
    men.
You treat me proudly in words and looks,
while showing gentleness to all the others.

I marvel at your arrogant presence
confronting me; for I have good reason to grieve.
It's unjust that another love tears you from me.
Whatever she may say — however she may welcome you —
Remember the beginning
of our love. Please God that I'm not at fault
for this parting of ours!

The great prowess that lodges in your heart
and your striking pride both make me unhappy.
For I don't know of any woman, near or far,
who wouldn't be drawn to you — if she were ready
    for love.
But you, dear friend, are so knowing, that you
ought to recognize the truest woman.
Remember the verses we exchanged at our parting.

My merit, my high rank should count for something,
and my beauty, and my faithful heart above all.
And so I'm sending you — there to your great house —
this song that serves as my messenger.
I want to know, best and dearest of noble friends,
why you show yourself so fierce, so savage to me.
I don't know if it's arrogance or ill will.

Messenger, I wish you to tell him this besides:
that lofty pride damages many a man!

3. *Estat ai en greu cossirier*
I've been in great anguish
over a noble soldier I once had,
and I want everyone to know, for all time,
that I loved him — too much!
Now I see I'm betrayed
because I didn't yield my love to him.
For that I've suffered greatly,
both in my bed and fully clad.

How I'd yearn to have my soldier
naked in my arms for one night!
He would feel a frenzy of delight
to have only me for his pillow.
I'm more in love with him
than Blancheflor ever was with Floris.
To him I'd give my heart, my love,
my mind, my eyes, my life.

Beautiful, gracious, sweet friend,
when shall I hold you in my power?
If I could lie with you for one night,
and give you a kiss of love,
you can be sure I would desire greatly
to grant you a husband's place,
so long as you promised
to do everything I wished!

4. *Fin joi me don alegranssa*
Perfect joy brings me delight!
This is why I sing the more gaily,
and neither harbor heavy thoughts
nor give a thought
to base and lying slanderers.
For I know they're trying to damage me.
Their spiteful speech doesn't frighten me —
it makes me live twice as gaily!

I have no faith
in wicked-tongued gossips,

for you can't keep your honor
if you deal with them.
They're in every sense
a cloud that spreads
until the sun loses its rays.
That's why I don't like false people.

And you, jealous people with your barbed tongues,
don't imagine that I falter,
or that joy and youth don't give me pleasure:
let your grief over that destroy you!

5. *Amics en gran cossirier*
Friend, I'm in great torment
because of you, and in great pain.
I believe that you scarcely feel
any of the ill I'm suffering.
Why, then, do you play the role of lover
since you leave all the wretchedness to me?
For the two of us do not play an equal part.

Lady, Love's ministry is such
that when he enchains two lovers,
both of them feel suffering and joy
in their own fashion.
I think — and I'm not a braggart —
that the heart's bitter anguish
has been altogether mine.

Friend, if you had felt a quarter
of the pain that harrows me,
you would well appreciate my burden.
But you scarcely care for the damages I suffer,
and when I can't avoid them,
it's a matter of indifference to you
that I endure both well and woe.

Lady, since there are slanderers
who have reft me of my sense and breath
and who are warring bitterly against us,

I am leaving you — not out of true desire —
but because I'm not near you. Their braying
deals us such a mortal blow
that we cannot taste a day of joy together.

Friend, I don't feel grateful to you
that these evils prevent
you from seeing me — since I long for you.
If you set about guarding my good name
more than I myself wish,
I'll consider you more zealously loyal
than a knight of St. John the Hospitaler.

Lady, I strongly fear that
I'll lose my gold and you'll lose the arena,
and that through the gossip of these slanderers
our love will be spoiled.
That's why I must be more guarded
than you, by St. Martial,
for you are the thing of greatest value to me.

Friend, you are so careless
in matters of love
that I think you have changed
from the cavalier you once were.
I feel I must say this,
for you seem to be thinking of someone else,
since my sorrow means nothing to you.

Lady, may I never again carry a sparrowhawk,
or hunt with falcon,
if — since you first gave me complete joy —
I have ever desired another woman.
I'm not such a liar,
but envious and disloyal people
have made me seem that way and have maligned me.

Friend, should I have such trust in you
that I can believe you'll always be faithful?

Lady, from now on I will be faithful to you,
and I'll never again think of another woman.

Almuc de Castelnou and Iseut de Capio

Here is a *tenso* between Lady Iseut and her friend Lady
Almuc. While one defends and the other accuses, both are
really sizing up and judging a male culprit. Iseut pleads with
Almuc to pardon Gui de Tournon after Gui has been found
guilty of wronging Almuc. In this lyric, with its play on
religious language — prayer, sacrament, repentance, mercy,
conversion — Iseut acts as an intercessor before the wrathful,
all-powerful, but ultimately merciful Almuc. Perhaps
Almuc's last-minute willingness to "convert" places her
again on an earthly plane with her lover.

6. *Dompna n'Almucs, si'us plages*
Lady Almuc, if it pleases you,
I would very much like to pray to you in this
   manner:
put aside your wrath and ill will,
and show mercy
toward him who sighs and groans,
and dies as he languishes. He laments
and most humbly seeks your pardon.
Perform the sacrament for him
if you want everything finished with him,
so that he'll be guarded against further failings.

Lady Iseut, if I knew
that he repented truly of the very great deception
that he committed against me,
it would be right for me
to show him tender mercy. But it doesn't suit me —
since he doesn't refrain from his wrongdoing,
nor does he repent of his fault —
to show indulgence toward him.
Yet, if you can make him repent,
you might convert me to his favor.

Bieris de Romans

Unique among the *trobairitz* is this love lyric from one woman to another, incorporating all the conventional praises and humble pleas for solace. Beatrice addresses a gracefully adoring poem to her friend Maria, after cataloguing her graces. Beatrice doesn't fail to sing her own praises as well, both as a lover and a poet.

7. *Na Maria, pretz e fina valors*
Lady Maria, your worth and excellence,
joy, understanding, and exquisite beauty,
the warmth of your welcome, your excellence and
    honor,
your elegant conversation and charming company,
your gentle face and amiable gaiety,
your gentle gaze and amorous mien —
all these things are yours, without deviousness.
And these things have drawn my truant heart to you.

For this reason I plead with you — if true love
    pleases you
and my joyfulness and sweet submission
should elicit from you the succour I need —
then give me, lovely woman,
if it's pleasing to you,
the gift in which I have most joy and hope.
For in you I have fixed my heart and desire,
and from you I have derived all my happiness,
and from you — so many times — my painful yearning.

And since your beauty and worth enhance you
above all women, so that no other is superior,
I plead with you — please! It would bring you honor
too, not to love some suitor who'd betray you.

Glorious lady, woman enhanced by worth, joy,
and gracious speech, my verses go to you.
For in you are gaiety and happiness,
and every good that one demands of a lady.

Alaisina, Iselds, and Carenza

An interesting three-way *tenso* among "sisters" upholds
the advantages of the unmarried life. Women are better off
wedded only to an allegorical gentleman named "Crowned
with Learning." Ideas of knowledge, learning, and wisdom
are scattered throughout. The spirit of the cloister, or at least
of the educated female community reigns, invested in the
form of the troubadour lyric, as Alaisina and Iselda seek the
advice of their senior sister Carenza.

8. *Na Carenza al bel cors avinen*

Alaisina:

Lady Carenza, you of the graceful and lovely body,
give counsel to us two sisters.
And since you know best how to sift over the best,
counsel me according to your own wisdom.
Shall I take a husband from among our acquaintances?
Or remain a virgin? That would please me,
since I don't think much of having babies,
and being married seems too depressing to me.

Iselda:

Lady Carenza, having a husband would agree with me,
but I think having babies is a great penance.
Your breasts hang right down to the ground
and your belly is burdensome and annoying.

Carenza:

Lady Alaisina and Lady Iselda, you have a good
    education,
reputation and beauty, youth and fresh color;
you have understanding, courtesy and merit —
above all the other ladies of my acquaintance.
For this reason I counsel you, in order to get
    good seed,

Take Coronat de Scienza[1] for your husband.
From him you'll have the fruit of glorious
    children.
Those who marry him will remain virgins.
Lady Alaisina and Lady Iselda, your remembrance of me
is a guarantee that you'll be shielded.
When you arrive, pray to the Glorious One:
On my departure, may he keep a place for me
    beside you.

Anonymous

One of the earliest troubadour lyrics, anonymous but
attributable to a woman writer, is the following *balada,* or
dance song. Basically it is a "chanson de mal mariée," a
complaint about a husband, comparing him unfavorably to
a lover. Its refrain is meant to be sung by a chorus of dancers,
but it contains a wider appeal in its closing verse to the
community of learned women everywhere to perpetuate the
song.

9. *Coindeta sui, si cum n'ai greu cossire*
I'm lovely but miserable
because of a husband I don't want or desire.

I'll tell you why I'm someone else's lover:
    (I'm lovely but miserable)
I'm fresh and young, I've a dainty body,
    (I'm lovely but miserable)
and I ought to have a husband who can make me glad,
someone I can play and laugh with.
    (I'm lovely but miserable
    because of a husband I don't want or desire.)

---

[1]Literally, "Crowned with Learning."

God knows I'm not the least in love with him.
    (I'm lovely but miserable)
I've little wish to make love with him.
    (I'm lovely but miserable)
I'm filled with shame to look at him.
I wish that death would do him in.
    (I'm lovely but miserable
    because of a husband I don't want or desire.)

But let me say one thing:
    (I'm lovely but miserable)
this friend of mine makes it up to me in love;
    (I'm lovely but miserable)
I indulge in fondest, sweetest hopes;
I cry and sigh when I don't see or gaze at him.
    (I'm lovely but miserable
    because of a husband I don't want or desire.)

And let me say another thing:
    (I'm lovely but miserable)
since my friend has loved me a long time,
    (I'm lovely but miserable)
I'll indulge in love
and fondest hopes, for the one I crave.
    (I'm lovely but miserable
    because of a husband I don't want or desire.)

I've made a pretty dance song to this tune,
    (I'm lovely but miserable)
and I ask everyone to sing it, far and wide.
    (I'm lovely but miserable)
And let all learned ladies sing it too,
About my friend whom I love and long for.
    (I'm lovely but miserable
    because of a husband I don't want or desire.)

Further Reading on the Women Troubadours

Texts:
Gabrielle Kussler-Ratyé, ed. "Les chansons de la comtesse

Béatrix de Dia." *Archivum Romanicum* 1 (1917), 161-182.
Oskar Schultz-Gora, ed. *Die provenzalischen Dichterinnen.* Leipzig, 1888.

Pierre Bec. "'Trobairitz' et chansons de femme. Contribution à la connaissance du lyrisme féminin au moyen âge." *Cahiers de civilisation médiévale* 22 (1979), 235-262.
Meg Bogin. *The Women Troubadours.* New York, 1976.
J. Boutière and A.H. Schultz. *Biographie des troubadours.* 2nd ed., Paris, 1973.
Glynnis M. Cropp. *Le vocabulaire courtois des troubadours de l'époque classique.* Geneva, 1975.
Margarita Egan, tr. *The Vidas of the Troubadours.* New York, 1984.
Marianne Shapiro. "The Provençal *Trobairitz* and the Limits of Courtly Love." *Signs* 3 (Spring 1978), 560-571.
Jules Véran. *Les poétesses provençales.* Paris, 1946.
James J. Wilhelm. *Seven Troubadours, the Creators of Modern Verse.* University Park, Pa., 1970.

12   A *Lai* of Courtly Romance and Two Fables

Marie de France (Twelfth Century)

Marie was a nobly born woman, originally from France, who lived and wrote in England during the last half of the twelfth century. She had connections with the English court, dedicating one of her books to King Henry II, and another to a Count William, perhaps the William Marshal, Earl of Pembroke, who was called the "flower of chivalry."

As for Marie's precise identity, it eludes us. She may have been Marie de Champagne, a daughter of Eleanor of Aquitaine. Possibly she was an abbess of Shaftesbury, half-sister to King Henry II, hence an illegitimate daughter of Geoffrey Plantagenet. Other Maries have been proposed. She simply tells us that Marie is her name in three of her works, each of a different literary type: in the *lai* of *Guigemar,* in the epilogue to her *Fables,* and in her *St. Patrick's Purgatory.*

Her writings consist of a dozen narrative *lais* with love as their subject; the 102 fables entitled *Isopet,* from Aesop, are short exemplary tales about animals, or things, or people; and the translation from Latin of an underworld and paradisal journey, earlier than Dante, is about the adventures of the knight Owein.

With certainty it can be said that Marie de France was the first of the great and well-educated French women writers. She flourished in the period now recognized as a renaissance of thought, learning, literary ferment, and a growing sense of the individual. The signing of one's work is one of the symptoms of this tendency, especially if a powerful patron had commissioned it and the author wished to show gratitude; earlier medieval work had tended to remain anonymous.

Much of the literature of the twelfth century, like the theology, had as its chief subject love in all its heavenly and earthly manifestations. Marie wrote of love from a secular, aristocratic, and female point of view. Her writing on love is clearly influenced by the cult of love that could be abstracted from the lyrics of Provence and northern France. But where the troubadours had made an august and remote figure of woman, Marie, like the *trobairitz*, explores the emotional tenderness and susceptibility of women under the stresses of love. Their voices, though less polished, resemble those of the troubadour women. Marie moreover rejects any body or code of rules where love is concerned. Her lovers are individuals caught in straits peculiar to them.

Marie also writes in reaction against the extremely popular genre of the *chanson de geste,* brawling embattled celebrations of war, full of wrangling barons, the play of weaponry, and male valor and devotion exercised in the carving out of history. Instead of portraying her male characters as heroes or heroic villains, Marie shows them as luckless and landless soldiers of fortune, struggling against the actual hazards and miseries of the profession of arms in their lives of restless raiding and tourneying. Marie rejects the mentality of this male military world entirely, finding in it the sources of feminine unhappiness. Instead of praising heroism, she is more attuned to the psychologically nuanced aspects of the romance world.

Marie's appeal and popularity in her day are reflected by a disgruntled rival, Denis Piramus, who complains that audiences, and women especially, admire the *lais* of *dame Marie.* These are, he maintains, "patently untrue in content, though artfully composed, and court audiences love them." The nobility is said to enjoy delightful stories "because they remove and discard sadness, tedium, and weariness of heart, and make people forget their anger and banish troublesome thoughts."

It is true that Marie's *lais* afford entertainment. They are full of elements of the marvelous and the surreal — humans who change into animals, magic potions, a curiously decked ship that conveys the hero to his destined mistress, for instance. But the *lais* are also noteworthy for their psychological interest; Marie introduces characters whom she identifies as admirable, and then allows them to fall into problem situations that force them to reveal their deeper, crasser natures. She realistically explores the initiation into adulthood as well as the dilemmas and hardships created by different kinds of love. Adolescent sexuality, tenderness, lust, jealousy, married love, adultery, and sacrifice are matters that she reports with her characteristically understated simplicity and economy, leaving the reader to make a final judgment.

The *lais* often center on a symbolic object, such as the nightingale in the *lai* translated below. The nightingale has been invented by the enamored wife of the tale to explain her nocturnal absences from her husband's bed. When a nightingale does materialize, its song, pathetic death, and costly embalming offer a rich, concentrated comment on the fantastic and doomed eroticism that is being celebrated, while realistically revealing the husband's brutality. The woman's bloodstained gown also provides an unforgettable, sexually-charged image.

Marie's writing has none of the rambling tendency and chattiness so common in medieval narrative. She goes straight to the heart of a situation, making of the *lai* a genre comparable to the short story rather than to the novel, which medieval romance resembles. Her poetry is succinct and bare, even strenuously so, and marked by a certain brusque cynicism that saves it from sentimentality. Despite their brevity, however, the *lais* are richly detailed as to foreground; events seem to float in an unspecified space that is left vague and mysterious.

While the *lais* leave the reader to reflect upon possible meanings, the even shorter fables from *Isopet* provide a moral conclusion that is often allegorical. Many show Marie's preoccupation with feudalism, chivalry, the quest for honor and power, in short, aristocratic concerns. Some deplore human imperfection. The fables translated at the end give a harsher, earthier view of love than is found in the *lais*. While one is about a knight and a worthy woman, and the other about a peasant couple, both demonstrate the fleeting nature of fidelity and the realities of adult sexuality. The first, an old Milesian tale which has an analogue in the *Satyricon* of Petronius, claims to illustrate the way of the world generally, but like the second it really singles out the lustfulness of women. The second fable contains a commonplace found in other narratives, notably in Chaucer's *Merchant's Tale,* that a woman caught in adultery will usually extricate herself with a clever, far-fetched answer. There is a resemblance between shrewd young May and the well-bred wife in the following *lai*: challenged, she quickly produces the alibi of the nightingale. An examination of a fuller range of Marie's works will reveal her pairing of motifs and themes in works that seem on the surface to be dissimilar.

In the following *lai,* Marie frames her story about the nightingale with two allusions to Breton singers, harpers and storytellers. These itinerant performers are credited by Marie and others, such as Chaucer and the writers of Arthurian romances, with having brought their short, sung narratives from the French province of Brittany to England. The word *lai,* like *lied,* means a musical composition of a narrative nature, meant to be sung.

Because the Bretons are thought originally to have migrated from England many centuries earlier during the Saxon invasions, these narrative *lais* apparently preserve ancient British and Celtic legends that have acquired a French setting. There are no "Breton *lais*" in existence, since they always belonged to oral performance, although there are some 36 poems that call themselves *lais* and possess their characteristics. Marie tells us in several of her *lais* that she has heard these sung, and that hers are written versions.

1. A Breton *Lai*

The Nightingale: Laüstic

I am going to tell you an adventure about which the Breton singers have composed a lay. It's called "Laüstic"; I believe that is what they call it in their country. It's "Rossignol" in French, and in plain English, "*Nightingale*."

In the Breton country of Saint Malo there was a famous

city. Two knights were living there in two strongly fortified houses. It was the excellence of these two barons that gave the city its good name. One had married a wife who was well-behaved, courteous, and elegant. It was wonderful to see how she arrayed herself to advantage in decorous keeping with the custom and style. The other young man was a bachelor knight, unmarried, well known among his peers for his bold exploits, his worthiness, and his readiness to conduct himself honorably toward people. He took part in tournaments, and spent money lavishly. He was generous with what he had.

He fell in love with his neighbor's wife. He begged so hard and pleaded with her, and he was so excellent a man, that she came to love him more than anything in the world. It was because of the good things she heard about him and because he lived close to her. They loved each other prudently and discreetly. They took care to conceal their behavior and to guard against being perceived, disturbed, or suspected.

They succeeded in this since they lived near each other. Their houses, with all the chambers and dungeons, were in close proximity. There was no barrier, nothing to separate them except a high wall of darkened stone. From the chambers where the lady slept she was able, when she stood at the window, to converse with her friend on the other side, and he with her. They were able to exchange their love tokens by tossing or throwing them. There was nothing to mar their pleasure; the two of them savored their happiness even though they could not come together to fulfill their desires. For the lady was closely guarded when her husband traveled throughout the country. Day and night their sole recourse was to talk together. No one could prevent them from going to the window to gaze at each other.

For a long time they were in love, until summer came, when woods and fields grow green again and orchards bloom. Small birds sing sweetly from the flowering treetops. It's not surprising that whoever longs for love can think of this and nothing else. I will speak to you candidly about this knight: he yielded entirely to his feelings, and the lady did too, both in words and looks. At night when the moon shone and her husband lay sleeping, she would often steal from his side; with her cloak wrapped about her she would go to the window, for she knew her friend would be at his. This is how they lived, gazing at each other for most of the night. They derived pleasure from seeing each other, denied as they were a greater bliss. She stayed so often at the window, and would get up out of bed so often at night that her husband lost his temper, and more than once demanded to know the reason she rose this way and where she went. "My husband," replied the lady, "anyone who hasn't heard the nightingale sing has not experienced joy in the world. That is why I go to stand at the window. I hear its sweet voice in the night and it seems a very great pleasure to me. So much delight does it give me and so intensely do I long to hear it, that I cannot close my eyes to sleep."

When her husband heard what she said, he laughed with angry contempt. An idea occurred to him to trap the nightingale. He ordered the household servants to work on traps, nets, and snares and to set them in the orchard. There wasn't a hazel or a chestnut tree anywhere that was not hung with nets or smeared with lime. Eventually they captured the nightingale. They took it alive to the lord, who was over-joyed when he saw it. He went to the lady's chambers. "Madam, where are you? Come now, let us talk. I've limed this nightingale, the cause of your nightlong vigils. But now you'll be able to slumber in peace, as it will never bother you again." In hearing her husband speak this way, she grew anxious and distressed. She asked him to give her the nightingale, but in a fit of perversity he killed it. He villainously broke its neck with his two hands. He threw the dead bird at his wife so that the front of her gown was bloodied over her breast. Then he went out of the room.

The lady took the little corpse, and softly wept over it. She cursed those who had treacherously caught the nightingale and set the traps and snares for they had killed a great joy. "Alas," she murmured, "how miserable it is for me! I'll not be able to get up at night and stand by the window where I've been accustomed to see my friend. I know one thing — he will think that I've swerved from my love. I must do something. I will have the nightingale sent to him and he will know what has happened."

In a length of satin embroidered and inscribed in letters of gold thread she wrapped the body of the tiny bird. She called one of her servants and entrusted him with a message to her friend. He arrived at the knight's house on his lady's behalf, saluted him, delivered the message, and offered him the nightingale. When the messenger had said and shown everything, and the knight had listened carefully, the adventure filled him with sadness. But what he decided was neither hesitant nor vengeful. He had a little coffer made, fashioned not of iron or steel but of pure gold ornamented with precious stones. It had a closely fitting lid. In it he placed the nightingale. Then he had the chest sealed. He carried it with him always.

This adventure became the subject of a story, for it couldn't remain concealed very long. The Bretons have made a lay about it which they call "Laüstic."

2. Two Fables from *Isopet*

The Widow and the Knight

There's a story written about a man who had died and was buried. His wife mourned bitterly over his grave both night and day. Now in the vicinity a robber had been hanged for his crime. A knight who was a kinsman of his cut down the body and buried it. But a proclamation had been issued throughout the land that anyone who took down the robber's body would be given the same sentence. If discovered, he would be hanged.

The knight didn't know what to do to save himself, for it was widely known that he was a relative of the hanged man's. He went directly to the cemetery where that worthy woman was weeping copiously for her lord. The knight spoke to her very sweetly, urging her to be consoled; in fact, he would be very happy if she would love him. This worthy woman regarded him with immense joy, and said she would do as he wished.

Then the knight explained the plight he was in because of the robber he had taken down from the scaffold. If she couldn't give him some assistance, he would be forced to leave the country. The worthy woman responded, "Let us unbury my lord here, and if he is suspended there where the

other one was, it will never be noticed. The living man must
be rescued by the dead, for it is to the living that we look for
solace."

The moral of this story makes it clear to us how much the
dead can expect from the living. So false is the world and bent
on pleasure.

The Peasant Who Saw Another Man With His Wife

I want to tell you about a peasant who saw his wife heading
for the woods with her lover. He went after them, but they
escaped and were hidden in the bushes. The peasant went
back home, furious. Later he began to harass and abuse his
wife. She asked him why he spoke to her that way. Her
husband replied that he had seen her lecherous friend
accompany her to the woods, and shame and dishonor her.

"Husband," she said, "please, for the love of God, tell me
the truth. Did you see a man go with me? Don't hide
anything!" "I saw him," he said, "go into the woods."
"Heavens," said she, "I'm done for! I'm going to die
tomorrow, or even today. Such a thing happened to my grandmother and my mother too just before they died — I saw it
myself. Other people saw it plainly. Two young men were
seen leading them away and no one else was with them. Now
I know I'm close to my death. Husband, send for all my
relatives, for we'll have to divide up our belongings. I mustn't
remain here in the world. I'll have to take my share of the
property and retire to a convent."

The peasant heard this and cried out, begging her
forgiveness. "Let it be, my dear friend! Don't leave me this
way! I was lying about what I saw." "Wait," she said, "I have
to think of the welfare of my soul, especially with this great
disgrace you've done me by inventing such a tall story. You'll
be bringing it up constantly, saying I've viciously strayed.
You'll have to swear absolutely in such a way that our
relatives will be convinced, that you did not see any man with
me. Then you must swear on your faith that you will never
utter another word on the subject or reproach me with it."

"Gladly, lady," he acquiesced. Together they went to a
chapel, and he swore to everything she wanted and more
besides.

Because of this tale, men accuse women of deviousness. You can see how false they are — they're more crafty than the devil!

Further Reading on Marie:

Texts: A. Ewart, ed. *Marie de France: Lais.* Oxford, 1947. Rpt. 1965.

K. Warnke, ed. *Die Fabeln der Marie de France,* Halle, 1898. Rpt. Geneva, 1974.

Glyn S. Burgess. *Marie de France: An Analytical Bibliography.* London, 1977. Supplement, 1986.
—— and Keith Busby, tr. *The Lais of Marie de France.* New York, 1986.
Paula Clifford. *Marie de France: Lais.* London, 1982.
Robert Hanning and Joan Ferrante, tr. *The Lais of Marie de France.* Durham, North Carolina, 1978.
Philippe Ménard. *Les Lais de Marie de France.* Paris, 1979.
Mary Lou Martin, tr. with text. *The Fables of Marie de France.* Birmingham, Ala., 1984.
Emanuel J. Mickel. *Marie de France.* New York, 1974.

13   The Soul's Divine Marriage

Mechthild of Magdeburg (ca. 1207-1282/1294)

In the century after Hildegard and Elisabeth, German mysticism flowered among women visionaries who expressed their piety in imagery drawn from courtly love lyric, or Minnesang, and the divine nuptials of the Canticles. Mechthild's vernacular *The Flowing Light of the Godhead* is an ecstatic and prophetic work begun when she was forty-three; its seven books represent stages of her experience.

Glimpses of Mechthild's life can be had from the autobiographical parts of her writing and from the recollections of her younger companions, the nuns of Helfta. She was born in the diocese of Magdeburg, apparently to a well-to-do noble family. She received her first "greeting" — the courtly *gruss* of an amorous glance — from the Holy Spirit when she was twelve. At twenty-three she left her family to be nearer to God, living in relative obscurity as a beguine in Magdeburg.

The urban sisterhood movement of the beguines[1] that spread throughout France, Germany, the Netherlands, Belgium, and to some extent Italy, took no religious vows,

---

[1]Various efforts have been made to trace the word: beguines were named for St. Begga, or for Lambert le Bègue ("the stammerer"), a twelfth-century priest of Liège who protected an early female community, or for the gray cloth worn by the women.

embraced no order or specific rule, and sought no authority
from the church. They did not precisely renounce the world,
and did not always live in groups; they often kept homes and
carried on trades. The lack of formal affiliation was to bring
accusations of mendicancy and vagabondage, even heresy.
Their condemnation led to their being lumped together in a
later English source as "young wanton wenches, and beguins,
nuns, and naughty packs." Actually they were women who
chose a contemplative life in modest poverty and self-support
through labor, following an apostolic ideal.

Whether Mechthild lived independently or in a community
is not known. She did however attract hostile attention by her
outspoken warnings and denunciations of the clergy as
"wolves" and "goats." In danger of persecution, she took
refuge twelve years before her death with the nuns of Helfta
monastery, near Eisleben in Saxony. Helfta was an outstanding center of female piety and learning. Never formally
Cistercian, since they were kept from being part of the order,
the gray-clad nuns nevertheless followed the rule laid down
in eleventh-century Cîteaux. The rule stressed work, prayer,
study, and a balance between an individual inner life and the
group's well-being.[2] Mechthild had written the first six parts
of her visions, meditations, dialogues, lyrics, and allegories
outside the cloister; these were gathered and rearranged by
the Dominican Henry of Halle, who may have been her confessor. At Helfta, elderly, sick, and blind, she dictated the
seventh part to her companion nuns.

Unlike many medieval religious women writers, Mechthild
claimed she knew no Latin, and wrote in low German. Henry
of Halle later made a "smoother" Latin version of her first
six books. In the fourteenth century Henry of Nördlingen
turned the work into High German verse, helping

---

[2]The best known of the Helfta women were Gertrude of
Hackeborn, Mechthild of Hackeborn, and Gertrude the Great of
Helfta, of whom the last two also left a significant corpus of mystical
writing.

to spread Mechthild's cult among the mystics who were his followers in Basel. The Latin and High German versions are extant, but Mechthild's original is lost.

In addition to the poetic imagery of the celestial erotic embrace, Mechthild draws upon the medieval cosmic elements. Air, fire and water inform her visions of divinity, as in the fusion of soul's breath with heaven's purifying fire, or in "flowing light." Liquidity especially becomes a godlike quality, with the parched soul's thirsting for the Spouse's divine moisture — dew, rain, blood, honey, milk, and wine.

Chief among the personages in Mechthild's dramatic dialogues are God, his messenger Love — the courtly Minne — and Mechthild's own Soul. The Soul is feminine, a poor and lonely courting maiden, not passive but bold in her frank desire. Through Soul, the mystic's rapture burdened with spiritual torment finds voice in the language of Minne's dialectic — love's sweetness shot through with anguish — that began with the lyrics of the troubadours. God's messenger can be Frau Minne, a noble lady ranking high in heaven's court who is empowered to woo the Soul as a queenly bride for the Lord. At other times Minne appears as a beautiful young man in a garden or orchard, a jousting knight, a dancer, or a drinking companion.

In the first selection, after an exchange of greetings and bargainings, Lady Minne woos the Soul for God, not gently, but violently, stalking her prey as a huntress. In this guise Minne also appears in secular lyrics and romances. The hunt for love's quarry was a favorite medieval theme stemming from antiquity, notably Ovid's *Art of Love.* For Mechthild nothing less than the capture, clubbing, binding and slaying of herself as quarry will ensure her union with the heavenly Bridegroom on an Easter Day of joyous resurrection. The dialogue varies from hunt imagery to that of the letter and seal, images of enfeoffment seen in troubadour lyric.

The second selection tells of the Soul's arrival at court and the utterances of love between her and God. The third selection describes the Soul's preparation as a bride, and her divine dance of love.

In the fourth selection Minne is a seductive young man inflamed with longing for Mechthild's Soul. The metaphor is that of drunken revelers in the heavenly wine cellar. Soul, the woman, feels besotted, unresisting, and degraded. Love's delicious promises must be paid for. The dramatic situation of the tavern prodigals gives way to that of the Song of Songs, where the inebriated Bride enjoys the Bridegroom's caresses, but later wanders destitute and scorned through the streets looking for him.

1. The Greetings of Love and the Hunt of Love

Mechthild's Soul came to Minne and greeted her with deep intent, saying, "God greet you, Lady Minne."
Minne: "God reward you, dear Lady Queen."
Soul: "Lady Minne, you are very welcome to me."
Minne: "Lady Queen, I'm honored by your greeting."
Soul: "Lady Minne, you struggled a long time with the high Holy Ghost, and you conquered him so that he gushed all at once into Mary's humble maidenhead."
Minne: "Lady Queen, it was for your honor and delight."
Soul: "Lady Minne, you have taken from me everything I ever won on earth."
Minne: "Lady Queen, you've made a blissful exchange."
Soul: "Lady Minne, you've taken my childhood from me."
Minne: "Lady Queen, I've given you heavenly freedom for it."
Soul: "Lady Minne, you've taken my whole youth."
Minne: "Lady Queen, I've given you many holy virtues for it."
Soul: "Lady Minne, you've taken my friends and kin."
Minne: "Ah, Lady Queen, that's a worthless lament!"
Soul: "Lady Minne, you've taken the world from me, worldly honor, and all worldly riches."
Minne: "Lady Queen, in an hour I'll recompense you on earth with all you desire of the Holy Ghost."
Soul: "Lady Minne, you have so harassed me that my body is seized by sundry ills."
Minne: "Lady Queen, I've given you much high wisdom."
Soul: "Lady Minne, you have squandered my flesh and my blood."
Minne: "Lady Queen, by that you've been enlightened and raised up with God."
Soul: "Lady Minne, you are a robber woman. Pay me back for

that!"

Minne: "Lady Queen, then take my very self!"

Soul: "Lady Minne, now you have repaid me a hundredfold here on earth."

Minne: "Lady Queen, now have you claimed God and his whole kingdom!"

The Soul's Handmaids and Minne's Beating.

The holy Christian virtues are the Soul's handmaids. The Soul in sweet sorrow cries out her anguish to Minne.

Mechthild's Soul Speaks:
"Ah, dearest Lady,
you've been my lady-in-waiting, lurking so long,
now tell me what's to become of me?
You have hunted, seized, and tied me so fast
and wounded me so deeply
that I shall never be healed.
You have beaten me with a club.
Tell me whether I shall ever finally recover!
Shall I not be slain by your hand?
It would have been better for me if I had never
known you."

Lady Minne's Reply:
"I hunted you for my delight;
I seized you for my desire;
I bound you tightly for my joy;
When I wounded you, you became one with me.
When I beat you with a club, I became your strong ravisher.
It was I who drove out the Almighty from heaven's kingdom
and deprived him of his human life,
then gave him gloriously back to his father.
How could you, vile worm, think you could recover
from me?"

Mechthild's Soul:
"Tell me, my Queen, I thought a small medicine from heaven
that God had often given me
might help me to escape you."

Lady Minne:
"If a captive wants to escape death,
let her reach for water and bread.
The medicines that God has given you
are nothing more than days of grace in this life.
But when your Easter Day dawns
and your body then meets its death blow,
I shall be there, encircling you, piercing you,
and I shall steal your body
and give it to Love."

Mechthild's Soul:
"Ah, Lady Minne.
I have written this letter dictated from your lips.
Now give me your great seal to affix to it."

Lady Minne:
"She whom God has captured for himself
knows where the seal must be pressed.
It lies between the two of us."

Mechthild's Soul:
"Be quiet, Minne, give me no more advice, I and all earthly
    creatures bow to you.
Oh my dearest Lady,
tell my friend his couch is ready,
and I am lovesick for him.
If this letter is too long, I have plucked a few
blossoms from its meadow.
This is its sweet lament:
Whoever dies of love shall be entombed in God."

2. The Soul Comes to Court

The courtly journey of the Soul to whom God shows himself.
    When the poor Soul comes to court she is prudent and well-
behaved. She joyfully gazes at her God. Ah, how lovingly she
is welcomed there! She keeps quiet, but is extravagantly
eager for his praise. And he shows her with great yearning his
sacred heart. It is like red gold burning in a great coal-fire.

And God lays her in his glowing heart so that the high prince and the little maidservant embrace and are made one like water and wine. Then she is annihilated and takes leave of her senses so that she can do no more, and he is sick with love for her as he always was, for he neither grows nor diminishes. She says, "Lord, you are my solace, my desire, my flowing stream, my sun, and I am your mirror!" This is the journey to court for the enamored Soul, who cannot live without God.

How God comes to the Soul
"I come to my love
as a dew upon the blossom."

How the Soul welcomes and praises God
"Ah joyful sight! Ah loving greeting! Ah minne-like embrace! Lord, the wonder of you has wounded me! Your favor has quelled me! O you lofty rock, you are so nobly cleft; none may nest in you but your dove and nightingale."

How God receives the Soul
"Be welcome, darling dove; you have flown so fervently over earth's kingdom that your feathers rise strong to the kingdom of heaven."

How God compares the Soul to four things
"You taste of the grape, you smell of balsam, you glitter like the sun, you are the increase of my highest love."

The soul praises God in five things
"O you, God, gushing forth with your gifts!
O you, God, flowing in your love!
O you burning God in your desire!
O you melting God in the union of your love!
O you God resting on my breast, I cannot be without you!"

God compares the soul to five things
"O you fair rose in the thornbrier!
O you fluttering bee in the honey!
O you pure dove in your being!

O you lovely sun in your shining!
O you full moon in your sphere!
I can never turn away from you."

God caresses the soul in six things
    "You are my pillow, my minne-bed, my secret resting place, my deepest desire, my highest honor. You are a delight of my godhood, a solace of my manhood, a brook for my burning heat."

The Soul responds to God in six things
    "You are my mirror — mountain peak of perfection — a feast for my eyes, a losing of myself, a storm of my heart, a ruin and scattering of my forces, and my highest safety!"

3. The Arraying of the Soul as a Bride

    Our Redeemer has become our Bridegroom! The Bride has become drunk with the sight of his noble face. In her greatest strength she takes leave of her senses; in her greatest clarity she is both dead and living. The longer she is dead, the more joyously she lives. The more joyously she lives, the more she journeys. The more she tastes minne, the more she is flowing. The richer she grows, the poorer she becomes. The deeper she dwells, the wider she ranges. The more she offers herself, the deeper are her wounds. The more she storms, the more minne-like is God toward her. The higher she floats, the more beautifully she shines from the glance of the godhead as she comes nearer to him. The more she labors, the more softly she rests. The more she grasps, the more quietly she falls silent. The more loudly she cries out, the greater wonder she works with his power and her might. The more her desire grows, the greater the wedding feast, the more enclosed the minne-bed. The tighter the embrace, the sweeter the kisses of their mouths. The more lovingly they gaze at each other, the harder it is to part. The more he gives her, the more she squanders, the more she has. The more humbly she takes her leave, the sooner she comes back. The more ardent she is, the more she glows again. The more she burns, the more gloriously she shines. The more enveloping

God's praise of her, the more avid is her longing for him.

The Bridegroom's beauty, and how the Bride shall follow him
  "*Vide, mea sponsa*! See, my Bride! How beautiful my eyes
are, how fair is my mouth, how fiery is my heart, how gentle
are my hands, how swift my feet —
and follow me!

  "You shall be martyred with me, betrayed through envy,
tracked to an ambush, seized in hatred, bound through hear-
say, your eyes bandaged so that you won't recognize truth,
beaten by the world's rage, dragged to judgment through
confession, beaten with sticks, sent to Herod with mockery,
stripped with banishment, scourged with poverty, crowned
with temptation, spat upon with abuse. You shall carry your
cross in the hatred of sin, be crucified in the denial of all
things by your own will, nailed on the cross with the holy
virtues, wounded with minne, die on the cross in holy steadfastness, your heart pierced with indwelling oneness,
released from the cross in true victory over all your enemies,
buried in paltriness, raised up from death to a blessed end,
carried to heaven on a draught of God's breath."

God asks the Soul what she brings:
"You hunt sorely for your love.
Tell me, what do you bring me, my Queen?"

The Soul answers:
"Lord, I bring you my treasure:
It is greater than the mountains, wider than the world, deeper
than the sea, higher than the sky, more beautiful than the sun,
more manifold than the stars, it weighs more than earth's
whole kingdom."

God speaks: "Ah, Soul filled with minne, do you wish to know
where your path lies?"

The Soul: "Yes, dear Holy Ghost, teach it to me."

The Holy Ghost: "You must overcome the sorrow of

contrition, the pain of confession, and the labor of repentance, the love of the world, the temptation of the devil, the luxuriance of the flesh, the destruction of your own will which so fiercely drags down many souls that they never can come back to true love. Then when you have beaten down most of your enemies and are so tired that you cry out, 'Beautiful youth, I'm longing for you — where shall I find you?' the young man will say:

"I hear a voice
that speaks a little of minne.
I have courted her many days
but her voice has never come to me.
Now I am stirred,
I must go to her.
She is the one who bears pain and minne together.
In the morning, in the dew, there is the sheltered secret
that first enters the soul."

Her chambermaids, the five senses speak:
"Lady, you must gown yourself in many colors."

Soul: "Love, where shall I go?"

The senses:
"We have heard it rumored
that the Prince is coming to you
in the dew and in the lovely song of birds.
Ah, lady, do not delay!"

So the Soul dresses herself in a shift of gentle humility, so lowly that she can endure nothing under it. Over it a white gown of clear chastity, so pure that she can endure neither thoughts nor words nor sentiments that might spot it. Then she covers it with a mantle of holy reputation, which she has gilded with all the virtues.

Then she goes into the wood, which is the company of blessed folk. There the sweetest nightingales sing in harmonious union with God, both day and night, and she

hears many sweet voices there of the birds of holy understanding. But the young man still does not come. He sends
her messengers, for she wants to dance. He sends her
Abraham's faith, the Prophets' yearnings, and the chaste
humility of our lady St. Mary, all the holy virtues of Jesus
Christ, and all the goodness of his chosen ones.

And so a lovely dance of praise will take place. Now the
young man comes and speaks to her:
"Maiden, as gallantly as you follow the dance, now, my
chosen partner, you will lead the dance!" But she says:
"I cannot dance, lord, unless you lead me.
If you want me to leap ardently,
you must yourself first dance and sing.
Then I will leap into minne,
from minne into understanding,
from understanding to enjoyment,
from enjoyment to far beyond all human sense.
There shall I stay and whirl still dancing in a ring."

4. The Heavenly Wine Cellar

As the dialogue opens, Mechthild's Soul is already drunk
with divine love. Minne invites her to drink further, and
reveals his own desire for her:

Minne speaks:
"If you'll come with me to the wine cellar
it will cost you a great deal.
Even if you buy a thousand marks' worth of wine
your money will be squandered in an hour.
"If you want to drink wine straight, without water, you'll keep
spending more than you have, and the tavern-keeper won't
pour you the full amount. You'll be poor and naked, despised
by all those people who'd rather seek pleasure in a pool of
muddy water than waste their wealth in the lofty wine cellar.
"You'll also have to suffer
when those people who go with you to the wine cellar envy
    you.
How scornful they'll be of you

because they dare not risk the huge expense,
preferring to drink their wine diluted with water!
Darling lady bride, I'll go to the tavern,
and eagerly spend all that I have,
and let myself be dragged through hot coals of love,
and submit to being beaten with the fiery brands of love's
    slanderers,
so that I can go often to that blessed wine cellar!"

Mechthild's Soul answers:
    "I choose eagerly to go there, since I can't do without love.
While he torments and insults me — this one who pours out
the tavern-keeper's wine for me — still he has been drinking
it too.
"I've become so drunk with wine,
that I am truly thrall to all creatures,
and it seems to me in my human disgrace
and my new-found wantonness
that no man ever treated me so badly before —
he can do any kind of sin with me, unblessed woman
    that I am.
And so I would not take vengeance on my enemies for my
sorrow, even though I know they might break
God's law against me."

Minne comforts the Soul:
    "Dearest playmate, when it happens that the wine cellar
is locked, you must take to the street, hungry, poor and
stripped bare, and so despised that nothing is left for you of
holy feasting. Then you can still have love, for that is never
spoiled.
"Lady Bride, I have such hunger for the heavenly father
that I forget all sorrow.
And I have such thirst for his son
that it takes all earthly yearning from me.
And I have for both of them such a ghostly need
that it goes higher than all I can grasp
of the father's wisdom.
And I can endure all the work of the son,
and all the solace of the Holy Ghost

that befalls me.
Whoever is seized by this torment
must always — however unworthy — hold fast
to God's holiness."

Further Reading on Mechthild:

Texts: P.G. Morel, ed. *Offenbarungen der Schwester Mechthild von Magdeburg oder Das fliessende Licht der Gottheit.* Darmstadt, rpt. 1963.
Revelationes Gertrudianae ac Mechtildianae. Vol. II. Ed. the monks of Solesmes. Paris, 1878.

Jeanne Ancelet-Hustache. *Mechthilde de Magdebourg: Etude de psychologie religieuse.* Paris, 1926.
Brenda Bolton. "Mulieres Sanctae." In *Women in Medieval Society,* ed. Susan Mosher Stuard. Philadelphia, 1976.
Caroline Walker Bynum. *Jesus as Mother: Studies in the Spirituality of the High Middle Ages.* Berkeley, 1982.
James C. Franklin. *Mystical Transformations: The Imagery of Liquids in the Work of Mechthild von Magdeburg.* Madison, N.J., 1978.
Ernest W. McDonnell. *The Beguines and Beghards in Medieval Culture.* Rpt. New York, 1969.
Lucy Menzies, tr. *The Revelations of Mechthild of Magdeburg or The Flowing Light of the Godhead.* New York, 1953.

14   An English Anchoress
Julian of Norwich (1343-1416/1419)

On the morning of Friday May 13, 1373, three days after being struck down with the illness she had prayed for, a woman of thirty who was called Julian of Norwich experienced sixteen visions or "shewings" in rapid succession. These lasted twelve hours, from four o'clock in the morning until four o'clock in the afternoon, in the presence of her mother and close friends. Her priest held the crucifix before her eyes, for she fully expected to die. Nearly twenty years later, in February of 1393, Julian received certain inner teachings that enabled her, as she wrote, to understand these showings more fully. Her revelations have been left to us in two versions: the short text records the original experience, and remains in a single manuscript. The long text, set down much later, represents not only the experience of the visions themselves, but her thoughts about them, illuminated and amplified after prayer and meditation. This long text is extant in a printed version and five manuscripts.[1]

Julian may have been born in the East Riding of Yorkshire between Beverley and the sea. She lived as a recluse, an

---

[1]Complete information about texts and manuscripts is found in Edmund Colledge and James Walsh (eds.), *A Book of Showings to the Anchoress Julian of Norwich.* Vol. I, pp. 1-18.

anchoress with one servant Alice, in a cell attached to the
church wall of St. Julian in Conisford at Norwich, whose
name she took for her own. At what age she became enclosed
is not known. Evidence of her living as late as 1416 comes
from the four wills of money made to the anchoress of St.
Julian's Church.

Norwich was a large, important English city in the fourteenth century. It had a flourishing religious and intellectual
life, supported numerous convents, and possessed an
excellent library. Facing Julian's anchorhold across the lane
was a house of Augustinian friars. There seems to have been
ample opportunity for learning; Julian perhaps received
further training from a tutor or a community of sisters, such
as the nuns at the Benedictine priory of Carrow. In 1377
Carrow consisted of eleven nuns, and Julian's anchorhold
came under its patronage. Her disclaimer in the long text that
she was a "symple creature unlettred," belies Julian's
achievement. Her adopting a humility formula in her later
work even betokens a certain literary sophistication, placing
her in the company of such accomplished rhetoricians as
Chaucer. Or, it may be a device intended to point to Christ
as the ultimate teacher. In either case, it should not be
accepted at face value.

While Julian's language is wonderfully crisp and plain,
and she emphasizes an affective rather than a theologically
intellectual piety — preferring simple images and homely
exempla — she shows that she was well read in Scripture.
She concentrates especially on the Psalms, the gospels, and
the epistles of Paul and John. She reveals an acquaintance
with William of St. Thierry, with *The Cloud of Unknowing*,
The Scale of Perfection, the *Ancrene Riwle*, and quite
possibly with Chaucer's *Boece*, translated in 1380. Her
Shewings often have a highly visual and tactile quality which
evokes the arts in her time. As she writes, the "payntyngs
of crucifexes" have made her familiar with the appearance
of Christ's sufferings.

During her life, Julian must have gained a reputation for
sanctity and wisdom. At the age of 71, she was visited by the
English mystic Margery Kempe, who was seeking spiritual
guidance from her, wondering whether the devil or God was
acting upon her soul. But Julian does not seem to have

informed Margery about her visions or her writings.

Although far fewer manuscripts of Julian's *Shewings* have survived than of her contemporary mystics, such as Richard Rolle and Walter Hilton — and indeed her work was nearly forgotten until the seventeenth century — there is today a remarkable upsurge of interest in her on three fronts: literary, feminist and mystic. Julian is a rhetorically adept author and a literary figure of great charm. She emerges as an inspiring feminist, who develops on the basis of maternal roles a pervasive imagery of the motherhood of God, notably through Christ, the second person of the Trinity. And, contemporary mystics have turned to her for guidance, for she provides vital lessons in spirituality. A glance through any issue of the *Mystics Quarterly*, published at the University of Iowa, turns up increasing evidence of passionate activity on Julian — spiritual, artistic, and scholarly. Books, articles, dissertations, and plays devoted to Julian are being produced. Cherida Campion has established an Archive/Repository in Norwich, and an Order of St. Julian has been founded in Norwich, Connecticut, by Father John Swanson, editor of *JuliaNews*. And the British novelist Iris Murdoch has a modern Julian character in *Nuns and Soldiers*, whose visitation from Christ is modelled on Julian's.

The first group of passages from Julian's work given below tells of her wish for sickness, often regarded as a softening and purification that would enable the soul to receive, wax-like, the experience of God's love, and embark on the contemplative life.

The second passage focuses on Julian's optimism in the face of sin, including the refrain which is the best-known statement in her writing, "All shall be well." While sin has no substance, Julian writes, it has a purpose. We may be reminded of Boethius's justification of evil, which teaches, exercises, and corrects the sufferer. Julian is remarkable in speaking of the purpose of sin as self-knowledge. Knowledge of self is a theme that appears in several parts of her writing. Meditation on the Virgin's qualities, even death itself, are ways to "oure self clerely knowyng."

Julian's affirmation of the motherhood of God, illustrated by a broad selection of passages in the third group, is not unique, as recent scholarship has abundantly shown. But

Julian's use of God's maternity appears far more deliberate and enveloping than it does among her predecessors or contemporaries. Motherhood's functions appear "in a complete connected cycle of life from before birth through after death" as Jennifer Heimmel has demonstrated in her study of Julian. Christ's motherhood involves "enclosure and growth within the womb; the trauma of labor and birth; the suckling of the infant and feeding of the child; the care and education of the older child; the setting of examples and disciplining of the child; the washing, healing, forgiving, and comforting of the child as it matures; and the continual loving, touching, and guiding of the child even to the point of its own death."[2] After death the maternal God restores the child to rebirth and return to the divine womb.

The fourth group of passages centers on Julian's temptations when visited and tormented by the devil. This assault occurs after her feelings of sickness, barrenness, and delirium have cast her down. Despite his recurrence, the devil is rendered ultimately powerless. Julian is given to understand by God that she will never be overcome.

The fifth set of passages below concerns Julian's image of the soul as a city in which God sits enthroned. While he reveals himself as reigning both in heaven and on earth, God's only real dwelling place is in the human soul. When the city is uninhabitable because of sin, the Lord willingly sits on the ground to wait. The city provides a reciprocal image to that of the maternal God. Just as we are enclosed in God's womb, so is God enclosed in the city of our hearts.

Finally, there is the simple powerful message of love, explaining the visions' meaning, which concludes the *Shewings*.

---

[2]*"God is Our Mother": Julian of Norwich and the Medieval Image of Christian Feminine Divinity*, pp. 54-55.

Preface by a Scribe

Here is a vision shown by the goodness of God to a devout woman, and her name is Julian, a recluse at Norwich, and still alive in the year of our Lord 1413. In this vision are very many comfortable words, greatly stirring to all those who desire to be Christ's lovers.

1. *Julian Tells of Herself and Her First Showing*

I desired three graces by the gift of God. The first was to be mindful of Christ's passion. The second was bodily sickness, and the third was to have, through Christ's gift, three wounds. Now the first came to my mind with devotion; I thought I had great feeling for Christ's passion, but yet I desired to have more by the grace of God. I thought I wanted to be, that time, with Mary Magdalene and with others who were Christ's lovers, so that I might have seen bodily the passion of our Lord that he suffered for me, and so that I might have suffered with him as others did who loved him. To be sure, I believed solemnly — to the extent that human understanding can reach — all the pains of Christ as Holy Church shows and teaches, and as do the paintings of crucifixes that are made, by the grace of God, according to the teaching of Holy Church, in the likeness of Christ's passion. Yet notwithstanding this true belief I desired a bodily sight, wherein I might have more knowledge of bodily pains of our Lord, our Savior, and of the compassion of our Lady, and of all his true lovers who believed in his pains at that time and since that time. For I wanted to be one of them and to suffer with them.

Julian's First Gift of Bodily Sickness

And when I was thirty and a half winters old, God sent me a bodily weakness in which I lay three days and three nights; and on the fourth night I received all my rites of Holy Church, and believed I would not live until day. And after this I languished further two days and two nights, and on the third day I believed oftentimes that I was about to pass away. And those who were about me thought so too.

But in this I was really sorry, and thought it was loathsome to die. It was not for anything on earth that it seemed pleasant to live, nor was it for anything that I feared, for I trusted God. But it was because I wanted to have lived so as to have loved God better, and for a longer time, in order that I might, by the grace of that living, have a greater knowledge and love of God in the bliss of heaven. For I thought all the time that I had lived here was so little and so short from the viewpoint of endless bliss. I thought this way: Good Lord, does my being alive no longer honor you? And I was answered in my reason, and through the feelings of my pains, that I must die; and I assented fully with all the will of my heart to conform to God's will.

So I endured until day, and by then my body was dead from the middle downward, as to any feeling I might have. Then I was stirred to ask to be set upright, leaning, with clothes behind my head, so as to have more freedom of heart to conform to God's will and think about him while my life should last. And those who were with me sent for the parson, my curate, to be present at my life's ending. He came, and a child with him, and brought a cross. And by then I had fixed my eyes, and was not able to speak. The parson set the cross before my face and said, "Daughter, I have brought you the image of your Savior. Look upon it and be comforted by it, in reverence of him who died for you and me."

I thought then that I was well, for my eyes were cast upward towards heaven, where I trusted I was to come. But nevertheless I agreed to fix my eyes on the face of the crucifix if I could, so as to endure the longer until the time of my ending. For I thought I might endure longer by gazing directly forward rather than upward. After this my sight began to fail and it was all dark about me in the chamber, and murky as if it had been night, save that in the image of the cross there remained a common light, and I never knew how. Everything but the cross was ugly to me, as if it had been thickly occupied by fiends.

After this the upper part of my body began to die, as far as I could feel. My hands fell down on either side, and also because of my weakness my head sank down to one side. The greatest pain I felt was shortwindedness and the failing of life. Then I truly thought I was at the point of death.

In a sudden instant all pain left me, and I was completely hale, and especially in the upper part of my body, as much as I ever was before or after. I marveled at this change, for I thought it was a secret working of God and not of Nature. And yet because of this feeling of ease, I trusted I should live no more. Nor was this feeling of ease fully easy to me, for I thought I would as lief be delivered of this world, for my heart was willing.

Julian's First Showing

And in this sudden instant I saw the red blood trickle down from under the garland, all hotly, freshly, plentifully, and vitally, just as it seemed to me it was in that time that the garland of thorns was thrust upon his blessed head. Just so, as both God and man, did he suffer for me. I grasped truly and mightily that it was himself that showed it to me without any go-between; and then I said "Thanks to the Lord!" This I said with reverent meaning and in a strong voice.

Her Understanding of God's Kindly Love

And at this same time that I saw this bodily sight, our Lord showed me a spiritual sight of his homelike loving. I saw that he is all things good and comfortable to us for our help. He is our clothing, for love wraps us and winds around us, hugs us and teaches us everything, hangs about us — for tender love — so that he may never leave us. And so in this sight I saw truly that he is everything good, as I understand it.

And in this he showed me a little thing, the quantity of a hazel nut, lying in the palm of my hand, and to my understanding it was round as any ball. I looked upon it and thought: What may this be? And I was answered generally this way: It is all that is made. I marveled how it might last, for I thought it might fall into nothing because of its littleness. And I was answered in my understanding: It lasts and always

shall, for God loves it; and so all things have being through
the love of God.

2. Sin is Examined: "All Shall Be Well"

After this our Lord brought to my mind the longing that
I had for him before; and I saw that nothing had prevented
me but sin. And so I beheld sin generally in us all, and I
thought to myself, "If sin had not been, we would all have
been clean and like our Lord, as he made us." And thus in
my folly before this time I often wondered why, through the
great foreseeing wisdom of God, the beginning of sin had not
been prevented. For then, I thought, all would have been well.

Steering my thoughts this way was a course I should have
forsaken. Nevertheless, I mourned and sorrowed without
reason or discretion. But Jesus, who in this vision informed
me of all that was needful to me, answered in these words,
and said: "Sin is behooveful, but all shall be well, and all shall
be well, and all manner of things shall be well."

In this naked word "sin" our Lord brought to my mind
generally all that is not good, and the shameful scorn and the
utmost tribulation that he bore for us in this life, and his dying
and all his pains, and the passion of all his creatures, spiritual
and bodily. For we have all a part in trouble, and we shall
be troubled, following our master Jesus, until we are fully
purged of our mortal flesh, and of all our inward affections
which are not very good.

And beholding this, and all the pains that ever were or
ever shall be, I understood the passion of Christ in its greatest
and surpassing pain. And yet, all this was shown in a
moment's touch, and was readily passed over, replaced by
comfort. For our good Lord did not want the soul to be afraid
of this ugly sight. But I saw not sin, for I believe it had no
kind of substance, nor any part of being, nor might it be
known except by the pain that is caused by it. And this pain
in my view *is* something for a time, for it purges us and
enables us to know ourselves and ask for mercy. For the
passion of our Lord is comfort to us against all this, and so
is his blessed will. And through the tender love that our good
Lord has for all who shall be saved, he comforts readily and
sweetly, meaning this: "It is true that sin is the cause of all

this pain, but all shall be well, and all manner of things shall
be well."

These words were shown very tenderly, showing no manner of blame to me nor to any who shall be safe. So it would
be a great unkindness on my part to blame or wonder at God
because of my sin, since he does not blame me for it.

3. The Motherhood of God

And thus I saw that God enjoys that he is our father, and
God enjoys that he is our mother, and God enjoys that he is
our true spouse, and our soul his beloved wife. And Christ
enjoys that he is our brother, and Jesus enjoys that he is our
Savior.

We Are One With God

And in our making God knit us and "oned"[3] us to himself,
by which "oneing" we are kept as clean and noble as when
we were made. By virtue of each precious "oneing" we love
our maker and like him, praise him and thank him and
endlessly have joy in him. And this is the working which is
continually wrought in each soul that shall be saved, and this
is the godly will we have spoken of earlier.

And so in our making, God Almighty is our kindly father
and God All-Wisdom is our kindly mother, with the love and
the goodness of the Holy Ghost, which is all one God, one
Lord. And in the knitting and in the "oneing" he is our very
true spouse and we his beloved wife, and his fair maiden, and
he was never displeased with this wife, for he says, "I love
you and you love me and our love shall never part in two."

God's Motherly Bearing, Feeding and Tending

Our natural, kindly mother, our gracious mother — for he
wished to be wholly our mother in all things — laid his ground-
work most low within the maiden's womb, and gently. And he

---

[3]Julian's English verb "to one," meaning to make one, is more
pleasing than the Latinate "to unite."

showed this from the first when he brought that meek maiden before the eye of my understanding, in the simple stature she had when she conceived. That is to say, our high God, the sovereign wisdom of all, arrayed himself in this lowly place, and decked himself very readily in our poor flesh, in order to do the service and office of motherhood himself, in all things.

The mother's service is nearest, readiest, and surest: nearest for it is the most natural, readiest because it is the most loving, and most secure since it is the most faithful. This office might never and could never be done to the full by any but by him alone. We know that all our mothers bear us to pain and to dying. Ah, what is that? But our true mother Jesus, he alone bears us to joy and to endless living — blessed may he be! Thus he sustains us within him in love and labor, up to the full term when he would suffer the sharpest thorns and most grievous pains that ever were or shall be, and he died at the last. And when he had finished, and had borne us to bliss, yet none of this could sate his marvelous love.

He showed this in these high, surpassing words of love: "If I were able to suffer more, I would suffer more." He could not die again, but he would not stint of his working.

Therefore, it behooves him to find us, for the precious love of motherhood has made him our debtor. The mother may give milk to her child to suck, but our precious mother Jesus may feed us with himself, and does so most courteously and most tenderly with the blessed sacrament that is the precious food of true life. And with all the sweet sacraments he sustains us most mercifully and graciously, and this is what he meant in these blessed words where he said: "I am what Holy Church preaches to you and teaches you. That is to say — all the health and the life of the sacraments, all the virtue and the grace of my words, all the goodness that is ordained for you in Holy Church — I am these things."

The mother may lay her child tenderly to her breast, but our tender mother Jesus may lead us, in a homelike way, into his blessed breast through his sweet open side, and show us there a part of the godhead and the joys of heaven with the spiritual surety of endless bliss.

The Word "Mother"

This fair, lovely word "mother" is so sweet and so natural and kind in itself that it cannot truly be said about anyone or to anyone but about and to him who is the true mother of life and of all. To the property of motherhood belong nature, love, wisdom, and knowing — and this is God. For although it is true that our bodily bringing forth is only a little thing, low and simple, compared to our spiritual bringing forth, yet it is he that does it in the creatures by whom it is done. The kind, loving mother that knows and understands the need of her child cares for it most tenderly, according to the nature and condition of motherhood. And always, as it grows in age and in stature, she changes her way of working but not her love. And when it has grown older, she allows it to be chastised in order to break down its vices, so that the child may acquire virtues and grace. All that is fair and good in this work, our Lord does in those by whom it is done. Thus he is our mother in nature by means of the working of grace in the lower part, out of his love of the higher. And he wills that we know it, for he wishes to have all our love fastened to him.

And in this I saw that all the debt that we owe to God's bidding to fatherhood and motherhood is fulfilled in truly loving God, a blessed love that Christ works in us. And this was shown in all, and namely in the high, plentiful words where he says: "I am this that you love."

We Are Sometimes Allowed to Fall

The mother may allow her child to fall sometimes and be hurt in various ways for its own benefit, but she may never allow any kind of peril to come to her child because of her love. And though our earthly mother may allow her child to perish, our heavenly mother Jesus may never allow his children to perish. For he is mighty, all wisdom, and all love, and so is none but he, blessed may he be!

But oftentimes when our falling and our wretchedness are shown us, we are so sorely worried and so greatly ashamed of ourselves that we scarcely know where we can hide ourselves. But then our courteous mother does not wish us to flee away, for nothing would be more hateful to him. But he wishes us to assume the condition of a child. For when it is hurt and afraid, it runs hastily to the mother, and if it can do no more, it cries to the mother for help with all its might. So does he will us to act like a meek child, who says: "My kind mother, my gracious mother, my precious mother, have mercy on me. I have made myself foul and unlike you, and I may not and cannot amend it, except with your help and grace."

He Is Our Nurse

The sweet, gracious hands of our mother are ready and diligent about us, for in all these workings he assumes the true office of a kind nurse, who has nothing else to do but to tend to the salvation of her child.

4. The Devil Assails Julian

And in my sleep at the beginning I thought the fiend set himself at my throat, putting forth a visage very near my face that was like a young man's and it was long and wondrously lean. I never saw anything such as that. The color was red, like a tile-stone when it is newly burnt, with black spots on it like freckles, fouler than tile-stones. His hair was red as rust, not sheared in front, and with sidelocks hanging over his temples. He grinned at me with a shrewd expression, showed me white teeth, and looked so much the uglier, it seemed to me. His body and hands were not in any way shapely, but with his paws he held me by the throat and would have stopped my breath and killed me, but he was not able.

Another Visitation of the Devil

The fiend came again with his heat and with his stench, and caused me great anxiety, as the stench was so vile and so painful and the bodily heat so dreadful and burdensome. Also I heard a bodily talking as if it came from two bodies, and both — to my thinking — talked at one time, as if they had held a parley, and all was in soft whispering. And I understood not what they said, and all this was to stir me to despair.

5. The City of the Soul

He made man's soul to be his own city and his dwelling place, which is most pleasing to him of all his works.

Julian Perceives the City of her Soul

And then our good Lord opened my spirit's eye and showed me my soul in the midst of my heart. I saw the soul as broad as if it were a vast stronghold, and also as if it were a blessed kingdom. In the midst of that city sits our Lord Jesus, a true God and true man, a person fair and tall of stature, highest bishop, most solemn king, and Lord most worthy of worship.

And I saw him solemnly clothed in honor. He sits within the soul righteously in peace and rest, and he rules and guards heaven and earth and all that is. His humanity together with his godhead sits in rest; the godhead rules and guards without any instrument or exertion. And the soul is all occupied with the blessed godhead that is sovereign might, sovereign wisdom, and sovereign goodness.

The place that Jesus takes in our soul, he shall never move away from, without end, in my view. In us is his most homelike home, and his everlasting dwelling.

And the highest light and the brightest shining of that city is the glorious love of the Lord, in my view.

6. Love Is His Meaning

And from the time that this was shown, I desired to know what was our Lord's meaning. And fifteen years after and more, I was answered in spiritual understanding, with these words:

"What, would you know your Lord's meaning in this thing? Know it well, love was his meaning. Who shows you this? Love. What did he show you? Love. Why does he show it to you? For love. Hold yourself to this, and you shall know more in the same. But you shall never know anything else from this — without end."

So it was that I learned that love is our Lord's meaning. And I saw very surely in this and in all, that before God made us he loved us. This love was never slackened nor ever shall be. And in this love he has done all his works, and in this love he has made all things profitable for us and in this love our life is everlasting. In our making we had beginning, but the love in which he made us was in him from time without beginning. In this love we have our beginning, and all this we shall see in God, without end.

Thanks be to God.

Here ends the book of the revelations of Julian, anchoress of Norwich. May God have mercy on her soul.

Further Reading on Julian

Text: Edmund Colledge and James Walsh, eds. *A Book of Showings to the Anchoress Julian of Norwich.* Studies and Texts, No. 35. Toronto: Pontifical Institute of Medieval Studies, 2 vols., 1978. Vol. I, pp. 201-202; 207-209; 210-211; 212-213; Vol. II, pp. 404-407; 594-598; 598-600; 604-606; 608; 648; 525; 639-641; 643; 732-734.

Ritamary Bradley. "Julian of Norwich: Writer and Mystic."
    In Paul E. Szarmach, ed. *An Introduction to the Medieval Mystics of Europe.* Albany, 1984, pp. 195-216.
Jennifer P. Heimmel. *"God Is our Mother": Julian of Norwich and the Medieval Image of Christian Feminine Divinity.* Salzburg, 1982.
Patricia Mary Vinje. *An Understanding of Love According to the Anchoress Julian of Norwich.* Salzburg, 1983.
Clifton Wolters, tr. *Revelations of Divine Love.*
    Baltimore, 1982.

15 Poet of the Court of France

Christine de Pizan (ca. 1365-ca. 1430)

As a child, Christine was brought from her native Venice to Paris. Her father was Tommaso di Benvenuto, whose family hailed from Pizzano; he had studied medicine and astrology at Bologna, and came to hold a respected post at the court of Charles V of France. Although Christine felt she was denied a formal education because of her sex, she had access in these royal surroundings to a considerable library which the enlightened king had amassed. In fact her reading program in mythology, philosophy, and history shaped her encyclopedic literary output.

Married at fifteen to Etienne du Castel, a notary and secretary to the king, Christine enjoyed a period of happiness with her beloved husband; they had three children, two of whom survived. But by 1390, Etienne had died of a contagion while traveling with the king, leaving the widowed Christine at twenty-five to support her children, her aged mother, and a niece. Three years earlier her father had died in near poverty after losing his position at court. Grief-stricken and burdened with financial hardships, Christine turned in this dark phase of her life to writing as a means of solace and income. The resulting lyric poems that are among her earliest work form an autobiographical document of her own love, as well as a foray into imagined situations for the pleasure of her royal and noble patrons. Among these are her sprightly "games of barter" — *jeux à vendre* — of which a part of one is translated here.

Between 1393 and 1402 Christine composed about 20 virelais, 70 rondeaux, and 300 ballades, her favorite lyric genre, with which she experimented continually. These poetic forms, evolving from early dances, used variously the refrains that were once assigned to a chorus. An example of one of these dance songs is the anonymous *balada* above in the section on troubadour women.

As a beneficiary of the corpus of courtly love literature that had been developing since the troubadours, Christine explored in her elegant lyrics, Poems 1 to 7 below, every possible angle of the man and woman in and out of love: the advances and retreats, the pleas and rejections, praises, joys, sufferings, recriminations, partings, reunions, and inconsolable losses. Love's ending is her poignant specialty. Deeply personal are her poems of her widowhood, to which she brings the language of *amour lointain* — the faraway, or unattainable love of Jaufré Rudel. Another early genre in which Christine composes some pleasantly raucous complaints is the song of the *mal-mariée*, the wretched wife, exemplified in Poems 8 and 9.

Love outside marriage also appears in the lyrics, as in the *Dit de la pastoure* (1403), "The Tale of the Shepherdess," and in the *Livre du duc des vrais amants* (1403-1405). This interesting book, combining poetry and prose, including many letters, centers on the agonized devotion of a princess and a duke, told chiefly from the male viewpoint. In its form and concern with the life of the emotions it anticipates early novels like *La Princesse de Clèves*, and ultimately the epistolary novels of Samuel Richardson. A portion of one of the letters, from Lady Sebille de la Tour, is given below, in which she counsels the princess on her conduct. Lady Sebille seems to transcend the formality of the advice-giving genre; from her loquacity something like a novelistic character wonderfully emerges.

Mindful of women's vulnerability to criticism, Christine's deep resentment against the pervasive misogyny of the day, and specifically as it surfaced in the *Roman de la Rose*, impelled her to attack male writers who maligned women. The *Roman* was a thirteenth-century love allegory of which Guillaume de Lorris had composed the shorter first part, where a dreaming youth discovers a rose garden. There he is stalked and pierced with arrows by the god of Love. The Rose that he seeks to pluck represents the desired woman. Jean de Meung, the continuator of the *Roman*, wrote an encyclopedic work containing lengthy invectives against women, whose roles he regarded as properly serving Nature through the continuation of the species. At the end the Lover plucks the Rose.

The quarrel over the *Roman de la Rose* involved a number of learned people in Christine's day. Jean Gerson, chancellor of the University of Paris, was one of those who agreed with Christine's view, and fueled the debate with his sermons in 1402. In her moral poem of advice to her son Jean du Castel, (for whom she may also have written Othea's letter of advice to young Hector) she urged him never to read either Ovid's *Art of Love* or *The Romance of the Rose*. Two of her lyrics, which are given here as 10 and 11, address the famous quarrel.

Christine's defenses of women are pervasive. Her *Epistre au Dieu d'Amour* (1399) assails male attitudes of scorn for women. The *Book of the City of Ladies* (1404-1405) helps to rehabilitate women's good name by gathering lives of heroines from history and from her own time. It presents Raison, Justice, and Droiture as three female figures who seek Christine's help in building a city to shelter such virtuous ladies. She wrote a tribute to the living warrior-saint, Joan of Arc, glowingly celebrating Joan's victory when she compelled the English to raise the siege at Orléans and inspired the French to crown the Dauphin, Charles VII. The *Dittié de Jehanne d'Arc* (1429) seems to be Christine's last work; she probably did not live to know of Joan's martyrdom.

Besides the war with England, there were rival factions in Paris for the throne that led to uprisings and massacres. Christine's concern for France's plight had moved her to compose works of history and moral allegory. Some of her political works include the *Livre de la paix*, the *Epistre de la prison de la vie humaine*, offering solace to women of France, and the partly autobiographical *Livre du chemin de longue estude*. Here Christine follows the Cumaean Sibyl, guided like Boethius by Lady Philosophy or Dante by Virgil. The purpose of the journey will be to secure wisdom for

France and Europe. Christine was also commissioned to
write a biography praising the dead monarch Charles V.

When Paris became dangerous in 1418, Christine and her
son Jehan left the city. Jehan, a royal secretary, finally died
in exile. Christine took refuge, probably ending her days in
the abbey of Poissy where her daughter was a nun; in an
earlier happier time she had celebrated a visit there in the
Livre du dit de Poissy.

1. Je vous vens la passe rose:
  Jeux à vendre.
She:
"I'll sell you a hollyhock."
He:
"Lovely one, I don't dare tell you
how much Love draws me to you.
You can see it all without my saying it!

I'll sell you a trembling leaf."

She:
"Many false lovers put up a front
to make their huge lies seem true.
One shouldn't believe everything they say.

I'll sell you the paternoster."

He:
"You know very well I'm yours;
I never belonged to anyone else,
so don't refuse me,
beautiful girl that I love, but without delay
grant me your love!

I'll sell you a parrot."

She:
"You're fine and good and gallant,
Sir, and well-bred in every way.
But I've never learned to love:

and I still wouldn't want to learn
how to fall in love or to be made love to!"

He:
"I'll sell you a turtle dove."

She:
"Left all alone and by herself—
led astray by a man who's fled—
That's how I'd live.
I'd never feel any joy in that,
no matter what I had."

He:
"I'll sell you a pair of wool gloves."

She:
"It would be too vile of me
to refuse your love;
since my love would willingly — if I dared —
be given to you;
I'd be loved by you,
for you're worthy of having
Helen, and even her lovely person.

I'll sell you the dream of love
that brings either joy or sorrow
to those who've dreamed it."

He:
"My lady, the dream I've dreamed
at night would come true
if I could win your love.

I'll sell you the soaring lark."

She:
"Your charming speech
and your fine and gentle manner,
gentle friend, make my heart joyful,

and so I can't refuse you—
I'll be yours without a quarrel!"

2. *Doulce chose est que mariage:*
   Autres Balades
A sweet thing is marriage;
I can prove it from my own experience:
it's true for a woman who has a husband
as wise and good as the one God found for me.
Let him be praised who has willingly
protected me, for I feel
the great worth of his conduct.
And surely my sweet one loves me very much.

The first night of our marriage
I could straightaway appreciate
his great worth, for he never treated me
          presumptuously,
or did anything to make me unhappy.
But as soon as it was time to rise,
he kissed me a hundred times, giving me pleasure,
demanding nothing rude of me.
And surely my sweet one loves me very much.

And he said in such gentle words,
"God permitted me to come to you,
sweet friend, and in order to serve you
I think he allowed me to prosper."
That is how he ended his reverie
throughout the night, and that is how he comported
          himself
steadfastly, never changing his mind.
And surely my sweet one loves me very much.

Prince, loving makes me lose my senses
when he tells me he is wholly mine;
and I'm bursting with sweetness—
and surely my sweet one loves me very much.

3. Ce moys de May tout se resjoye:
   Cent Balades d'Amant et de Dame
In this month of May everything rejoices,
it seems to me — except for poor, wretched me!—
who doesn't have the one she used to have.
For this reason I sigh in a small stifled voice.
He was my fair love, my sweeting,
who now is so far away from me.
Ah, come back quickly, my dear friend!

In this sweet month of May when everything's
      greening,
let us seek our joy on the tender grass
where we'll hear the joyful singing
of the nightingale and many a lark.
You know the place! In a small clear voice
I beg you, saying,
"Ah, come back quickly, my dear friend!"

For in this month when Love often captures
his prey, I think it's the duty
of every lover to take his pleasure
with his lady, his sweet little darling.
He shouldn't leave her all, all alone,
it seems to me, even for a day and a half.
Ah, come back quickly, my dear friend!

My heart's breaking in half for love of you;
Ah, come back quickly, my dear friend!

4. Pour quoi m'avez vous ce fait:
   Rondeaux
Why have you done this to me,
handsome one? — You've only to reply.
You know the martyrdom I'm suffering,
and I never did you any harm.

And indeed you went away
not deigning to say good-bye to me;
why have you done this to me?

I took my complaint to the God of Love,
concerning this wrong, saying, "Lord God,
you made me choose my sweet friend,
who's rewarded me so cruelly.
Why have you done this to me?"

5. *Source de plour, riviere de tristece:*
   Rondeaux
A fount of tears, a river of grief,
a flood of sorrow, a sea full of bitterness:
these engulf me and drown my poor heart in great
   pain—
my heart that feels overwhelming loss.

They drench me, plunge me violently,
for around me swirls
more forcefully than the Seine,
a fount of tears, a river of grief.

And their great tides break over me in a great
      deluge,
as Fortune's wind drives them
upon me, dashing me so low
that I can scarcely rise again, so harshly do they
      stifle me—
a fount of tears, a river of grief.

6. *Quant je voy ces amoureux:*
   Autres Balades
Whenever I see these lovers
casting such tender looks
between them — looks of sweetness —
and trading such tender glances,
laughing with joy, and drifting off
together, apart from the rest, with their special
      games,
it would take little to melt my heart!

For when, because of them, I remember
the one from whom I can never be parted,
my heart hungers

to bring him back to me.
But my sweet love, my kind friend,
is far away. For him I mourn so deeply
it would take little to melt my heart!

So my heart languishes
in heavy sorrow.
It brims with aching sighs
until he comes back to me—
whom Love caused to please me so much.
But with the grief that harries me
it would take little to melt my heart.

Prince, I cannot keep silent
when I see lovers two by two
giving each other solace—
it would take little to melt my heart.

7. *Seulete suy et seulete vueil estre:*
    Cent Balades
Alone am I, willing to be alone,
alone, my sweet love has abandoned me;
alone am I, I have no friend or lord.
Alone am I, in sorrowful distress;
alone am I, languid, ill at ease;
alone am I, more adrift than anyone;
alone am I, I live without my love.

Alone am I, in the doorway, by the window;
alone am I, hidden in a corner;
alone am I, nourished by my tears;
alone am I, whether sorrowing or calm.
Alone am I, nothing can delight me.
Alone am I, locked fast within my chamber;
alone am I, I live without my love.

Alone am I, everywhere, every place;
alone am I, whether I walk or rest;
alone am I, more than any earthly thing.
Alone am I, abandoned by everyone.

Alone am I, harshly bowed down,
alone am I, suffused with frequent tears.
Alone am I, I live without my love.

Prince, now my sorrow is beginning:
alone am I, appalled by my mourning.
Alone am I, in colors duller than dun.
Alone am I, I live without my love.

8. Que ferons nous de ce mary jaloux?: Cent Balades

8. Que ferons nous de ce mary jaloux?:
   Cent Balades
What shall we do with this jealous husband?
I pray to God he gets skinned alive!
He goes about keeping such a close watch on us
that we can't get near each other.
We could hoist him in a tough noose,
the filthy, ugly churl — all twisted with gout—
who gives us so much trouble, so much grief!

Let his wolfish body strangle.
It's of no use to him — it's only a hindrance.
What good is this old man, full of coughs,
apart from scolding, scowling, spitting?
The devil can love him and cherish him.
I hate him too much, the twisted old hunchback,
who gives us so much trouble, so much grief!

Hey, he deserves to be cuckolded by us,
the baboon who does nothing but search
through his house. Hey, what's to be done? Shake
his pelt a little to make him crouch.
Or let him — not walk—
but quickly fall down the stairs, the suspicious churl,
who gives us so much trouble, so much grief!

9. Dieux! on se plaint trop durement: Autres Balades

9. Dieux! on se plaint trop durement:
   Autres Balades
God! Everyone complains too bitterly
about these husbands. I've heard too many slanders
about them, and how they're ordinarily

jealous, snarling, full of wrath.
But I could never say such a thing,
because I've a husband exactly to my liking—
fine and good; he's never against me.
He wills absolutely whatever I will!

He wants nothing but enjoyment,
and scolds me when I sigh.
And he's pleased — unless he's lying—
to have me amuse myself with my lover,
if I happen to choose someone besides him!
Nothing I do makes him doleful.
Everything pleases him; he's never against me.
He wills absolutely whatever I will!

So I must live merrily,
for such a husband is enough for me,
who — in all my behavior—
never finds fault with anything.
And when I'm drawn to my lover,
and welcome him sweetly,
my husband laughs about it — the gentle lord—
he wills absolutely whatever I will!

God help me! Don't let this husband
change for the worse. He has no peer,
for whether I want to sing, dance or laugh,
he wills absolutely whatever I will!

10. *Jadis avoit en la cité d'Athènes:*
Autres Balades
Once long ago in the city of Athens
dwelt the flower of zeal for sovereign learning.
But despite certain noble sentiments
arising from their great philosophy, an excessively ugly error
misled them, so that they wished to have
several different gods. For their own good
someone should have preached to them what they
should have known:
that there is only one God, but this wasn't

well-received by them.
One is often scourged for saying what is true!

The very wise Aristotle, versed in
esoteric learning, was a fugitive from this same city
full of such error; he suffered many griefs
because of it. Socrates, who was the fount
of reason, was driven from the place.
Many others were slain by indivious men
for telling the truth; and everyone can plainly see
that everywhere under heaven
one is often scourged for saying what is true!

So that is the way the world's wisdom goes.
For this reason I say that many people are angered
with me. Because with vain words,
with dishonor and dubious ill-fame,
I dared to find fault in young and old,
and with the *Romance* — pleasant and quaint—
of the Rose — a book that should be burned!
Yet for that opinion, many would leap at my eyes.
One is often scourged for saying what is true!

11. *Mon chier seigneur, soiez de ma partie:* [1]
    Rondeaux
My cherished lord, be partisan of mine!
They have openly attacked me in all-out war—
the allies of the *Romance of the Rose*—
because I've not converted to their ranks.

Against me they have waged such cruel battle
that surely they think they have me under siege;
my cherished lord, be partisan of mine!

Despite their onslaught, I will not retreat
from my position. But it's a common fact

---

[1] Kenneth Varty suggests that Christine is addressing Louis duc
d'Orléans, father of the poet.

that people will fall upon one who dares defend
 what's right.
Still, if my understanding is tro weak,
my cherished lord, be partisa.1 of mine!

12. The letter of Lady Sebille de la Tour, to the beloved lady of the Duke of True Lovers: *Le Livre du duc des vrais amans*

My very revered lady:

Once I have presented my humble respects to you, may
it please you to know that I've received your very kind and
friendly letter, for which I thank you with all my simple heart.
You do me so much honor by recalling the slight services that
I have rendered you in the past — services not at all worthy
of what your excellent and noble person merits. I am more
grateful than I can ever deserve in all my life.

My dear lady, as for visiting you at present, please excuse
me, I humbly beg you. Upon my faith my daughter is very
seriously sick, so that I can in no way leave her. God knows
how distressed I am over this particular illness.

My very revered lady, since I cannot talk with you as soon
as I would like, and I'm bound to advise you as one who has
been in my charge from childhood until now — though I
haven't been worthy of this — it seems to me I would be
wrong to keep silent on a subject that I know might bring
harm to you if I didn't mention it to you. And so, dear lady,
I'm writing upon the following matters. I humbly beg you that
no ill will can impel you to hold it against me, for you can
be sure that my very great love and the desire for your
increasing noble reputation and honor move me to do this.

My lady, I've heard certain news of your behavior, about
which I'm pained with all my heart, for fear of the loss of
your good name — since it seems to me that the news
concerns this. For it is correct and reasonable that every
princess and high-born lady — since she is exalted in honor
and rank above all others — should surpass them in goodness,
wisdom, mores, position, and manners. And she should excel
in these in order to serve as a model for other ladies and even

for all women to pattern their behavior on her.

And so it's fitting for her to be devout toward God. She should have an air of assurance, calm and self-containment. She should be temperate and not extreme in her pleasures. Her laughter should be low, and not pointless. She should have a dignified bearing, a modest look, a noble expression, a gentle rejoinder and a friendly word for everyone. Her clothing and attire should be rich, but not excessively ornate. She should welcome strangers with formality and self-possession, without too much familiarity.

She should be deliberate in her judgment and not flighty, never appearing severe, wicked or spiteful, or overly proud when served, but humane and kindly to her waiting-women and servants, not too arrogant, but reasonably generous with her gifts. She should know how to recognize which people are the worthiest as to goodness and prudence, and which are her best servants. These she should draw to her, both maids and menservants, and reward them as they deserve.

She shouldn't put credence or faith in flatterers, men or women, but if she spots them, she should drive them away from her. Let her not believe lightly-carried stories, nor be in the habit of whispering with strangers or close friends, secretly or in seclusion — even to one of her servants or women — so that none of them think they know her secrets more than anyone else does. She should never laughingly say anything to anyone at all in front of other people which isn't comprehensible to all, so that those who hear it may not suppose there to be any silly secret between them.

She shouldn't keep herself locked in her chamber and too isolated, nor should she be too commonly seen by people, but should sometimes be withdrawn and other times in company.

Now, while these conditions and all other kinds of behavior proper to a high-born princess used to be observed by you, it's been said that you have changed. You've become more pleasure-loving, more animated in your conversation, even lovelier than before. When outward behavior changes, people commonly judge that the heart too has changed. Now you want to be alone and away from people, except for one or two of your women and some of your servants with whom you confer and laugh even in the presence of others, and talk covertly as if you understood one another quite well. And only their company pleases you. No one else can serve you to your liking. These things and mannerisms stir envy among your other servants, and they judge that your heart is enamored or whatever.

Ha! my very gentle lady — for the love of God, take care of who you are, and the high rank to which God has exalted you. Don't forget your soul and your honor for any foolish pleasure, and don't indulge in vain notions that several young women have who allow themselves to believe that there's nothing wrong in being passionately in love as long as there's no coarseness involved — for I'm certain you would prefer death to this! — and that it makes life more delightful and that it makes a man valiant and renowned for good. Ha! my cherished lady, it's quite otherwise, and for God's sake don't deceive yourself about it.

Take the example of such great mistresses that you have known in your time, who, simply because they were suspected of such love — even though the truth was never known about it — lost both their honor and their lives. And yet, I am convinced, upon my soul, that they were guilty of no sin or vulgar wrongdoing. And yet their children saw them reproached and maligned. And as dishonorable as such foolish love is in every woman, rich or poor, how much more unseemly and injurious it is in a princess and a lady of rank — the more highly born she is, the worse it is.

There is good reason for this. A princess's fame is carried everywhere throughout the world; and so if there is any stain on her good name it becomes more widely known in foreign countries than that of ordinary women, and also because of her children, who will rule over lands and become princes of other people. It's a great misfortune when there is any suspicion that they may not be the rightful heirs and great misfortune can come of it. For even if there hasn't been any physical wrongdoing, nobody will believe it who has heard it said, "This lady is in love." And because of a little foolish glance, cast perhaps in one's youth and without naughty intent, wicked tongues will judge and will add things that were never done or thought of. So the tale that goes from mouth to mouth is never lessened but keeps on growing.

Further Reading on Christine

Text:
Maurice Roy, ed. *Oeuvres poétiques de Christine de Pisan.*
3 vols. Paris, 1886-1896. I, 187; I, 237; III, 287; I, 183; I, 182;
I, 244; I, 12; I, 78; I, 216; I, 250; I, 249; I, 162-165.

Diane Bornstein. *Ideals for Women in the Works of Christine
    de Pizan.* Michigan, 1981.
Jacqueline Cerquiglini, ed. *Cent Ballades d'Amant et de
    Dame.* Paris, 1982.
Alice Kemp-Welch, tr. *The Book of the Duke of True Lovers.*
    London, 1908.
Sarah Lawson, tr. *The Treasure of the City of Ladies, or The
    Book of the Three Virtues.* New York, 1985.
Enid McLeod. *The Order of the Rose.* London, 1976.
Earl J. Richards, tr. *The Book of the City of Ladies.*
    New York, 1982.
Kenneth Varty, ed. *Christine de Pizan: Ballades, Rondeaux,
    Virelais.* Leicester, 1965.
————. *Christine de Pizan: A Bibliographical Guide.*
    London, 1984.
Charity Cannon Willard. *Christine de Pizan: Her Life and
    Works.* New York, 1984.
Josette A. Wisman, ed. and tr. *"The Epistle of the Prison of
    the Human Life," with "An Epistle to the Queen of
    France," and "Lament of the Evils of the Civil War."*
    New York, 1985.
Edith Yenal. *Christine de Pizan. A Bibliography of Writings
    By Her and About Her.* London, 1982.

The Garland Library
of Medieval Literature